Theatre Professionals say...

Finally! A book for actors about the real world of professional theatre. Bravo Mary McTigue! *Arthur Storch, Artistic Director, Syracuse Stage and Chairman of Theatre Department, Syracuse University (1974-91)*

Everything you've ever wanted to know about becoming a theatre performer ... thoroughly entertaining and useful. *Janet Hayes Walker, Artistic Director, York Theatre Company, New York City*

Thanks to Mary McTigue, the artist and the ambitious business person—once great natural enemies—can finally integrate comfortably within the same human being. From the amateur's very first dream of a career as an actor, to the hard-core professional artist, *Acting Like a Pro* handles every possible step, its problems and its solutions. It is a definitive work. *Michael Hartig, Michael Hartig Agency, Ltd., New York City*

A terrific resource and inspiration for the young performer! So many books purport to teach acting—*this* book teaches how to get hired and re-hired, and gives actors a healthy respect for the profession. *Rita Litton, Director, ACTeen Professional Video School, New York City*

At last, a straightforward how-to manual for novice actors seeking professional tips, from the first audition through a final production. Mary McTigue does not waste the reader's time with abstract observations; rather, she describes the actual process of bringing a play to life for the actor. *Penny Potenz Winship, Community Theatre Director*

Acting Like a Pro is a truly comprehensive collection of useful insights which will benefit any aspiring actor who contemplates a future in professional theatre. ... highly recommended. *C. Ronald Olauson, Ph.D., Professor of Theatre, Mankato State University, Mankato, MN*

Acting Like a Pro is a much-needed addition to the list of books that can so help earnest beginners in this profession. What to expect, how to prepare, and where to spend energy and time are all thoroughly and thoughtfully covered by Ms. McTigue. Well done! *Stephen Stout, Professional Actor and Director, New York City*

Acting Like a Pro

Who's Who, What's What, and the Way Things *Really* Work in the Theatre

792.028
M

Mary McTigue

BETTERWAY PUBLICATIONS, INC.
WHITE HALL, VIRGINIA

Published by Betterway Publications, Inc.
P.O. Box 219
Crozet, VA 22932
(804) 823-5661

Cover design by Rick Britton
Typography by **Designations**

Library of Congress Cataloging-in-Publication Data

McTigue, Mary
    Acting like a pro : who's who, what's what, and the way things
really work in the theatre / Mary McTigue.
    p. cm.
    Includes index.
    ISBN 1-55870-223-7 (pbk.) : $14.95
    1. Acting—Vocational guidance. 2. Acting. I. Title.
PN2055.M39 1992
792'.028'023--dc20   91-41419
                                                            CIP

Printed in the United States of America

For Aspiring Actors

Whatever you can do, or dream you can, begin it.
Boldness has genius, power and magic in it.
Goethe

Foreword

If a young American actor opens most introductory acting texts to the final chapter, he or she will more than likely discover helpful advice on the business of acting; i.e., the audition process, rehearsal procedures, or perhaps a few details on photos and résumés. All the authors of these manuals recognize how vital this information is to the aspiring actor, but invariably the lessons are abridged and sometimes awash with generalities. Finally, with *Acting Like a Pro*, by Mary McTigue, the subjects of professional etiquette and the craft of the working actor are fully addressed.

The training of the American actor has progressed from the laboratories of the 1930s through the urban studios of the 1950s into the university programs of the last several decades. The path traveled has been productive in many ways, but it has also led the young actor-in-training further from the professional arenas and away from the centuries-old apprenticeship tradition of the art. The fledgling artist once learned his craft by performing under the watchful eye of a master actor. Academic programs are constantly grappling with this "professional distance" by attempting to balance the student's artistic technique with craft process and procedure. Ms. McTigue's book offers invaluable insight and should prove to be a definitive source connecting the student actor to the profession.

Her discussions of craft matters, the do's and don't's of working in this highly ritualized art, are clear, no-nonsense, and tempered in experience. The writing style is concise and conversational. As I was reading, I imagined myself sitting backstage in a green room overhearing a veteran actress challenging and encouraging an enterprising intern.

The chapters are organized in a logical fashion, guiding the actor from the initial work on auditions, through pre-rehearsal tasks and the rehearsal process. The author even includes a valuable introduction to basic techniques employed in period plays. Ms. McTigue's work is remarkable for its thoroughness and specific detail. The actor will discover how to work, whom he is working with, and what he should be working on. Information ranges from scanning iambic pentameter to the appropriate use of false eyelashes. Her final chapter supplies the reader with career options, craft tools, and definitions of professional unions. (Teachers, do your students know anything about industrials? Voice-overs? AEA? AFTRA? SAG?)

In short, anyone interested in the craft of acting (actors, acting coaches, directors) should find this book a necessary companion to every rehearsal. In fact, if all American actors simply obeyed Ms. McTigue's "Ten Commandments of Theatre" and diligently practiced her "MASTERTRACK for Actors," the theatre would be a saner, more productive working place.

Richard Warner
Professional Actor/Director
Head of Acting, Department of Drama
University of Virginia

Contents

Acknowledgments

The completion of this book would not have been possible without the help of my husband Frank Tooni, who not only took care of Patrick and did laundry, but also read every word and offered helpful editorial comments. Special thanks too, to Bob Neu and Carol Wolfe, for their suggestions and review of technical and musical sections. I am grateful to all manuscript readers in both academic and professional theatre for their encouragement and outright endorsements. Lastly I wish to acknowledge the people with whom I have worked over the years (you know who you are), both the exemplary professionals from whom I learned so much, and the beginners whose mistakes were the inspiration for this book.

Introduction

BEAUTY IS NOT ENOUGH

So many actors are convinced that if they are talented and beautiful and intelligent, they will automatically be successful in theatre, everyone will love them, and they will win fame and fortune just as soon as they get the right breaks. They take acting classes, attend schools, and develop concrete theories on how to approach a role. Then they want to know, "Now, how do I get an agent so I can get a job and become a star?" And many schools and books offer advice on how to get into show business. There's a big gap here. Actors never get the chance to learn how they are expected to behave in a real-world situation, never see an overview of how professional theatres operate, never get exposed to how to work with the people in the business, and don't know the professional lingo.

Perhaps you've been to drama school, or have done lots of academic and community theatre plays—doesn't that give you the knowledge and experience you need to know how to get the role and do it right? NOT REALLY. Why? Because the subject has largely been ignored; because there's a whole world encompassing the professional experience that is simply not addressed in any book or any course.

Acting Like a Pro is designed to help you learn the procedures and behaviors that are expected of professional actors, the "unwritten rules" of rehearsal and performance, some of the secrets that pros use to get their roles and to work happily within a company, appropriate backstage behavior, and important theatrical superstitions. Even if you have no intention of pursuing acting as a career, all the material in this book will help you find success and happiness in your avocation as an actor, because all the professional secrets that are shared here also apply to working in community and academic theatre.

WHO CARES?

Why are these things important? Because you can be a fabulously talented actor and not get the part simply because you weren't properly prepared for the audition. Because you might get the role, but then be miserably unhappy in rehearsals because everyone's not doing things your way. Because your work might be excellent, but you lose favor with directors because you don't understand how *they* work. Because you may be brilliant, but nobody likes working with you because you don't know how to memorize lines or keep your performance together. Because you might look gorgeous in those costumes, but the crew finds you "difficult" to work with.

Wait a minute, you might be thinking. I know how to "prepare" for a role; I know how to be "professional" at rehearsals; I know how to deal with the director; and I don't care what other actors or the crew think as long as I'm great. Besides, I'm an "artist," and we are always allowed a little temperament. WRONG. That kind of thinking might not get you fired, but you would be amazed at how many future jobs or coveted roles you stand to lose because of your ignorance and indiscretion.

THE ONES THAT GOT AWAY

Let me give you some real-life examples of what I'm talking about. A couple of years ago I was the "reader" at auditions for a Broadway play. (The reader is a professional actor who is hired to read the scenes with the actors who are actually auditioning.) I was delighted to see a woman I had known years previously who had become very successful. She'd won a Tony award for her performance on Broadway in a long-running comedy, and had since appeared in terrific roles in numerous films, including a recent Woody Allen hit.

This professional and very talented actress literally "blew" the audition. Her reading may have been brilliant, but unfortunately the auditors could hardly hear her. She had worked in film and TV for so long that her voice, actions, and character were geared to the diminutive dimensions of those media, and would never "work" in a Broadway house. Nobody asked her to do it again, "bigger and louder." They simply said, "Thank you," and she left the room. After she did, one of the producers said, "Well, that's sad. She's lost it." In fact, this actress did work again on Broadway several years later, but for this particular audition, she simply wasn't prepared.

Years ago I was at a theatre in Chicago when a friend of mine flew out of his audition, gave me a huge bear hug, and announced that the director had asked him to understudy the leading man in the theatre's current comedy. Bruce had done some children's theatre, but was at the time unemployed and delighted to have the job. The role called for a muscular "macho man," and Bruce was a pretty skinny kid at the time, so he started to work out every day at a gym in preparation for the role, even though he was "only" the understudy.

A couple of weeks later, the leading man was dismissed for "disciplinary reasons," and Bruce went into the part. Shortly thereafter the show was moved to New York, and Bruce had the lead in a Broadway play. It only lasted a week, but that was enough time for one of the top theatrical agents in the business to see the performance, ask Bruce to sign with him, and the rest is history. Bruce went to California, did many films and TV movies, and even became the star of a successful TV series. I often wondered what happened to that actor who was dismissed, and what exactly those "disciplinary reasons" were, but it doesn't matter—I've never heard *his* name in the business again.

A director friend of mine has always regretted casting a particular actor in one of his Off-Broadway plays. When the actor first came in to audition, the director was elated—here, finally, was an actor who looked perfect for the role and had just that indefinable quality the director was seeking. His first reading was terrific, and he seemed enthused about the play. But as rehearsals progressed, it became clear that the actor was on an incredible ego-trip, and worse, that he didn't have any intention of trying to behave professionally, much less humbly. He wouldn't (or couldn't) take direction, was constantly disrupting rehearsals to work on his own special problems, and ultimately undermined any possible feeling of "ensemble" with the rest of the cast. This particular actor was very successful in commercials, and perhaps because he made a lot of money, he felt that he was better than anyone he was working with, including the director. However, in this instance, he not only destroyed any chance of working with that director again, he also ruined what might have been a pleasant, if not successful, Off-Broadway run.

WHAT YOU DON'T KNOW CAN HURT YOU

OK, so now you're thinking, well, I wouldn't do any of those things. Besides, what I don't know I will learn from directors and experienced actors as I go along. WRONG AGAIN. Why not? First of all, because there's too much to learn; that's why this is a book and not a pamphlet. Second, because people in theatre who know better and might teach you probably will not.

Why wouldn't more experienced actors share their secrets with you? Simply for the good of the show. Experienced actors know that a good working relationship with everyone in the cast is paramount to a good production. They also know that jobs are carefully delineated, and would never presume to take over the director's or stage manager's role. They will always try to maintain a good working relationship with *everyone* in the cast, because they have to work with them ON STAGE. People who start criticizing and disciplining soon find that less experienced actors get resentful, take offense at the criticism, and might even sabotage the scene with the actor who gave it. Pros are always more concerned with the show than with teaching. Additionally, so many young actors are so filled with their own sense of importance and ego that older, more experienced actors often take the attitude that they should "learn from their own mistakes." Unfortunately, they rarely do.

As for directors, you simply can't count on them to tell you everything. Aside from the actual all-consuming work of directing the play, directors will rarely make an actor aware of what mistakes he or she is making regarding procedures or behavior. They don't have time. It's all the director can do to try to get all the other elements of the play in working order, and the actors are only one of the problems. Directors have to make decisions about the costumes, the sets, the lighting, the concept, and the play as a whole. Plus, contrary to what individual actors may think, there's usually more than one actor in a play, and each one of them presents a unique problem to the director. Directors just don't have the energy to spend a lot of time on any one individual.

In addition, if an actor is disruptive or temperamental, the director will usually do everything in his or her power to "understand," and try to "bring the actor along." Most good directors know that if they spend all their time disciplining and teaching, they won't have any time to direct the play. And good directors will never jeopardize their play by becoming angry or criticizing too much—they really can't afford to ruin their working relationship with the actor, no matter how difficult it is. They will just have the patience of Job throughout rehearsal and performance, kiss the actor goodbye and thank him, and never, ever, hire him again.

WHAT CAN YOU DO?

Acting Like a Pro is written *by* an actor *for* actors, to help them learn what is expected of them in all theatrical situation—from auditions to closing night.

In this book, actors will find everything they need to know about working in professional theatre, and everything they need to know to act *like a pro* in any theatre at any level. The author shares with the reader all those "unwritten rules" of professional theatre that can't be found anywhere else. They were learned through twenty years of professional experience in more than fifty professional productions, working with hundreds of other professional actors and directors in New York and throughout the country. *Acting Like a Pro* contains the tips and techniques that professional actors use to win roles, to make rehearsals productive, to keep performances alive and fresh, and to maintain a pleasant and professional backstage atmosphere.

Acting Like a Pro is NOT an acting theory book per se, but it contains a great deal of good advice about how professional actors approach auditions and performances. This is NOT a book about getting work as a professional actor, but you will find many guidelines used by the pros that will help you get jobs, as well as an overview on how to get started in a career. This is NOT a book designed *only* for aspiring professional actors—it's for actors working anywhere in any play, and it applies to all theatrical situations because it's so practical. This is NOT a book that comprehensively covers film and television work, but because other media have their basis in theatre, most of the procedures and vocabulary apply to other media work.

WHAT'S IN IT FOR YOU

Acting Like a Pro contains examples of how professional actors prepare, work, and behave in theatre. The amateur or student actor will not only learn what goes on in professional theatre, he or she will gain a great advantage in auditions, rehearsals, and performance by knowing the "professional edge"—what experienced actors do to make their work constantly exciting.

• THE AUDITION: GETTING THE ROLE spells out what professional actors do when they really want to win the role.
• THE REHEARSAL PROCESS: READ-THROUGH TO PRE-VIEW provides a full explanation of the entire process of rehearsing the play, and also presents a professional approach to rehearsals, which illustrates the difference between rehearsing productively and wasting time.
• THEATRE PERSONNEL AND CREW: HELPING THEM HELP YOU identifies the crew and office people actors need to know and how to work with them. There is also specific advice on dealing with the departments of costumes, props, lights, sound, and the set.
• THE TEN COMMANDMENTS OF THEATRE give the actor the basics of performance discipline—how the pros constantly work to maintain their own performance throughout the run.
• VOICE AND VERSE, PERIOD AND STYLE offers the reader an introduction to the importance of voice work and Standard American Speech. There is a special section on verse performance and a

discussion of the major types of plays, historical periods, and basics of style.

• THE MASTERTRACK FOR ACTORS is a unique methodology designed by the author, based on experiences and observances of how professionals work in rehearsal and performance. An easy-to-remember acronym, MASTERTRACK offers a comprehensive approach to the acting experience.

• In BACKSTAGE PROCEDURE AND THEATRICAL SUPERSTITIONS, you will learn what the calls are and how to respond to them properly, as well as "eyelash etiquette" and green room protocol. Perhaps even more important are theatrical superstitions—why you should never whistle in the dressing room, or use real flowers, or quote from a certain play.

• ACTING AS A CAREER spells out what areas of work the three unions cover and their membership requirements. Agents and managers are defined, and there is advice on professional tools such as pictures and résumés. For those who are interested in acting for film and television, there is a discussion of work in those areas.

WHO NEEDS THIS BOOK?

This book is written for actors, students, apprentices, interns, Equity Membership Candidates, teachers, stage managers, and directors. Its application is theatre performance in colleges and theatre schools, community theatres, summer stock *and* professional theatre, from children's theatre to repertory companies, from dinner theatre to dramatic stock. Beginners with no experience will benefit from the basics contained in *Acting Like a Pro*; aspiring actors will benefit from the techniques and advice; and young pros will learn many things they didn't know.

It should be noted that this book is not exclusively written for young people. I have known and worked with many actors who didn't even begin a career until they had retired after numerous years in another profession. Many people have aspired to be actors in their youth, only to get married and have a family, or pursue another career for a number of years. Then they find themselves with the opportunity to return to their "first love." This book is for them too.

Teachers will find *Acting Like a Pro* of great benefit to actors of all ages in their theatre classes, drama clubs, and workshops. Directors might consider the book required reading for all cast members in their productions. Colleges and professional schools may wish to incorporate this new subject matter into their theatre curriculum. Because even if you're not a professional actor, by *Acting Like a Pro*, your auditions, rehearsals, work, and performance will be better, smoother, happier, and certainly more professional—and by *Acting Like a Pro* (if you really want to), you'll take the first and most important step toward *becoming* a professional actor.

1

The Audition:
Getting the Role

PREPARATION

In order to get work in the theatre, your audition has to be great. Not good, not good enough, it has to be GREAT. Some inexperienced actors feel that the director and/or casting people have good imaginations, and all you need do is show up—they can tell if you have the look and the talent needed for any particular role. Not true. Your job is to help them as much as possible to *see* you in the play, the period, the role. You *have to* work at it. If you don't, that's your decision. Unfortunately, somebody else will give it the time and effort and use all the tricks, and that person will probably get the role, sometimes simply by virtue of the fact that she is showing the director that she really *wants* it.

I know one professional actor in New York who really spends time preparing his auditions. I've often seen him backstage reading a script, going over lines, and asking others to read through scenes with him. He said to me once, "I don't want to embarrass my agents, so I always spend time preparing for my auditions. Even if I don't get the part, the word will get back to my agent that I gave a terrific reading."

Your audition has to be even better than a performance. Why? Because if you don't get cast, you'll never get a chance to give a great performance. You might be saying, "But the more I prepare, the more nervous I am." That's sometimes true. But if you are well prepared, *and* you learn how to deal with your nerves (which is discussed at the end of this chapter), you will give a far greater audition than if you just go in "winging it."

The Play's the Thing

The minute the casting notice for a play or season is posted, there's one thing you will want to do first: READ THE PLAY. If you've already decided you want to audition, read the play. Even if you think you know this play because you've seen it in the theatre or on television, read the play. Before you decide *not* to audition, read the play. Maybe you've been invited to audition (an enviable position!), but you have some other conflicts right now—you've just done a play, you're very busy with other projects, you're not terribly interested. Don't base your decision *not* to audition on outside factors. Here's why. If you're really an actor, you might just read the script and find out that this part is the one you've been dying to do, that the play is so fascinating you would love to work on it, that you are tremendously challenged by the theme or the style.

One very important note here: READ THE ENTIRE PLAY. Don't just look at the role you're interested in and/or the scenes in which your character appears. For two reasons: one, it's impossible to get a feeling for the character you're auditioning for by just reading his or her lines and scenes. You must have an idea of the entire setting for your character, and you must be aware of the background of other characters (the ones you will be working with), and you must know what other characters say about yours. There's another important reason for reading the entire play: the director may ask you to read for another character. If you've read only the scenes in which the character *you* want to play appears, you won't have a clue. There is no substitute, and there are no shortcuts to reading the entire play. It usually takes a couple of hours at most.

Where to Get the Play

Check the library first. If you live in a college or university town, check all the libraries. Call the local bookstores to see if they carry it. In larger cities, there may be bookstores that specialize in theatre and related books. If you want to and can afford it, *buy* a copy —an actor will never waste money on scripts—and start building your own library. Classic plays by Shakespeare, Shaw, O'Neill, Inge, Williams, Coward, Miller, etc., are almost universally available in either single copy or anthologies.

If possible, try to find out the edition or translation of your particular production. For example, there were many "editors" of Shakespeare, some of whom actually changed some of the words and punctuation. I have found that there are even differing editions of Noel Coward plays, which is odd because his plays are fairly recent and written in English. It seems some of them were rewritten (probably by Coward himself) for American production. It would be helpful if you knew the exact edition that the director plans to use. ("Edition" can refer sometimes to the name of the editor, such as the "Harrison" Shakespeare, or the name of the publisher, such as the Samuel French *Present Laughter* by Noel Coward.)

Regarding plays originally written in another language, particularly classics by Molière, Ibsen, Chekov, etc., there are often many available translations. You place yourself at a great disadvantage if you do not find out what translation is being used, because they can differ tremendously. Still, if you cannot find the exact edition of the play (or cannot find out what edition or translation is being used), read *any* edition or translation you can get your hands on. Having some idea of the overall picture is better than none at all.

For more contemporary plays, you can write or call the publisher to obtain a copy if you can't find it at the library or local bookstore. Be sure to ask first for the "Acting Edition" of a play—these are the editions created specifically for actors and are generally softcover, smaller, easier to use, and cheaper than hardbound editions. Often the Acting Edition will also include some "stage manager's notes," which are the parenthetical italicized staging directions used in a premiere production.

Bookstores that carry plays include: the Drama Book Shop, 723 7th Ave., New York, NY (212) 944-0595, and Applause Books, 211 W. 71st St., New York, NY (212) 496-7511. Plays may also be obtained directly from publishers: Samuel French, 45 W. 25th St., New York, NY (212) 206-8990 and Dramatists Play Service, 440 Park Ave. So., New York, NY (212) 683-8960.

What if the play is original and has not been published, or what if you can't find a copy or afford one? Then you can always ask the casting director or director (or whoever is handling the auditions) whether scripts are available to read. Be sure to call the appropriate office to arrange a time, and ask in advance if the plays may be removed from the premises. Often they cannot, in which case you would go to the office and read the play (plan to spend at least two hours). It is always wise to call again before you arrive to make sure there is a copy of the play available for you to read; sometimes they are all "checked out," or being read by others.

Sides are usually available for actors, and you should always ask about them. Sides are the photocopied pages of the actual scenes (arranged by character) you will be reading for the audition. If the producer/director/casting person does not have sides, you should always ask what pages or what scenes your character will be reading. If you do not have the exact translation or edition, you may ask them to clarify exactly where the scene begins (first line) and ends (last line). I have found that it is helpful to obtain sides *in addition* to reading my own copy of the play. That way I'm covered even if the play is a different edition or translation. It is rarely helpful to read a summary of the play, and character descriptions are very often misleading. Don't rely on them.

Elements of the Play

On the first reading, try to avoid drawing any conclusions and don't get hung up on your character or your scenes. Just read it through. My most important piece of advice is READ FOR COM-PREHENSION. Read for the meaning of the whole play, the setting, the characters, the period, the style. Read it like a *story*. As you read you will become aware of certain elements of this particular play:

- the locale (where the play is set)
- the period (the time period)
- the type of play (comedy, tragedy, etc.)
- the style (realistic, absurdist, etc.)

If the play is set in England in the 1920s and revolves around rich, decadent people as you might find in a Noel Coward play, for example, your approach will be very different from the way you tackle a Neil Simon play that takes place in Yonkers, New York in 1939.

Once again, in making your decision for an audition, your research is important. You can't always rely on the play alone to give you all the answers regarding locale, period, and style. Sometimes a director will place a classic play in a different locale and period—I've seen Shakespeare's *As You Like It* set in American pre-Civil War South, and *Julius Caesar* transported to 1970s Washington, DC. Often a director who plans to change the locale and period (and thereby the style of the play) will post this information on the audition notice. Be aware of these elements—it could change your whole approach, and it's critical to know before you get into the audition itself.

Why is all this important? Because *for your audition*, you will have to determine how to dress, what accent to use, what style is appropriate in order to present yourself in the best possible light.

What to Audition For

Michael Shurtleff, author of a very important book called *Audition*, advises that actors should audition for everything, every chance they get. I agree. Unless you're really very wrong for the play and/or all the roles, you will have the benefit of learning and working on a new piece, the experience of "getting it out there," the opportunity to meet new directors and casting people, and the chance to give a "mini-performance."

In addition, when you give a fabulous audition, even if you are not cast, the director (or perhaps assistant director or casting director) will notice and remember you. You will never waste your time or effort by auditioning well.

Don't assume that you are wrong for a play because of your race, creed, religion, or sex. A friend of mine played the next door neighbor in *Death of a Salesman* on Broadway—he's black. In other productions I've seen a black Brutus in *Julius Caesar*, a black Luciana in *The Comedy of Errors* (whose sister Adriana was played by a white actress), and a Hispanic father and son (Proteus and Antonio) team in *The Two Gentlemen of Verona*.

Hamlet has frequently been played by women, and recently a female star played Falstaff at the Folger Theatre in Washington. As artistic director of the New York Shakespeare Festival, Joseph Papp was noted for his use of Affirmative Action casting (the use of "non-traditional" types of actors in various roles). I have always thought that the Chorus in *Henry V* could effectively be played by a woman.

With regard to age, it is important to at least look approximately the age or type of the character. If you're short, with youthful features, you can probably play ingenues and juveniles well into your twenties. If you're tall, you can do older roles, and will probably not be cast in the much younger roles unless everyone in the play is about the same age. I worked with a director who consistently cast me older than my actual age, which was fine with me, because I had the chance to do some really great roles for him. Asked about this, he replied, "Well, you're tall."

Remember that on stage everything is relative. Let's say there are a mother and daughter in the play. If the mother is cast older than the play calls for (which is often the case) then the daughter will be older too—so the mother won't look *too* old. If you are in a college or university situation in which the casting pool is all students of about the same age, you may have the chance to play the older, and often more interesting, roles.

Just a few years after arriving in New York (when I was still quite young), I auditioned for the young Anne in a production of *Richard III*. At the second callback, the director asked me if I would play the role of Margaret. I had to think a minute, because I had not auditioned for what Shakespeare describes as an "ancient old hag." However, I did it, and it was a wonderful experience.

A final note: If you really don't like the play, don't have the time, or are truly not interested, then don't audition. (Note: I once declined an audition for a showcase because I decided after reading the play that I hated it. When I saw the production, it turned out to be quite good, good enough to move eventually to an Off-Broadway paying contract.)

But back to the point: no one who commits to a play should be reluctant to devote the time and energy required to do a good job. If the director has specifically posted a notice that "only actors who are absolutely right for the parts should audition, and don't waste our time," then think twice (but only twice) before you plunge in. You can always go to the audition and let *them* make the decision.

I once went to an open audition for a musical, which for me was pushing it since I have never been known as a fabulous vocalist.

Before I opened my mouth to sing, the director asked me if I was familiar with a comedy that was scheduled next in his season. I wasn't, but he asked me to come back in a couple of hours to read for the lead. Though it was midwinter, I scrambled for a script, hustled back, and got the role. Two days later I was on a plane to Florida, and that director was fond of saying about me, "I found her in a snowdrift in Chicago."

Memorization

To memorize or not to memorize? This is an age-old question, and one that is difficult to answer definitively. I say: prepare, prepare, prepare. There is simply no better way to get your face "out of the book" than knowing the lines. But absolutely do not get paranoid about this! And DO carry the script and use it at your audition.

If you study the script diligently, every day, reading for comprehension and reading aloud, by the time you get to your audition your lines will be *very nearly* memorized. Many professional actors believe that they can't really act until they get "off book," so they plunge into preparation for an audition with an incredible concentration. If memorization is easy for you, here's a professional trick: memorize funny lines, very dramatic lines, last lines of long speeches, and short lines.

Those people who have trouble with memorization should not try to memorize at all for the audition. They could spend all their time trying to learn the lines by heart, rather than doing the real work of studying the character and emotional content. You have to decide what's best for you; however, if you read somewhere that you *should not* memorize, you may not do the kind of complete preparation you could.

A word of warning about preparation: don't look at your own lines and ignore everybody else's. One of the most common mistakes that neophyte actors make is concentrating *only* on their own lines. They don't know the cues, they don't know the action or intention, they have no idea of what's really going on.

Again, *read for comprehension*. What is my character really saying? What is the other character saying? What is my response, my reaction? How do I really feel? How does the other character feel?

Acting is two-fold: it involves REACTION as much as ACTION. If you're only playing your own action, then you're only doing one-half your job playing one-half your character.

Go over and over the lines until you feel very secure. Try them lots of different ways, with different emotions. Try different characters, different accents. Do all sorts of outrageous things. Only by experimenting can you find what will "work" for you.

For the audition, always carry the script. (Even if you have done the play before and have the lines "cold.") The director wants to see a performance, but if you don't have the script in hand he will *expect* a performance. Carrying the script is a good reminder that "this is only an audition." Your audition with script will be even more impressive than without.

In addition, even if you have tried to memorize some lines, don't rely on your memory in an audition. It's a strange situation, in a strange place, you're reading with people you don't know, and you'll probably be nervous. Even if you have had the opportunity to study the script for several weeks and feel very confident, do not concentrate on memorization.

Concentrate on being as "into" the character, scene, and moment as possible, just as you do in rehearsal or performance: what the other character is saying, how you would really react, what is actually happening. If you tend to get nervous, concentrate on relaxing.

GENERAL AUDITIONS

General auditions are "set" pieces prepared in advance, usually a monologue or two. Sometimes general auditions are used to screen people for a particular play, and the actual play auditions follow the generals. Frequently, theatres or schools have general auditions just to see new people, when casting for a season, or when selecting actors for degree programs or Equity Candidate internships.

Professional actors always have plenty of monologues and are prepared to do "generals" in almost any situation. Often, general auditions are composed of two contrasting pieces. Sometimes the theatre or auditors will define exactly what they mean by "contrasting"; i.e., a classical piece and a contemporary piece, or a tragedy and a comedy. On the other hand, "contrasting" may be the actor's choice: the selections might be contrasting in period (a Shakespeare and a Simon), or in style (a Noel Coward and a Tennessee Williams), or in content (a comedy and a tragedy). If the audition specifically requests a classic piece, *usually* the auditors are looking for something in *verse*. This could be a verse speech from Shakespeare, a Molière speech translated into verse, or a verse piece from any number of classical plays. If you are requested to do a classical piece, it may be wise to clarify whether or not they want verse by asking, "When you say 'classical', does that mean verse?"

Where to Get Monologues

Where do you get material for monologues? One of the best ways is to see plays, in live theatre or on TV. Watch for the parts that you like and think you could do, keeping a special ear for a longer speech. Then get a copy of the play and find that speech. One of my favorite monologues developed after I saw Diana Rigg in a touring production of *The Misanthrope*.

Many people leaf through plays looking for the long speeches, or they check out a book of monologues that also provides a brief character description and synopsis of the scene. Before choosing a speech from a collection of monologues, consider that hundreds of actors are using the same resource books, and the material presented is probably overused. If you must do one of these monologues, be sure to get a copy and read the entire play.

Here's a professional secret: do a monologue from a play you've done. You will be much less nervous, and you will benefit from all the weeks of rehearsal and direction that you received in the play. Here's another tip: find a play that you like, and a scene you like, and put together a monologue from *dialogue*, using only your character's lines. Often there's no need to incorporate the other character's lines in order to make sense. One of my favorite monologues appeared in a Neil Simon play as dialogue. One day I sat down at the typewriter and wrote out my own lines as a single speech, deleting the other character's lines completely. With no additions or corrections, it worked. I ended up with a terrific and unique monologue that I used for numerous general auditions.

Selecting and Preparing Monologues

What to choose for your monologues? Do your *best stuff*. Do the tried and true monologues that you have studied in class or done in a production over and over. Don't try out new pieces for the first time at important auditions. If you have several monologues to choose from, pick the ones that are most appropriate to the season that you are auditioning for. If you know, for example, that the summer stock company is doing a Molière and an Arthur Miller, then do a French farce and a dramatic American monologue. It isn't necessary to do monologues from the *specific* plays, and often wiser not to. But if you can select something similar in style and period, it often helps.

General auditions are always memorized and "blocked." On rare occasions you may work with a partner, but most often you will be out there alone. You will have to make quite a few decisions on your own. Here are some DON'Ts:

- DON'T wear a complete costume and full theatrical makeup.
- DON'T bring tons of props to use.
- DON'T rely on furniture except the barest essentials such as one or two chairs.
- DON'T introduce your piece by giving the auditors a synopsis of the play or the characters or the scene.
- DON'T bring or use taped music or a sound track.

Your general auditions should work in an office as well as a theatre, and should take a minimum amount of time. The important thing is YOUR WORK. If you rely on lots of extraneous junk, it will just be distracting.

A note about *time*. Often in professional theatre, when general auditions are being held, there is a time limit posted. You must time your piece, preferably before you memorize it (otherwise you may memorize ten minutes when you only need three). Use a watch with a second hand, read the piece through with as much emotion as you can possibly summon, and time it. If it times out too long, cut it before you memorize it. When you have the piece fully memorized, time it again. If you don't, you'll end up going too long because of the time added when you started "acting." Why worry so much about time? Here's why. Because someone at the audition may (honestly) have a stop watch, and they will stop you after the three or five minutes, no matter where you are.

I once did an audition as a partner for someone who was trying to get into the Actors Studio in New York. The entire piece depended on the very last line, which revealed that the character I was playing was actually dead. (It was a "Twilight Zone" kind of scene: Was my character really dead? Was she a figment of the other character's imagination? Was she a ghost?) Needless to say, the scene was too long, we were stopped, and the whole surprise ending went right out the window along with the scene.

And another note about time. Choose to make your piece(s) shorter, rather than longer. Most directors can tell what you can do in one or two minutes. You don't get brownie points for memorizing the longest piece. Spend more time getting a really great piece and working on it than on memorizing a long and difficult one.

Example of a General Audition

Here's how a general audition might go. You come in, and if you are not introduced, you will say, "Hello, I'm Johnny Jones. I will be doing Mercutio from 'Romeo and Juliet', and Hal Carter from 'Picnic'." Then you will "take stage" (find your position), take a moment (but only a moment), and begin. When you take stage, find the light. Many auditions are held in dimly lit theatres, and if you're not in the light, you just won't be seen. If you are doing a general audition that involves two pieces, pause briefly between the first and second, just enough time to let the first piece "sink in," and then proceed directly with the second piece. Again, it is not necessary to set the scene or give any kind of exposition for your second piece. At the end, pause after your final line, "hold the moment" (by freezing for just a second), resume a natural posture (do not bow), and say "Thank you." Then leave, unless you are requested to stay.

Do not comment on your audition, do not apologize if you think you "screwed up." I have seen students do a perfectly acceptable audition, and then make a face, say something like "that was terrible!", or slump their shoulders and slink out. That is not professional and will only hurt your chances.

What happens if you really do screw up? For instance, what do you do if you "go up" (forget your lines)? Here's what professionals do: GO ON. If you have forgotten the line, take a breath, concentrate, and say the next line that you can remember. Chances are, once you get back into it, you'll be OK. It really doesn't matter whether or not you make complete sense. I don't recommend saying "I'm sorry, may I begin again?" If you do that, you're really setting yourself up. You not only will be terribly embarrassed if you "go up" again, but the second time the auditors have already heard some of what you've done and they're bored. If you cannot remember anything, then retrieve your script and use it.

How Do You Get to Carnegie Hall?

This leads me to a general recommendation about generals: practice, practice, practice. Go over your lines during the day, on the bus, in the car, mowing the lawn, doing the dishes. Use your family or friends, your roommate or fellow actors as "audience" and perform it for them. You'd be surprised at how your memory will vanish the minute you have an audience. It is not necessary to get comments or criticism from your audience. Just ask if you can take a few minutes of their time, and don't be embarrassed to do it. (Just think how much more embarrassed you would be if you screwed up at the audition; and if you think you'll be nervous in front of your family or friends, multiply that by ten and you'll have an idea of audition panic.)

Many professional actors will hire an audition "coach." I have worked with several teachers and many directors who are willing to spend the time (in exchange for some bucks) to work with me on my monologues. This may be well worth your money if you are auditioning for something you consider very important. The coach directs your monologues, or simply helps choose pieces and gives notes or comments on the work. Your coach is your audience. Some teachers or directors or qualified friends may even be willing to coach you for free.

Looking at the Auditors

Should you *look* at the auditors? This question will come up more when doing generals than for play auditions, so I'll address it here. Many monologues are written to be delivered to another character on stage with you, so you set up your other character and try to deliver the lines to this imaginary person. However, some plays specifically call for the actor to "break the fourth wall," and address the audience. You'll find this often in Shakespeare plays (in fact, many of the soliloquies or "asides," are intended to be delivered to the audience). Choosing a monologue that is written to be delivered to the audience is great—it gets your face out to the house.

However, in a general audition, a monologue should NOT be delivered directly to the auditors, for two reasons: 1) it is even more difficult for the actor to deliver a speech directly into someone's eyes than simply into a vast sea of faces; and 2) it asks the auditors to become a part of your performance, thereby creating a "dialogue." This will make your auditors uncomfortable *and* take away their ability to judge you objectively. They are so busy being a part of your work that they can't sit back and see it from a distance. Then where do you look? Look out to the house, but not directly at your auditors. Look slightly above their heads or to an empty space right next to them.

Once I did an audition for a very important casting director and thought it would be very clever to "use" her as my other character in my second monologue. I even warned her in advance of what I was going to do. Unfortunately, by the time I got to my second piece, she either forgot or didn't realize exactly what I was up to. I delivered the first line right to her, and she started talking back to me, as though I were just making conversation. This is funny now, but it wasn't then, and I think she was probably terribly embarrassed. After the fact, so was I, and even worse, I've never seen that casting director again.

Accents

Doing accents is fun and challenging for most actors. It helps create the character and adds flavor to the play. In addition, many plays that are written for a specific type, or in a special locale (particularly if the author has a good ear for regional speech) sound better when done with the proper accent. Consider, for example, how important an accent is to a Noel Coward play (British), a Tennessee Williams role (Southern), and many of Neil Simon's funniest characters (New York).

Should you do an accent for an audition? Sure, why not give it a try? Several weeks before the audition, listen to movies or tapes of characters speaking in those accents. (Don't listen to a tape or movie of the exact play you are reading for; you don't need to parrot every line, and you certainly don't want to give a vocal carbon-copy of someone else's performance.) Try to get the flavor and the feel of the accent, including not only words and inflections but also rhythmic patterns. Then try practicing your own lines in the accent. Also, try speaking in that accent all the time—talk to yourself, chat with your fellow actors in that accent. If you have enough time to practice, and begin to get comfortable and even have fun with it, then do it at your audition.

There is an excellent book called *Foreign Dialects*, by Lewis and Marguerite Shalett Herman, which is very helpful with numerous dialects and accents. There are also records and tapes available at some of the specialty theatre bookstores. Many professional actors will spend the time and money to work with an accent coach just for an audition. For example, I have a friend in theatre who is British. Whenever I have an audition for a British play, I call George and we work together for an hour or so. This type of one-on-one coaching is terrific.

When should you do accents? 1) When the play specifically calls for one, meaning that if the play is done as written, and the locale is England or Georgia, etc., then it is safe to assume that all the major characters in the play will have the accent of that locale or region; 2) when the character description leads you to believe they are *from* a locale that is usually associated with an accent, even if nobody else in the play is; and 3) when the casting notice or director has stated that the play will be set in a particular locale that you *know* would require an accent.

This last example can sometimes be confusing. Let's say they are doing a production of Shakespeare's *Twelfth Night*, and the director has indicated that the setting will be turn-of-the-century Barcelona.

Do you do a British accent (because it's Shakespeare) or do you do a Spanish accent (because it's Spain)? When in doubt, ASK. Many of the classics, wherever they are "set," will be done in Standard American Speech, which is the generally accepted speech for most of Shakespeare in the U.S. (Standard American is the speech that most newscasters use—without any recognizable accent, and with excellent diction. Practice and learn it.) Sometimes some of the characters will have an accent, while others will not (example: good guys/bad guys, one family and another, persons from one locale vs. another, etc.).

Many professional actors will think about (and use) an accent when they feel that the character isn't "working," or that the fun of the play or character might be enhanced with an accent. For example, I was auditioning for a summer stock production of a melodrama called *The Torchbearers*. The small role I was reading for wasn't really "fleshed-out" by the author, and I was having trouble getting a sense of her from the few lines in the scene I had to work with. Finally I tried a Judy Holiday doing *Born Yesterday* (ex-chorus girl from Queens). The role immediately came to life and became really fun. I got the part, and the accent gave me a "handle" (touch-off point) for the entire role.

A note of caution: Don't just plaster an accent on a character without doing your homework first. All the work that you do to create a real character and real emotional sense should not go out the window if you are doing an accent. Don't spend all your time perfecting the accent and not doing the acting. Try to get the flavor of the locale and character with the accent, and try to be comfortable enough with the accent that you can forget it while you're concentrating on the really important things. And be careful that your accent is not so "thick" that you can't be understood. It's far more important for your words to be clear than for your accent to be authentic.

About accents in general. Actors should have a variety of accents they can do comfortably at all times. These include for "all-American" types: British (King's English and Cockney), Irish, French, German, and various American regional accents such as Brooklyn, Southern, Midwest, etc. If you have somewhat of an "ethnic look," you might be better off concentrating on accents you would be more likely to use, such as Italian, Spanish, Greek, Arab, and Oriental. (This advice is not meant to discriminate, just to be practical. For example, if you're blonde-haired and blue-eyed, and look generally WASP, the chances of being cast as Italian or Spanish are fairly slim, and vice versa. Know thyself.)

Have fun with accents, practice them (meaning just speak in the accent) when you're *not* auditioning, with fellow actors or friends. Choose to work on characters and monologues that require accents. The more comfortable you are with an accent, the greater your chances of being cast in a variety of roles and the greater your choices when working on different types of characters in numerous plays. Look at the number of characters and accents that a small group of people use in a show like "Saturday Night Live." Wouldn't it be fun to be able to do that?

About your *own* accent. If you are from the South or the major metropolitan area of New York, and/or if you are Black, Asian-American, or Hispanic, you may very well have an accent. If your first language, or the language your parents speak is other than English, chances are you will have a noticeable accent. In addition, if you're from the Midwest or California, your speech will probably have the regional twang, country slang, or nasality common in folks from those areas. Get rid of it. Work with a speech teacher constantly. This is number one priority. You can't expect to be cast in a variety of roles if you have an accent. (See Chapter 5.)

WHO'S WHO AT AUDITIONS

Part of your preparation for auditions may be to find out who is going to be present at the auditions—the director, the casting director, and (if it's a musical) the choreographer and musical director. Sometimes you will see the names posted on the audition call sheet or this information may be available by asking. It would be helpful to know, for example, if the director is someone you've worked with, or someone you'd particularly like to work with. It is *not* absolutely necessary to know who will be watching your audition, but many professional actors make it a point to find out.

When you walk into an audition, you may see several people there. Don't expect to be personally introduced to each one of them, and for heaven's sake, don't go shaking everyone's hand and personally introducing yourself. It just isn't necessary and takes valuable time away from your audition. Here is a list of people who might be watching your audition:

The Director—He or she makes all major decisions regarding the entire production including design, look, style, etc. Because the director has artistic responsibility for the production, he or she usually has the final say about who gets cast.

The Casting Director—In professional theatre, the production or theatre often hires the services of a casting director. These people do the screening of actors to determine who gets to audition, and often confer with the director as to who gets cast.

The Playwright—He or she wrote the script. Needless to say, important established authors don't go running around the country attending auditions. But if you are doing an original (new) work, the author will probably be present. The author usually does not have the final say in casting, but may have "casting approval," meaning if he doesn't like someone picked by the director or casting director, he can "veto" a casting choice.

Composer and Lyricist—If your musical is original, the composer (who wrote the music) and the lyricist (who wrote the words to the songs) may also be present. (In a play that has incidental or background music there may also be a composer, but in this case the composer usually doesn't attend auditions.)

The Choreographer—This is the person who, in musical theatre, stages all the dances. Sometimes there are separate dance auditions. There may also be a choreographer in plays with music, who stages the musical "movement," simple as it may be. In addition, if there is any kind of special physical activity involved in the play, there will probably be a Fight Choreographer, who teaches and stages the moves.

The Musical Director—This person is responsible for how the songs sound in musicals. He or she works directly with the cast (sometimes in separate sessions) to rehearse the singing and vocal production. The musical director will often have a say in casting; i.e., an opinion about who he or she thinks can actually handle the difficulties of a singing role. In a smaller theatre, the musical director may also be the conductor of the orchestra, and/or the pianist (the piano is often the most important and sometimes the *only* instrument).

The above list includes the people who are usually the most influential in making the casting choices. However, there are other important people who may be at your audition, and who may be directly involved in the casting process. They include:

The Producers—They are responsible for making sure the entire production goes on, and that means money. Producers get the funding for a show, and they're also responsible for all production elements such as total budgets for set construction and costumes, advertising and theatre costs. Obviously, producers work closely with directors and designers. On Broadway, producers are called Backers or Angels, and they might do nothing more than send in a check. (In that case, there is an Executive Producer who actually does the work.) In smaller theatres, however, the producer might be the person who owns the theatre, in which case he or she may have a great deal to say about which actors he or she wants to hire.

The Artistic Director—In regional theatre and resident stock companies there is an Artistic Director who is in charge of the entire season. These people run the artistic side of the theatre and work closely with the producers to set the season (choose the plays to be done). Artistic directors often direct one or two plays per season; for the plays they are not directing, they choose the additional directors.

Artistic directors may be directly responsible for casting an entire season in which a resident or repertory company will be utilized. This means that a corps of actors is hired to play most of the major roles in all the shows throughout the season.

Managing Director—This person may also be called the Business Manager or General Manager. Managing directors handle the business end of the theatre, which includes the box office, the "house," scheduling the theatre space (including rental to visiting companies or children's theatre), and hiring theatre personnel, including box office and house managers, subscription sales and publicity people.

To further confuse the issue, various theatres may have different titles for their VIPs, including Producing Director, Managing Producer, Producing Artistic Director, Executive Director, etc. The main thing to remember is that anyone who has a title with Manager, Director, or Producer in it is probably important.

THE APPOINTMENT AND THE INTERVIEW

What to Wear for Your Audition Appointment

Don't go out and find a costume for your audition. But it is always wise to wear something that *suggests* the time period of the play and the type of character you are auditioning for. For example, if the play is set in a time period before 1900, all the women would probably be wearing long dresses, so a woman who shows up in a leather mini just isn't going to "look" right. The dress does not have to be full-length; something that has a nice flow and a decent length will work. For a conservative look, a man can almost always wear a suit, but it wouldn't be appropriate if he's auditioning for Puck in *A Midsummer Night's Dream*, or a blue-collar longshoreman in *A View from the Bridge*. Be inventive with your clothes choices—if you're auditioning for Noel Coward, wear something that suggests the '20s.

A note of caution: don't go too far. Wear a basic outfit that you feel comfortable in and can forget about. Don't use wigs, hats, props, and other stuff that can only get in your way unless you think they're ESSENTIAL to your audition. Another note of caution: some actors will do anything to get cast, and show up for auditions in tight, low-cut, revealing clothes. Don't do this unless you are: 1) auditioning for the part of a prostitute, or 2) you want to give the director the impression that you are "available" for more than the play.

Here's a professional secret: if you have more than one audition in a day and can't get home to change, it is worth it to bring a change of clothes with you. If you need to look very glamorous and "upscale" in one audition, and very casual in another, pack your bags.

Have your clothes all ready, cleaned and ironed, the night before your audition. If you want to do your hair a special way, practice with

it a few times before the day of the audition. You have to be comfortable when you're preparing on the day of the reading. Allow
yourself plenty of time to get dressed and do hair and makeup.

Makeup and Hair

When making your makeup choices, it's important to know
where your audition will take place. If it's in a classroom or small
office, obviously you will not wear as much makeup as if the auditions
are held in a large theatre.

Women should wear makeup that is appropriate for the character. For most ingenues and leading ladies, street makeup is perfectly
acceptable. If you're auditioning for a role like Adelaide in *Guys and
Dolls*, you might want to put on the false eyelashes and rouge to
suggest her character—just make sure you practice wearing them
around the house beforehand.

Women's hair should also be appropriate to the role. If it's a
classical piece, hair is usually worn *up*. A note for both women and
men: there is nothing more distracting than trying to see an actor's
facial expression and eyes through a clump of hair. Get it off your face
and out of your eyes. Even if your character is sloppy, sexy, or super-
hip, you should challenge yourself to find other ways (costume,
stance, makeup, attitude) to express those qualities.

Men will usually not need to wear any facial makeup, even in a
theatre, for an audition. However, if there's a special role that
requires a very different look, and a man wants to try a mustache or
wig to show the director how perfect he can look, that would be
acceptable. For example, a bald-headed man who can sing very well
and is dying to do Curly in *Oklahoma* might enhance his chances if
he wore a really fine wig. Or you might want to add just that element
of villainous "sleaze" for Nicky Arnstein in *Funny Girl* with a
mustache. Again, notes of caution: 1) Be sure you practice with your
wig or mustache well in advance. 2) Your mustache, wig, sideburns,
or whatever MUST BE very good. If it doesn't look completely
natural or if you are not completely comfortable, don't do it.

Warming Up

It is very important to warm up, both vocally and physically, before an audition. This doesn't necessarily mean doing a series of boring voice exercises, or doing an hour of aerobics before your appointment. But getting out of bed and rushing sleepy-eyed to your audition is not wise. Your muscles and voice need to be awake and in condition to meet the physical demands of the theatre. Warming up is also essential in helping control your nerves. Aside from the many excellent vocal exercises you may learn in school and acting class, here are some additional suggestions:

• Sing—Even if this is not an audition for a musical, singing will warm up your vocal cords and give you a much greater range for vocal variety, character work, and accents. An actor I know who does a lot of Shakespeare warms up by singing opera.

• Dance—You do not have to do formal dance warm-ups (unless, of course, you are auditioning for a musical that will require you to dance). All you have to do is turn on a record and do your favorite "moves," whether contemporary break-dancing or old-fashioned cha-cha. Any type of physical movement will loosen you up. One professional I know gets out of the subway a stop early and walks to the audition.

• Read your lines OUT LOUD—If you don't have time to do the whole play, select the scenes you know you will be reading. You cannot warm up "silently, in your head." There is no substitute for doing your lines aloud. This should be done at home, before you get to the audition. It may be the only time you get vocal practice before the audition itself.

Your Appointment Time

There is a saying in professional theatre. "An actor is never on time—an actor is ALWAYS EARLY." It is critical for you to be on time. Better yet, be early. But not too early. Here's why. Theatrical auditions are notorious for running late. But "ours is not to reason why." Many professional auditions I have attended do run late, but often they happen on time, and sometimes they're ahead of schedule. It is very irritating for the auditors to be kept waiting.

At auditions for one Broadway show, an actor was scheduled for the last appointment just before the lunch break. The auditors waited for at least twenty minutes, and they knew WHO they were waiting for. Finally, tired and hungry after a full morning, they went to lunch, which was considerably shortened because of wasted time waiting for the actor. He finally did arrive after lunch, breathless and apologetic, but needless to say, he was not cast. So always start out early for your audition, leaving plenty of time to get lost or stuck in traffic. If you have an emergency and know you are going to be late for a scheduled appointment, at least call the theatre or studio and let them know.

Actually, in the cold, cruel world of professional theatre you would be considered very lucky to *have* an appointment time. In some theatres and schools you get to sign up for the time you want to audition. That's great! Just be sure to make a note of the time you've signed up for on your own calendar. Sometimes theatre personnel remove the sign-up sheets once they're filled.

Frequently, there are no appointment times given. The casting notice will just say "Wednesday 1-5 pm at the Brown Theatre." If this is the case, get there early. You may find yourself standing in a line behind fifty or a hundred other people just to sign up. You may be number 72, in which case you may not be seen for two or three hours. If you can, go away and come back; just be sure to return by the time your number is called. The reason I suggest that you go early is that if you don't want to miss out entirely, you can at least get on the list. If you arrive at 4:30 p.m., you may find that they have already signed up too many people and can't fit you in at all. You should be prepared to audition when you arrive, however. Casting calls are one of the most unpredictable things in the theatre—some that you expect to be packed will not, and others will have people lining up around the block.

There's a saying in the Army: "Hurry up and wait." That's how it is in theatrical auditions. It's very important to realize that this is common, that nothing can be done about it, so get used to it, expect it, and arrange your schedule so that you will have at least a couple of hours, if possible, from your audition time until your next scheduled appointment. Get in the habit of remaining calm and cool and concentrating on your character and your role while waiting. Sometimes you are told with whom you will be auditioning, so you can rehearse the lines with that person. If you wish to do this, always ask your partner beforehand if he or she wants to go through it. Some actors do not like to rehearse in this manner, preferring to "wing it." Please respect that—it will not hurt your audition at all if your partner doesn't want to rehearse.

Some actors wish to remain quiet and alone in the green room or waiting room. Respect that too—you may wish the same for yourself. Others prefer to chat and joke with fellow actors; it sometimes keeps their mind off the audition or their annoyance that the auditions are running so late. If you are one of the "chatters," try to keep the noise level to a minimum, or go into a hallway or other area where it won't be disturbing to other actors. If you are waiting backstage, near the backstage area, or in the audience, of course there will be no talking at all.

The Conflict Sheet/Questionnaire

You may be asked to complete a conflict sheet and/or question-naire when you arrive at the audition. This will include information such as your name, address, phone numbers (critical, both home and work), and other pertinent information the director needs to know.

The *conflict sheet* or conflict section refers to your class or work schedule, which you should complete in full, including any and all work or regular appointments that might *conflict* with the rehearsal or performance schedule. You should write down here all the *necessary* conflicts you would have if you should be cast. Let's say you have a part-time job, and you cannot afford to be in this production unless you can continue to work. You would then write down all your regularly scheduled work times (for example: Monday, Wednesday, Friday 1-6) on the conflict sheet.

On the other hand, if you can afford to take a leave from work and are planning to IF you are cast, don't write this down as a conflict. If you have singing lessons on Wednesdays at 3:00, and they are very important to you, write this in as a conflict. But if you can reschedule the lessons *around* the rehearsal schedule, then don't write it down. Use your head when filling in the conflict sheet.

The *questionnaire* will ask you for specific information such as your name, phone number, and prior experience. You should always fill this in completely; for now, it is your "résumé." Professional actors always have pictures and résumés to leave; however, if you are a student or newcomer it is absolutely not necessary. (Professional pictures and résumés are discussed in more detail in the last chapter. If you DO have a résumé, note on the questionnaire: "Please see résumé, attached.")

On the questionnaire, you would list any and all previous theatre experience. Be as detailed as possible: list the role, the play, and the theatre where it was performed. If you have little or no experience, that doesn't matter. "Experience" may also include any dance, singing, or musical recitals you have performed in. If you are auditioning for a musical as part of the chorus, but have no experience except singing or dancing lessons, list that, i.e., "Voice lessons/two years/with Hilary Brown" or "Ballet & tap/three years/ Singleton Studio."

If you have any special skills, list those. For example, if it's a production of *Barnum*, and you can twirl the baton and/or do acrobatics, don't forget to mention that. If there is a "special skills" section, list anything you can do that is unique or involves a certain talent, i.e., "do a great imitation of Mick Jagger," or "classical piano/ ten years/Bach to Beethoven." Don't use this section to be too inventive, but on the other hand, do let the director know what you can do, even if you think it's outlandish or doesn't apply to this audition. They want to know—that's why they give you a questionnaire.

The Interview

Sometimes your audition will be preceded by an interview. (Your first meeting with the auditors may be nothing more than an interview.) The initial interview is very important, and you should wear exactly what you are planning to wear for your audition. In professional auditions, the actor is often introduced by the casting director. If you are not introduced, it is OK to say, "Hello, I'm Marvin Jones."

If there is an appropriate chair set up for you to sit on, then do so. (This will depend on whether this is just an interview or an interview/audition. If a brief interview precedes your audition, there will probably not be a chair for you.) Be relaxed, but don't be too chummy. Whatever you do, don't ask personal questions of the director and don't talk too much. This is a business appointment, and your primary reason for being there is to allow the casting people and director to see if you're right for anything in their play.

Notice the use of the word "allow." You do not need to convince them or do a "hard sell." On the other hand, don't be a limp rag. Be bright, be interesting, be brief. Try to let them see enough of you to know that you would (a) be a nice person to work with and (b) be aggressive and confident enough to do some creative work. It is not necessary to talk about everything on your résumé or questionnaire—they can see it. Many interviewers do ask about your previous experience, and in that case, feel free to elaborate.

Some actors have a tough time with interviews for two reasons: 1) they are very shy and/or nervous and don't have anything to talk about or 2) they feel that they should be judged by their work, not by their personality (or lack of it). It's important to realize that interviews are often part of the audition process, and actors should learn to be comfortable with them.

If the interview is followed by your audition, take stage, find the light, take a moment (but only a brief moment) to "get into character," and then plunge in.

MUSICAL AND CHORUS AUDITIONS

In musical theatre, how you sing and dance will determine as much as your acting ability whether or not you get cast. Often the singing and dancing auditions are separate from auditions for the "book." You will wear something appropriate to your character, but that you can also comfortably move or dance in. A wise choice is to wear something you could combine with your dance clothes, just in case you are asked to sing again at the dance auditions, or read after your singing auditions. Of course, what you wear may be determined by whether or not you are primarily a singer who dances or primarily a dancer who sings.

You will usually be asked to sing something that shows your range. Though the singing audition may be only eight to sixteen bars, you should memorize and be prepared to sing the whole song. Tape your music together in an accordion-fold, so when it's opened up it is one long single sheet, easy for the pianist to follow. Always bring your music to your audition, handing it to the accompanist as you enter. You may speak briefly with the accompanist, explaining what you're going to do and even humming the tempo. (Warn them if you do something unusual, such as a laugh or scream.) Don't ask the accompanist to transpose—if you must sing the song in another key, have the music written out.

What should you sing? Anything from a musical is usually better than a currently popular song. American musical theatre is unique, with a style of its own. You'll stand a better chance with a song from a musical than if you come in sounding like a nightclub act. If the show is *Jesus Christ Superstar*, something from that show or something by the same composer (Andrew Lloyd Weber), would be appropriate. If it's Rodgers and Hammerstein, you have a lot to choose from. If it's Sondheim, be sure you can handle it.

Sometimes you will be specifically requested to prepare and sing a song from the show for which you are auditioning. In that case, try to arrange to rehearse with your coach or accompanist as frequently and as far in advance as possible. When you go in to sing, have your lyrics written on a separate sheet so that you don't have to peer over the accompanist's shoulder and try to find the words. Practice with this sheet in advance. And do your best.

For the dance section of the audition, wear appropriate dance clothing and shoes. Even if you are primarily a singer, if you are requested to attend the dance audition, wear the proper clothing. (Sometimes just by looking like a dancer, you can carry it off. In addition, you don't want to be tripping over yourself in a long skirt and boots.) By the same token, if you're really a dancer and they request that you sing, give it your best shot. Often there are featured roles in musicals that require a great singing voice or a great dancer, but those people must also be able to perform reasonably well in their weaker area.

If you are primarily an actor who can't really sing or dance, do some research on the musical to see if there are character parts or non-singing roles. There often are. Many times the character roles, even if they have a song, can get by with a fairly awful voice, or talk-singing. Check it out before you dismiss the musical and/or your own abilities.

Chorus Auditions

Anyone who has seen *A Chorus Line* can imagine the anguish of auditioning for the chorus of a musical. These folks are the real troopers of musical theatre, and their performances can make or break the show. Their auditions are heartbreaking and grueling, starting with the old practice of *typing-out*. This is the situation in which several hopefuls are called in at the same time and simply stand in a line. The auditors select which people they want to audition just by looking at them. Some are typed-out (asked to leave, "wrong type"), and the others are the lucky ones who have a chance to audition. It's degrading and demeaning, but sometimes the only way the casting people can get through the hundreds of hopefuls that show up.

You will be asked to sing, often in front of a group of other chorus auditioners, and often only sixteen bars of a song. Pick your best stuff, it's not very much. Professionals often do the section that contains the "money note," which is the note that shows off your voice so well it would sell tickets.

Then you will be asked to dance, but it's not a solo number. A group of people will be shown through the steps by a choreographer, and they have to imitate those exact steps. They're given a couple of times to practice (right in front of the auditors), and then they have to do it in a group *without* the choreographer. Good luck. People actually do get cast in musicals this way, but you've got to be good and you've got to be quick.

DEALING WITH NERVES

Nerves are an actor's worst enemy, but everybody gets nervous before an audition, even the most seasoned professional. The only attack of nerves worse than an audition is opening night. You may as well assume that you are going to be nervous, and learn how to deal with it. Here is a list of how some professionals deal with nerves:

1. Be prepared. The more confident you are, the less nervous you will be.
2. Warm up. Doing your vocal and physical exercises at home, before your audition, will help you feel immensely better. Warming up for singers and dancers is absolutely essential—it will help prevent injuries.
3. Breathe and stretch. Take deep breaths, close your eyes, bend over and touch your toes, do neck rolls and shoulder shrugs, pace around instead of sitting. A teacher I worked with at the Royal Academy of Dramatic Art in London used laughter as a relaxation technique.
4. Chat with others. If you are alone on the day of your big audition and getting nervous, call a friend and just talk. It warms up your voice and your personality, and it relieves tension. At the audition, chatting with other auditioners works for some people; it may work for you. Just be sure that the person you are chatting with doesn't mind, and remove yourselves from others and the auditions. If you find chatting distracts you from your concentration, DON'T DO IT, and don't get roped into talking with others. You will not be considered rude if you excuse yourself, saying, "I'm just going to go over my scene," and walk away.
5. Practice the scene with a partner. Find a place in a hallway, away from others and nowhere near the actual auditions, and read quietly through the scene. You may also find yourself chatting and establishing a rapport with your partner. Don't go so far away that you can't hear your name when called. Again, be sure to ask your partner if he wants to read through it beforehand.
6. Meditate or pray. It is often not advisable to go over and *over* your lines (if the audition is prepared) or over and *over* your scene (if you've had a chance to look at the script). You can calm yourself by doing a quiet meditation in which you boost your confidence (Say, "I'm a good actor") or by praying. My mother advised, "Say a Hail Mary and do the best you can."
7. Read over the scene. If you have not had the opportunity, for whatever obscure reasons, to prepare in advance, spend every

second you have reading over your sides. Do not attempt to read the entire play at this time, but read and study your scene. If you are getting it for the first time, take a deep breath, relax, and read for comprehension. Then look at your own lines. Does this technique help you deal with nerves? Absolutely. You have to concentrate. Even if you have only ten minutes before your audition and you feel that you will be "winging it," read over and make some quick decisions about how you can deliver a terrific audition.

8. Just say no. The worst thing in the world you can do to "loosen up" before an audition is drugs (alcohol is a drug). Drugs will negatively affect your concentration, speech, physical bearing, timing, and emotional state. Combine the drugs with your own adrenaline, and the result might be terrifying. The day of your audition it is highly inadvisable to have any beer, wine, or other alcohol, marijuana, cocaine, crack, amphetamines, or barbiturates. (Of course, I am not condoning the use of any illegal substances under any circumstances.) Professional actors even avoid any alcohol or drugs the *night before*, as well as the day of, an audition or a performance. It is common to have insomnia the night before a big audition, but no great harm will come from a little lack of sleep. It is far better to be tired at an audition than even a little hungover.

THE READING

At last, you are called in to do your reading from the script for the play. With all the time you've probably had to prepare, now is not the time to be surprised. Usually in professional theatre, the casting director, or whoever is running the auditions, will tell you when you are the person "on deck," which means that you will be next *after* the person who has just gone in. If this is not the case, FIND OUT who you will go after. If you have signed up in a particular order, ask around and find out who is just ahead of you, or ask the casting person the name of the person just ahead of you and remember it. That way you will not be shocked when your name is announced. Because you will not be shocked when your name is announced. Because when they call you, it's too late to go to the bathroom, apply lipstick, put on your bow tie, or do anything else.

When you go into the audition, leave your preparation behind. No deep breathing, stretching, or cracking knuckles once you get into the theatre or audition room. In professional readings, the name of the actor is usually announced as he or she enters the room, which avoids the whole issue of formal introductions. If your name is not announced, simply introduce yourself in a general way to the group of auditors.

Using the Sides or the Script

For your reading, should you use the sides or the script? If you have received sides in advance, and you've checked the sides to make sure they are the same as your script, use your own script for the reading. If you haven't received sides in advance, always check the sides or the script that is given out at the auditions—it may not be the same as your script. If their version is different from yours, use theirs.

I arrived at an audition for a Noel Coward play once, and found in looking at their script that it was considerably different from my own. I used their script. (I also got the part.)

Once you're sure your script is exactly the same, it will make you feel a little more secure to use your own script. For example, I always mark my script by underlining my character's dialogue in yellow highlighter, so it's easier to read. Plus, I am more familiar with where the words are in my own script, so I feel more comfortable with it.

Props

Don't use props at auditions. You will be carrying the script, and props will just get in the way. This is particularly true of lit cigarettes, because they can not only be dangerous, you will end up flicking your ashes all over the floor and searching for someplace to put the darn thing out. You can mime the action to the best of your ability, but don't even let that get in the way of your concentration and acting.

Who You Will Be Reading With

In the first round of professional theatre auditions, actors rarely read with other actors. The theatre has a *reader*, a professional actor who reads all the other characters for the actors who are actually auditioning. The theatre may also use a stage manager or ASM (assistant stage manager) to read with the actors. This practice has advantages and disadvantages. The disadvantages are obvious: stage managers are not actors, and their inability to read lines won't help your audition much.

The same is true of readers, even if they are professional— they usually don't "give" too much. (Don't forget, these people are reading the same lines from the same scenes over and over all day. It's a pretty boring job.) In any case, you're not going to get a lot of reaction, or acting, from your reader. Don't expect it.

The advantage of reading with someone other than an actor is that *you* are the only person auditioning at your audition. If the other person reading with you is also being considered for the show, his "hard work" may conflict with your own.

Many theatres do have actors auditioning together, and often you will know with whom you will be reading before you go in. If you can, and want to practice with that person before your audition, fine. If you have a friend who is also at the auditions, and you really want to read with him or her as your partner, don't ask to do so. You might get lucky and be paired with that person, but if not, read with the person to whom you're assigned. Often the director wants you to read with someone specifically to see how you "match up" with them. If you don't think your assigned partner is very good, or you don't get along with him, put that out of your mind. You cannot let personal opinions get in the way of your best performance.

You may walk into an audition and find one person there— the director. And you might be reading your audition scene with that one person. If this is the case, read directly into his eyes as if he were your scene partner. (Many directors were actors before they began to direct—trust them.)

Volume

It is difficult to make generalizations about volume because of the size of the space in which you'll be reading. Of course, you don't need the same volume in an office as you will need in a large auditorium. However, here's one generalization that will always be true: be absolutely sure you can be heard. The one thing an actor owes to himself, the auditors, and the audience is that his words can be heard and understood. It is better to err on the side of being too loud than too soft. There is a tendency today (in theatre and film) to whisper words in an attempt to be "real." Forget that. That is not acting—that's mumbling. Remember the story in the Introduction about the Tony Award-winning actress who missed her chance at a Broadway play because she couldn't be heard? Don't do it.

Reading for a Different Role

You have spent months preparing the lead in a play, really working on it and practicing, only to be asked to read for another, smaller role. Or you had your heart set on doing a role in a play you just love, and now you're asked to read for a completely different play. What do you do? Go for it. This has happened to me numerous times, and it always worked out well.

I once prepared for the lead in an Agatha Christie play, only to be asked to read for a supporting role. Not only did I get the role, I realized later it was more "my type" and infinitely more fun than the leading role. In another situation I thought I would be great as Fanny Brice (the Barbra Streisand role) in *Funny Girl*. (Have I mentioned that I'm not a great singer?) I didn't get it but I was cast as Mama Brice—a tremendous challenge and a show-stealing part, particularly when hamming it up in "Who Taught Her Everything She Knows?".

Don't be disappointed if you're asked to read for another role. The director likes you well enough to think you can do it, and actors don't always know what's best for themselves. We always want to do the lead, when in fact, the lead is not always the best role for us (or even the best role in the show). Trust the director to do his or her job, which is to cast you as you will best fit in the production.

On the other hand, if you have been assigned or requested to read for one role but you really want to read for another role, then it's up to you to ask. Most directors will not refuse. They have no way of knowing that you love the other role and you feel you can do it.

Perhaps you have a certain "look," and the director doesn't "see" you in another role, but you know that you can not only look the role, you have the quality and range to play it. Give the director a chance to see you by reading for it.

Taking the Role

A director once described a great audition as one in which the actor really "took" the role. The actor came in so well prepared, and with such confidence, energy, and enthusiasm, that the role seemed to belong to her the minute she walked in the room. You have to give it your all. You will never embarrass yourself by really going for it and letting the auditors know that you want it. The more you give to an audition, the more the director will *have* to determine whether or not you can actually do the role.

In my experience, there are times in auditions (and in performance) when the role "takes" the actor. By this I mean that the material is so perfect, and the audition so well prepared, that the actor can really be free to "let go," and let the character "happen." This is a very special kind of phenomenon; in sports it's called being "in the zone." If you have done your homework and are able to relax at the audition, you might just find this happening to you. Let it happen and enjoy it. I'm not talking about losing control or concentration. But being "in the zone" can also occur in performance, and when it does, it's great.

This happened to me when I went into an open audition for a production of a Neil Simon play, reading for a character I adored. I really had fun at the audition. I got the job, and only later found out that the role had been cast even before they held the required auditions, but they loved my audition so much that they gave notice to the actress who was supposed to play it and hired me instead.

Auditions are the most stressful situations actors will (almost) ever be in, and they strike terror in the hearts of otherwise brilliant performers. We all have to do them. Try to relax, let go, and enjoy it. This is particularly true if you're doing comedy, but even in a heavy drama your acting will be better if you are relaxed. Concentrate on DOING THE ROLE and DOING THE SCENE. Concentrate on the moment, not on what happens in the end of the scene.

Give to your scene partner, and listen to what he or she is saying. Forget the auditors. Forget what happened this morning. Forget your tension. Forget how high the stakes are and how much you want to impress these people. Forget what a star you will be *if* you get it. Just do it.

CALLBACKS

If you get called back to read again, rejoice! The director liked you and wants to see you again. Some directors have two or more callbacks, and this is common. Don't assume that the director has seen you and doesn't need to see you again. Directors need to match people up with the others they are seriously considering, and they physically need you there. In professional theatre, the auditors are often allowed one audition and *two* callbacks (that's three auditions). After that they have to pay the actors to audition again.

But I know one young man who had auditioned *seven* times for the understudy role in the Broadway production of *Biloxi Blues*. He was finally cast and went on a national tour with the show. I auditioned four times for one Off-Broadway production—I never got it. So if you are frustrated with all these auditions and callbacks, don't let it show.

Remember what you wore to the first audition? WEAR EXACTLY THE SAME THING. Many professional actors are very superstitious about this point, and will duplicate their exact same outfit right down to the lipstick and jewelry, socks and shoes. From the director's point of view, there's a very practical reason for this. He can't possibly remember everyone who came in the first time, so you will help jog his memory by wearing the same outfit. He called you back partly because he liked your "look." You made a good impression in whatever you were wearing, so why mess with success?

What if you're called back for a different role? Wear the same thing. Let's say you were reading for the role of a lawyer, and now they're calling you back for a blue-collar worker. Wear the suit you wore the first time, but take off the jacket, loosen the tie, unbutton the shirt, and roll up the sleeves. Women can drastically alter an outfit with the help of a scarf on the head or around the shoulders, costume jewelry, or different shoes.

There is always the exception. Sometimes the director or casting director will request that you wear something different. I once got a call from the director of a play who thought what I wore for my audition was lovely, but that the author thought the character should wear something a little "stronger" (meaning brighter, more colorful). And a friend of mine was told by one director that she looked "shapeless"—could she wear a dress to the callback that brought out her figure? In a case like this, wear what you're requested to wear. These people are trying to help you.

Professional actors also have superstitions about their callbacks; they say, "Read exactly the same way you did. They liked what you did at the first audition, so why change it?" That's a fine approach. If you've had some time between the first audition and callbacks, and have done some improvements in your performance, then by all means make it better. At a callback you may be lucky to be paired with a better actor who will enhance your performance. On the other hand, maybe your new scene partner isn't as good; try to make your audition even better in spite of that.

Finally, there is sometimes the feeling among the actors that the director and other auditors are somehow AGAINST them. This couldn't be further from the truth. I've sat in at auditions on the "other side of the desk" (usually as a reader), and I know that directors are dying to find the right people. They are delighted when the actors do well. They are really pulling FOR you, because they want a good cast. It doesn't matter what your experience is or how many credits you have; if you give a good audition, they will love you. And when the role is right, they will cast you.

Dealing with Rejection

Theatre folks joke about the stereotypical director's "Don't call us, we'll call you." (It's laughter through tears. It's also true.) Not only should you NOT CALL, don't sit by the phone waiting. In most professional situations, the actors never receive a call, even one that's a "No, thanks." Unless someone specifically says they will let you know one way or the other, don't count on hearing from them.

Go out and get yourself another audition.

On the other hand, if the results of the auditions are posted, always check the callboard, even if you think your audition was terrible. You never know.

Everybody gets rejected, even the best actors, so you might as well get used to it. Often the person who is cast is someone you consider to be not as good as yourself. Hold onto that thought. I often think to myself, that "if the director didn't see me in the role, then I don't want to be doing it." You might be a better actor than the person who was cast, but directors have their own ideas. And they're not always looking for the *best* actor. They are looking for the best combination of acting, looks, type, an "indefinable quality," and someone who will match up with the rest of the company. If you have done your best, your consolation prize is simply knowing that.

Another consolation (if you're looking for one) is that directors *do* remember actors who give great auditions. They will call you in for something else, and probably cast you when they can. A good audition is NEVER WASTED.

2
The Rehearsal Process: Read-Through to Preview

A PROFESSIONAL APPROACH TO REHEARSAL AND MEMORIZATION

Before the First Rehearsal

OK, so you got that magic call and you're cast. What do you do between the time you get the role and the time you go into rehearsal? For one thing, if you haven't already, get a copy of the script, making sure you have the correct edition or translation and (are you ready?) *read the play*. The theatre will usually provide you with a copy of the script once you are cast, but if they don't have them, invest the money and get your own copy.

Yes, read for comprehension, for the story, not just your own lines. Read all the stage directions. You may or may not be doing those directions, but it will help you get an idea of some of the actions required. Determine whether or not you will be using an accent or a character voice. Try to get a sense of the style of the piece, and look for places where there might be special business. Start thinking about who your character is, how that character looks, walks, talks.

Memorization

After you have read the play and have an idea of what's happening, you can begin work on your own role. Many actors mark their own lines in yellow (or another light color) highlighter. Then you can go ahead and memorize the lines. Gosh, you say, before rehearsal even starts? Yes, before rehearsal even starts. Professionals go into rehearsal with most of their lines down. They carry the book and mark for blocking, but they know the lines.

Admittedly, professional actors may have three or four weeks between the time they are cast and the first day of rehearsal. I realize that in many theatrical situations there is often little or no "lead time." You get cast, and a few days later you go into rehearsal. If this is the case, spend those few days concentrating and working as hard as you can on memorization.

Some actors object to this thinking for several reasons: 1) they can't really memorize until they get the blocking; 2) they don't know how the director will want them to deliver the lines (the emotional sense) and therefore they don't want to memorize until they get into rehearsal; or 3) they think the play will probably be cut and don't want to memorize lines that may not be there. These are just silly excuses.

For one thing, you can memorize without necessarily having the blocking. Once you get the blocking, you have two things to memorize: the blocking *and* the lines. One will not help you with the other. You don't need to have a complete emotional sense to memorize lines. Also, relying on what the director will "give" you isn't doing your job; you have to come in with something in order for the director to lead you one way or the other. Directors, no matter how much help they may be, still can't learn your lines for you. If your initial emotional sense is changed by the director, fine. You will find it easy to take the direction and do it many different ways if you have the lines firmly in your mind.

There's a theory that the human mind is like a computer. Memorization is nothing more than getting those lines into the database, so that they can come back to you easily. The more work you devote to memorization, the more time and effort and concentration you can spend on the emotional sense and the acting. Lines are absolutely essential. You can have great acting ability and wonderful feelings, but if you don't have the lines the play goes right down the tubes. Many an actor has experienced memory loss during rehearsals when things start to really "click" emotionally because the brain is trying to do too many things at once; the more emotion we put into the words, the more likely we are to forget the lines. Concentrating on memorization will ensure that no matter what is happening emotionally, the lines will be solid.

Another point about memorization. There are tons of things in a theatrical performance to remember besides lines: blocking, costumes, bits, props, and director's notes. Give yourself a break. If you can get one of these elements down early, you're ahead of the game. Here's another point: it's extremely difficult to memorize under pressure. The closer you get to performance, and the more stress there is, the more difficult it will be to concentrate. Don't forget that in rehearsal you've got a "mini-audience" (the cast) and a director watching; even if you have the lines at home, you'll find they're gone the minute you get up in front of real people. And if you think these real people cause stress, imagine what happens to your feeble brain on opening night when the house is packed. Memorize when you have ONLY ONE THING to do, when you have no audience, when you are relaxed, before you get bogged down with other things.

At least twice that I can recall I've come into a rehearsal with my lines down cold, only to find out that the first rehearsal would be "marking the cuts." Out went many of my (memorized) lines, my gems. So what. It was a heck of a lot easier for me to get rid of some lines I already knew than to start learning all my lines from scratch. The missing lines only bothered me from an ego standpoint; they didn't interfere with my performance.

A Memorization Method

Usually I begin memorization with nothing more than the script. I study the lines quietly and get them into my head, then try to go through them one at a time, word for word, to make sure I have the individual lines correct. This is important. Your first memorization is no time to "just get the sense," because that's what you'll end up with. Do not paraphrase, ever. Get the line right, exactly as written.

Once you have individual lines down, you can begin to string them together. At this stage I use an index card on my script, covering my lines but revealing the cue lines. This way you can double-check each line for accuracy immediately after you say it. Some actors rope friends and/or family into cueing them while they are trying to memorize lines. If you do that, be careful. Make sure you have the whole script (or at least a big chunk) well studied and memorized, and don't ask for too much time too often. Actors get so involved they will work a thing to death. But patience runs thin for the cuer, and you will rarely find your kind of dedication in others. This method also takes away the fun (for the helper) of seeing the show for the first time. Note: If you ask someone to cue you, ask for corrections if you paraphrase.

Once I have a long scene or an act pretty much memorized, I start to use my most reliable memorization friend: a small portable tape recorder. I take a couple of uninterrupted hours to record all the cues (all the *other characters' lines*) on the tape, leaving blank space (recorded silence) wherever my lines come in. I leave enough space to do my lines relatively slowly, so that if I have trouble, the tape recorder will give me a little extra time to remember the line or to correct myself when I am first starting to memorize. Later, this little extra time allows for emotional pauses (when I'm well into rehearsal and adding the acting).

This tape is wonderful to have, because you can also use it in your Walkman® or your car, making good use of your time wherever you are and not disturbing anyone else. (Anyone who sees you thinks you're nuts, that's all.) You can use this tape from the minute you start to memorize to the last performance.

Using this method serves another purpose: learning your cues. I've never heard anyone mention that they have to go home and work on their cues. I don't understand why. Actors must memorize their lines *and their cues*. If you don't know the cues, you don't know when to talk. Nothing is more irritating than working with someone who is always jumping on your lines because they know *what* they say next, they just don't know *when* to say it. Your tape will help you memorize your cues because you will *hear* them every time you practice with it.

After I've made my tape, I go back to working on the play line by line and scene by scene. I always try to work quietly and alone, using just the script and the index card method first. When I feel really confident that I know the lines of a whole section or scene, I work it with the tape recorder. Then I turn off the recorder and work the next scene. Every time I learn a scene I go back to the beginning of the tape and run everything I've previously memorized.

Don't try to do too much at once. If you try to work too fast, it will all be gone the next day. Do just one scene or one monologue a day. And always go back to refresh your memory on the parts you think you already know.

One of the standard "in" jokes of professional theatre is that after a tremendous performance, some excited audience member will come backstage and gush, "How did you ever memorize all those lines?" Most professionals know that the line memorization is the very *least* of their performance. Learn to memorize early and easily, and get on to the important things.

At Rehearsals

Those infamous two maxims of the theatre we talked about in the section on auditions also apply to rehearsals: "An actor is never on time, an actor is always early" and "Hurry up and wait." Actors should plan to arrive at the rehearsal hall well before "call" time (the time rehearsal is scheduled to begin, or the time you are supposed to arrive). You can get yourself a cup of coffee and schmooze a little with your friends prior to rehearsal, but you must be on time.

"Hurry up and wait" is unfortunately what happens in rehearsal. Good directors call cast members only for their own scenes, and try like crazy to stick to the schedule. But don't count on it. Acting and directing are creative processes—it's extremely tough to maintain a rigid timetable. Rehearsals for even the simplest plays are complicated in terms of scheduling—plays with crowd scenes and musicals are almost impossible. Use this sitting-around time to look at your lines, mark blocking in detail, and go over notes (yours and the director's) from previous rehearsals. Don't count on waiting time to learn your lines—it's usually too noisy and busy.

Bring your script to every single rehearsal, even after your lines are memorized. You will need it to make blocking changes and add notes. You will also want to go over your lines. You would be surprised how many lines are incorrectly memorized or (in a monologue) totally forgotten. Bring a *pencil* to every rehearsal and mark your blocking and other notes (such as direction, emotion, props) in pencil. Never use a pen. Blocking tends to change— frequently. It's so much easier to erase than to cross out indelible ink. Acting scripts have limited space to make notes. You will have to make the very best use of it.

Rehearsal Spaces and Markings

Rehearsals take place in rehearsal halls, rarely in theatres; there is usually another show's set in the theatre or they're busy building the set for your show. Rehearsal "halls" may be classrooms, lobbies, lofts, basements, dance studios, small auditoriums, or people's living rooms.

If you're in the same place for most of your regular rehearsals, the floor should be marked with masking tape to indicate where the walls, stairs, doors, and outer limits of the stage are. Large pieces of furniture such as couches, chairs, and tables may have been pulled from storage so you'll have some sort of furniture. Sometimes three folding chairs will represent a couch, a cardboard box might be an end table, a hat rack might be a standing lamp.

Use and respect your rehearsal space. Study it. It's the best you will have to work with until the real thing comes along.

Rehearsal Discipline

It is essential for actors to be quiet when they are in the rehearsal hall and rehearsal is taking place. If you are not in the scene that is being worked, go to another room or elsewhere to talk or run through your lines. People cannot concentrate when there is extraneous noise. Also, the director or stage manager will get angry and yell at you if you talk during rehearsals.

If you're in the scene and the director is directing someone else, keep quiet. Don't start goofing off with a friend. Pay attention—you may be brought into the discussion at any time. Have some respect for the director and your fellow actors. Your director may be very relaxed and informal, but you must still maintain a professional atmosphere at all times. Directors get very upset, and rightfully so, when their actors are disruptive, noisy, or inattentive.

When run-throughs begin, you must be aware of where your scenes occur and be prepared to go on. Don't be wandering around the halls or (worse) down in the cafeteria getting coffee. There is nothing more irritating to the stage manager than to have to stop to find some actor. When you are "on deck" be there, be prepared, be quiet. Even if the director is stopping the scene ahead of yours and giving notes, don't assume that you can "take a break." When the signal is given to resume, you are expected to be ready and waiting.

WHO'S WHO IN REHEARSAL

Most of the people who attended your audition (see Who's Who at Auditions) will be at the rehearsals, though not all of them all the time. Of course you will expect to see the director and there may be an assistant director. The casting director will not be present at rehearsals; his or her job is done once the play is cast.

Often the costume designer, lighting designer, and set designer attend early rehearsals. In a musical, you will see the choreographer and the musical director, plus a rehearsal pianist. If the play requires accents, there may be an accent coach at one or several sessions. Others who might drop in from time to time include VIPs such as the producer, the artistic director, the business manager, the company manager, and the press agent.

On the first day you will, of course, meet the rest of the cast. I find it helpful to write down their names on the script next to their characters' names. It is wise to do this immediately (though surreptitiously), when you can still remember their names. Some of these people will not be called at the same rehearsals as you are, and you may not see some of them again until run-throughs begin.

Be sure to write down the names *and phone numbers* of the stage manager and assistant stage manager (ASM). If you need to get in touch with anyone, it will primarily be these folks. You may also want to jot down the names of prop and costume people who are at the first rehearsal. Hopefully, there will soon be a *contact list* passed out, which lists all the actors' names, local addresses, and phone numbers, in addition to contact numbers of the stage manager, ASM, and company manager.

Besides the director, the one other person who will attend all rehearsals and who is essential to the production is the **Stage Manager**. Literally "Manager of the Stage," he or she oversees everything that happens on stage during the performance. Stage managers really run the production, and it's important for you to know who they are, to respect what they do, and to follow their directions. They have their authority straight from the top—the director.

The stage manager keeps the *master script*, which is a copy of the script, usually pasted up on 8 ½ x 11 paper (to add margin space), and placed in a three-ring binder. The stage manager writes in the margins all blocking and business, light and sound cues—everything he or she needs to run the production. From tech rehearsals on, the stage manager actually "calls" the show: with the master script, he or she cues lights and sound, actors and crew. At this point, the stage manager will usually be located in the "booth," which may be a fancy soundproof glass-enclosed room located at the back of the theatre above the audience, or may be a podium and stool backstage.

During rehearsals, if you have a real problem remembering your blocking (or if you can't decipher your own writing), the stage manager should have it noted. When you get *off book*, it's the stage manager (or assistant stage manager) who is "on book." Your SM is also the major conduit between actors and crew personnel—for any communication you have with the crew, contact the stage manager first.

In rehearsal, the stage manager is the director's "right-hand man" or woman. He or she helps the director by calling the actors to attention, scheduling the breaks, getting the actors "back in" after breaks, making the calls during performance, and coordinating schedules for the director, the cast, and the crew.

If you are going to be late for rehearsal or if you have a conflict, it's the stage manager you will call, or if your call time is changed, the stage manager will call you. The stage manager's job is enormous, so don't make it more difficult by giving him problems such as being late for rehearsals or entrances, forgetting your blocking, or making noise backstage.

The stage manager may have an **Assistant Stage Manager** ("ASM"), who helps the stage manager in all job functions and also fills in when he or she is not available for rehearsals. For example, the ASM may be assigned to "make the calls," (half-hour, etc.). Your ASM should be regarded with the same respect you give to the stage manager.

In professional companies, there may also be a **Production Stage Manager**. On Broadway and in larger theatres, the PSM oversees the stage management crew, including the show's stage manager and ASM. In rep theatres and summer stock, for example, the PSM will be on staff for the entire season, whereas individual stage managers may be "freelanced-in" (hired for just one or two shows). The PSM may or may not be present at rehearsals, and usually does not run the show. While you may not be dealing directly with a production stage manager, you should know what he or she does.

In production companies, regional theatre, and resident stock, there is also a **Company Manager**. This is the person who coordinates everything for the company members, from scheduling flights in and out of the city and arranging to pick up actors at the airport, to providing transportation around town, making sure housing meets standard requirements, creating local maps, etc. If you are cast in a show "on the road," the company manager will provide you with the information and amenities you need to help make your stay in another city comfortable. The company manager will not attend rehearsals, but will usually be available to the cast members. Often company managers work in the theatre office and (in smaller theatres) may be doing a variety of other jobs besides looking after the actors.

In addition to the stage management, there will be some crew people at rehearsal to assist with the technical aspects as your rehearsals progress. One of the most important is the **Property Master**. *Props* include all the myriad little things on the set that are used or moved around in the show, and all the things the actors carry around and use. Typical props are drinking glasses, silverware, table linens, cigarette boxes, magazines and books, guns, candles, etc. *Personal props* (used by actors) might include pipes, cigarette holders, canes, handkerchiefs or eyeglasses.

Also within the realm of the property department may be costume pieces that fall under the general heading of props by virtue of their needing to be pre-set or struck from the stage (example: hats, gloves, shawls, coats, capes). If these items are simply worn by the actor from start to finish, they are considered costumes. If a hat gets left on stage, or a coat needs to be pre-set, it becomes the responsibility of the props department.

THE FIRST REHEARSAL, READ-THROUGHS, AND DISCUSSION

The first rehearsal will begin with introductions of cast and crew and other theatre personnel, which was discussed in Who's Who at Rehearsal. Next, the stage manager or company manager offers general orientation and house rules, and other pertinent business will be taken care of. At this time you may be given a "due date" for your *bio*, which is a short summary of your theatre experience for the program (see Chapter 3).

The director will then take over, and frequently the first piece of business is showing the "model set." This is the set designer's miniature reproduction of the set created with balsa wood and matchsticks, painted and trimmed, complete with small-scale furniture. Many model sets I have seen are fascinating and beautiful —they look just like little doll houses. Meticulous set designers even place tiny little people in the model set to give an accurate sense of the relative scale of objects.

The set designer or the director will explain where the entrances are, where platforms and steps are, where furniture will be placed. The stage manager may then explain how the rehearsal space as marked matches up with what is on the set. If this is a Production (Broadway) contract, or otherwise well-established theatre, you may be shown sketches of the costumes (*renderings*), which have been drawn by the costume designer—swatches of the actual material to be used are sometimes attached to the sketch.

Sooner or later you'll get down to business. The director may begin by talking a bit about his or her approach to the play. Most read-throughs are informal, with the cast sitting around a large table. When you actually begin the read-through, take it seriously. Some actors feel that the read-through is "just a reading." Absolutely not. The director is looking for as much emotional sense as you can possibly bring to this first reading—accent, character, and all. It is not necessary to have full volume, obviously, but aside from that you should try to interpret your role as completely as you can. You will not be moving around at the read-through, but you can certainly use gestures, and attempt to look toward (if not *at*) scene partners.

If you have memorized your lines, don't let it show—it's not appropriate in this setting. Keep your book in hand at least until after the play is blocked. You'll need it to take notes and mark stage movement. (You also don't want to offend other actors who may not be as prepared as you are.)

After the first read-through, the director may open up discussion of the play, inviting actors to throw out ideas on elements of style, character relationships, and theme. If you have a generous rehearsal period you may spend more than the first day doing read-throughs and discussion. In one repertory company on a three-week (full-time) rehearsal schedule, we spent an entire week sitting around the "talk table."

In addition to general orientation, the traditional read-through, and discussion (depending on your allotted rehearsal time), at the first rehearsal you may also get the French scene breakdown and/or cuts in the script.

French Scenes

French scenes are derived from neoclassic French drama, in which every time a character entered or exited, it was called a new scene. Today's plays are divided into large acts, so using French scenes helps break the play into smaller rehearse-able scenes. The French scene breakdown is usually done by the stage manager or director. Considerate directors use French scenes in order to arrange rehearsals so that only the people who are in the scheduled scenes (as opposed to the entire scene or act) may be called.

French scenes are usually designated by a number following the act and scene number: hence, Act 1, Scene 2, French Scene 3 would be denoted as I:2,3. When you are given the French scene breakdown, mark your script carefully with the appropriate numbers as dictated—you have to know whether or not you're in the scene. Often the stage manager will provide the cast with a French scene breakdown, which will list the act, scene, and French scene numbers and the characters involved in each.

Cuts

In longer scripts, particularly Shakespearean or other classical pieces, it is not unlikely that the director will make cuts. Take them down exactly as dictated; the first rehearsal is not the time to protest. However, if you are heartbroken, or if you strongly disagree because you feel the cuts destroy the sense of your character, it is possible to approach the director with your own ideas.

In one of my forays into Shakespearean theatre, a great deal of my role was cut. Fortunately, the director had scheduled individual rehearsals for his principal players. When my turn came to work alone with the director, we sat down and talked about the cuts. I had really worked on the script, and instead of using the director's cuts (which were simply large sections of speeches), I offered an alternate script that cut the same number of lines, just in different places. He bought it. If you are going to protest the cuts, it would be wise to suggest "alternate cuts," rather than just insisting that all your lines be reinstated. Directors simply have to make cuts for time, and they don't like it any more than the actors do. You will have to learn to accept this.

In a show I did at Syracuse Stage, we received cuts from the first rehearsal right through until production week. I will admit it got to be a little frustrating, not to mention confusing. There was, naturally, some protest from the actors affected by the cuts, but generally they were taken with good grace. The result was a tighter, shorter, admittedly better play.

BLOCKING TERMS AND GUIDELINES

Terms

Once you are finished with read-throughs and discussion, you will start blocking. Blocking is the stage movement in plays, and in musicals it is the general movement that is not choreography. Blocking rehearsals are usually time-consuming, but good blocking is critical to the success of the play.

Almost everyone who has done a play has learned very quickly the basics of stage movement. The following terms are based on traditional blocking for proscenium stage. In proscenium, the set is composed of three walls, and the action of the play is viewed by the audience through the "fourth wall" (where the front curtain is).

Here is a general overview of the terms you will hear during blocking and throughout rehearsals:

Enter and Exit—These terms are used only when the actor actually comes on from the backstage area and goes off stage. You will enter and cross, and all other movement on stage will be referred to as "crossing." You won't "exit" from one room on stage to another—the exit is reserved for going offstage. *Exeunt* is the Latin plural of "exit," meaning "they go out."

Stage Right, Stage Left, Center Stage—As the actor faces the audience, stage right is to his or her right, stage left to the left, center stage is in the middle. Note: In some European countries stage right and stage left may be just the opposite of ours. Britain uses "Prompt" (SL) and "Opposite Prompt" (SR), noted in scripts as "P" and "OP." Heidelberg has the most unusual designations of all: "Neckar seite" and "Schloss seite," meaning "the side of the river" and "the side of the mountain."

Upstage, Downstage—As the actor faces the audience, upstage is behind him, away from the audience, toward the back wall of the set; downstage is towards the audience. The terms upstage and downstage derive from a literal usage: stages were once commonly *raked*, which means they were built on a slant for better audience viewing. The stage was highest at the point farthest away from the audience and gradually sloped down towards the house.

Two directives are usually combined, e.g., upstage left, downstage right, upstage center, etc. Here's a simple chart of the basic stage areas:

	AUDIENCE	
DOWNSTAGE LEFT	DOWNSTAGE CENTER	DOWNSTAGE RIGHT
STAGE LEFT	CENTER STAGE	STAGE RIGHT
UPSTAGE LEFT	UPSTAGE CENTER	UPSTAGE RIGHT
	BACK WALL OF SET	

Crossing and Countering—An actor's movement on stage is called crossing. Thus you may hear: "Cross downstage left," which simply means that's where you move to. *Countering* is an abbreviation of Counter-crossing; it means that the actor will move in an opposite direction to another actor. If you are requested to "counter downstage center," the move will primarily be to balance the stage relative to the other actors. You may be requested only to "counter" (without being given a specific place to go), which all professional actors understand as finding the best place on stage to balance the picture.

Shared Scenes/Profile—When you're working with only one other person on stage you will be "sharing the scene." It is critically important to be "on a line" with your fellow actor during shared scenes. Draw an imaginary line exactly parallel to the edge of the stage (in proscenium only). Both of you will be working on exactly the same line; hence, the audience will see two "profiles." Many amateur actors unconsciously upstage their partners during what is supposed to be a "shared scene." Don't do it. (See upstaging, below.)

Opening Up, Full Front, Taking Stage—These terms refer to getting your body or face out to the house. Opening up indicates that you should share your face/body with the audience more; full front means deliver it straight out to the house. The directive *take stage* gives you the liberty to move around the entire stage as you see fit to dominate the action and get focus. Taking stage amidst a group of your fellow actors will generally only be suggested for a scene or monologue in which you are supposed to be the center of attention. ("Take stage" can also be used in a more general sense to mean simply go on stage—or take a position as though you were on stage —and grab focus. See Auditions.)

Cheating—Cheating is not a derogatory term. It simply means that you move your body or face a bit so that the audience can see you better or so you'll be in a better position on stage. Cheating can refer to blocking movement or to the position of your body. In blocking, if you're asked to cheat, it means moving your body very slightly (and somewhat surreptitiously) in order to balance the stage picture, to make room for another actor or actors, or to give focus.

Cheating can also refer to the position of your body or face: cheating out means turning slightly towards the audience; cheating up means upstage; cheating away or toward refers to turning slightly away from or towards the action. The director will generally specify what type of cheating is needed; e.g., "cheat upstage" would mean move your whole body; "cheat your face upstage" would mean turn your face only; "cheat your body" would mean turn the body upstage but don't change your position.

Upstaging—Upstaging is a cardinal sin in professional theatre. The term refers to taking focus away from where it belongs. If you are literally upstaging someone, you are standing so far upstage from them that the audience will see only the actor's backside. In a shared scene you may be only an inch or two upstage of your partner, but you are still upstaging because your partner must face away from the audience to look at you.

Upstaging can also refer to doing bits or business, crossing or moving so that you inappropriately steal focus. Interestingly, this type of upstaging is also called *stealing focus*. You can also "upstage yourself," which is stupid. If the director tells you you're upstaging yourself, it means you are looking or facing upstage too much and should cheat out, open up, or move.

Turning Up, Giving Focus—Turning up tells you to purposely face away from the audience towards an upstage action; giving focus will require that your body and attention go entirely to the actor or action that should be the center of attention. Turn toward the action, look at it, and don't be doing anything else.

Shtick, Bits, Business—These terms refer to a special piece of on-stage action. Shtick is a bit of funny business. A bit is a little piece of stage business. Business is a defined piece of action. Sometimes these terms are used interchangeably.

Thrust and Arena Stage Movement

Stage directions can become very complicated if you are performing in thrust stage or arena stage productions. In thrust stage there is a back wall, but the entire stage "thrusts" out, with the audience on three sides. In arena stage (or theatre-in-the-round), the stage is in the middle of the auditorium, with the audience surrounding it on all sides.

Most directors give blocking in the vocabulary of traditional stage movement as noted above. Generally, for thrust and arena stages there is more movement, and it's usually more fluid than proscenium blocking, for the simple reason that you will *always* be blocked from someone in the house. You have to keep moving in order to share yourself with most of the audience. The single most important thing to keep in mind when playing thrust and arena stages is to "play the diagonal." Instead of facing your fellow actor straight on, you will move slightly to his left or right shoulder. That way you won't be blocking each other from the section of audience you are each facing.

Marking Blocking

As you are given blocking, jot it down quickly with pencil in your book, right next to the line on which you move. Using a large book (like the master script) or a separate notebook is not recommended—it's cumbersome and confusing. Some directors move very fast, so be prepared to take quick notes while you are walking and saying your lines. Use the following abbreviations:

Cross—X
Stage Areas
    Downstage Right—DSR
    Downstage Left—DSL
    Center Stage—CS
    Downstage Center—DSC
    Upstage Center—USC
    Upstage Right—USR
    Upstage Left—USL

When marking blocking try to be as specific as possible. Place yourself in relation to the furniture, the set, and other actors. For example, if you are directed to move downstage left to the right side of a chair, that's exactly what you should note: "X DSL to R of chair." Don't forget to write down what you do when you get there. Do you stand by it or sit in it? (Crossing to a couch or chair does not necessarily imply that you do sit.)

Let's say, for example, there are two chairs downstage right, and you are directed to cross and sit in the chair on the left. You mark in your book "X to SR chair." You see how murky this will be at the next rehearsal? Which chair? Stand or sit?

If you are directed to sit on a couch, note exactly where on the couch you are, i.e., "sit SL on couch." If there are two small couches together note which couch, i.e. "sit SL on SR couch." If you are given bits or business with costume pieces or props, write it down specifically: "take off hat, put DS end of hall table."

Obviously, it's going to be difficult to take very exact notes if the rehearsal is moving swiftly. Though it is perfectly appropriate to take a short moment to jot down your blocking, you don't want to hold up rehearsal constantly by stopping everyone to say, "I have to write this down." So here's a professional tip. After your scene has been blocked, and you are either offstage or on a break, sit down and go over the scene in your head (or if the stage is clear, on stage). Write down carefully and clearly everything you remember. I usually take quick, sloppy notes during blocking rehearsals, then when I'm going over it in detail I erase those notes and replace them with very exact, detailed, readable notes that I can follow at the next rehearsal.

Blocking Guidelines

1. Level of Performance —You will not be expected to give a full-out performance during blocking rehearsals. But neither should you just walk through it, mumbling your lines. That is absolutely unprofessional. Try to use the blocking rehearsal to give as much of a performance as you can. You will help yourself by getting ideas and stimulating the director to give you ideas if you are really working.

A great deal of blocking will come out of your character—if you're not playing it, you'll end up with moves that don't feel right later on when it's too late to change. In addition, lots of bits and business will be suggested by the kind of performance you're doing, the kind of character you're playing. If you're just "marking it" you won't get the full benefit that you derive from truly playing the scene. If your character isn't alive, and if you don't bring some spontaneous ideas into the rehearsal, the director will just move you around like a stick. At the same time, you should also be aware of the confines of blocking rehearsals. Most professional actors keep the volume down a bit, so that they can hear the director, who will constantly be stopping and starting. In addition, you will probably be holding back a little emotionally. If you are totally and completely involved in *playing* the scene you'll resent being stopped all the time. So find a happy balance, and use what works best for you at this level.

2. Use the Upstage Hand—When you are directed to do something with your hand, you should almost always use the upstage hand (the one closest to upstage), rather than the downstage hand. Let's say you're standing stage right, smoking a cigarette. As you face center stage, the upstage hand is your left hand, so use that one to hold the cigarette and smoke it. Using the upstage hand will open you up to the house; using the downstage hand will block your face from the audience.

3. Cross on Your Own Lines—Generally you will cross or move on your own lines, and not on someone else's. There's a good reason for this: moving takes focus. So if you're speaking and crossing at the same time you are pretty much guaranteed to have the audience's attention. It follows that crossing on someone else's line usually steals focus. If *you* have input into the blocking process, cross on your own lines. On the other hand, if you are directed to cross when someone else is speaking, do so; some directors feel that it's perfectly OK to ignore this "rule." (Note: Crossing on another actor's line is not the same as "countering," described in blocking terms.)

Blocking: Whose Job is it Anyway?

I have heard that some directors block the entire play prior to the first rehearsal and dictate it to the actors. Some actors even feel that this is the director's job and expect it. On the other hand, most of the many fine professional directors I've worked with do no blocking beforehand at all.

I did a production once in which the director had not blocked the show prior to rehearsals. His leading man, a veteran actor with more than twenty years of professional experience, expressed to a fellow actor that he was extremely disappointed and had "lost faith" in the director because "he had not done his job." Actors who feel like this are only hurting themselves.

Throughout most of my professional experience the director has *not* blocked the show. At Hudson Guild, an Off-Broadway theatre in New York City, I had the pleasure of working with Craig Anderson, a brilliant director. He never gave blocking, and at one point late in rehearsal, I blurted out in frustration that I thought maybe I should move on a particular line, maybe not, what should I do? Craig calmly replied, "Mary, whatever makes you feel most comfortable."

Most often the director hires a bunch of good actors and encourages them in the early blocking rehearsals to "stumble through it." If the actor has read the stage directions as well as the script, he or she will find numerous crosses and moves that are necessary and/or logical. For example, the stage direction might say "crosses to bar and mixes drink," followed by the line, "Well, here's to us." Who couldn't figure that out? The actor is obviously going to have to get to the bar, mix a drink, and toast before he says the line.

Another reason directors sometimes don't give blocking is that they want to see what comes out of the actor's instincts as he or she is playing the character. This may seem like a terribly undisciplined and chaotic way of getting the blocking, but if actors are professional and cooperative, it can often be easier than the director plastering his ideas on them without giving them a chance to "feel it out."

A director I worked with frequently not only never did blocking, he didn't believe in preliminary read-throughs. We'd arrive at the first rehearsal and he'd say "OK, let's do this play." The blocking was always good and his shows were always successful. Of course, we only had a week to rehearse, he hired professional actors, and he trusted them to do their work. If we hadn't read the play prior to rehearsal and done our homework, we were all in trouble.

Often in professional theatre, blocking is a concerted effort, a combination (or compromise) of actors' instincts and director's ideas. The director will see what the actors are doing and make suggestions as they go along. If you have a director who works this way, have fun and enjoy the process. Naturally, this type of work assumes that the actor will come into rehearsal with some ideas of when and where he enters, to whom he is speaking, where he needs to go, and the emotional sense of the character and the scene. *Do your homework.* The more you can give to the blocking rehearsals, the more the movement will be "your own" and flow naturally from your character.

Finally, however, it's the director who gets the last word. No matter how many brilliant ideas you have, no matter how strongly you feel that you absolutely have to be in one place, if the director wants you elsewhere, that's where you go. Be aware that the initial blocking rehearsals are a "rough draft," and that the blocking may change as you go along. Trust your director. Even if you don't agree with the blocking he or she requests, try your hardest to make it work. There are other people on stage, and the director sometimes needs you to be in a certain place for the stage picture, not just for you. The smart directors will admit when something is not working and change it. When you're given definite blocking, it's your job as an actor to integrate it into your character and make it look as though you chose to be there.

SCENE WORK, WORK-THROUGHS, AND RUN-THROUGHS

Once the play is blocked, the type of rehearsals you have next will depend on the director. I've worked in situations in which run-throughs began right after the play was blocked. In most rehearsal schedules, however, the director will do some scene work, followed by work-throughs, followed by run-throughs.

Scene work involves working a particular scene over and over for blocking and acting values, and also to practice special choreography or business with props and costume pieces. Scene work will probably *not be in the order* in which it is written; for example you may work Act 1 (Scene 2), and Act 2 (Scenes 1 and 3) at one rehearsal. The schedule for scene work will usually be to the actors' advantage, calling only people who are in specific scenes together. This is where your French scene breakdown, if you have one, will be used.

During scene work you will polish and rework the blocking, and really get down to the nitty-gritty of the emotional sense. Scene work is often done early in the rehearsal schedule immediately following blocking rehearsals; however, if a scene is not working it may be individually scheduled in late rehearsals as well.

In musical theatre, early rehearsals will be of three different types: dance, musical, and scenes. Dance rehearsals concentrate on learning and working the dance steps and choreography, and they are run by the choreographer. (If the choreographer is busy elsewhere, the *dance captain* may run a rehearsal. One of the dancers in the show, the dance captain is appointed by the director or choreographer, and he or she may also run brush-up rehearsals to ensure that the dances stay in shape.) Musical rehearsals, run by the Musical Director, are devoted to vocal production and interpretation of the songs. The director will be in charge of scene rehearsals, which may not incorporate music and dance numbers.

Work-throughs are rehearsals *in order as written*, but there will be stopping and working. Work-throughs are usually long, and it's difficult to schedule actors to arrive just in time for their scene. Once again, be prepared to wait. On the other hand, if you do not appear in the play until Act 2, it's possible your call will be considerably later than the call for people in Act 1.

Run-throughs are rehearsals in which you "run through" the entire play from start to finish. Once you get into run-throughs you will usually not be stopping unless there is a problem. The closer you get to dress rehearsal, the less likely it is that you will be stopped, or that it will be permissible for YOU to stop. Generally you will know (or you should find out) what the correct procedure will be for that particular run-through. Ask the director or stage manager if stopping is acceptable and under what circumstances (i.e., props not in place, technical problems, lines). There are times when you may be stopped by the director for technical problems but you may not stop the rehearsal as an actor. Directors need run-throughs to get an overall sense of the play and to time it.

Actors must be in place and ready to go directly from one scene to another during a run-through. If you are not in the theatre and cannot wait backstage, you will wait at the sides of the marked set in the rehearsal hall. The director will be very upset if you aren't in place ready to go for your entrance or scene, and the stage manager can't be running all over to find you. If you are in a theatre that does not have an intercom (also called a "squawk box") that goes from the stage to the dressing rooms, then you will have to wait where you can hear. "Places" is only called for beginning of acts, not for scenes, so be prepared to go on with all your proper rehearsal costumes and props.

Usually there will be at least one final run-through (just before dress rehearsal) in which there will be NO STOPPING. This means exactly that, no matter what happens. Whether or not you forget your lines, are missing props, or your costume isn't in place, you will go on. If the set falls down, you will go on. If someone else forgets his lines, you will go on. There's an obvious reason: once you get into production, no matter what happens you will have to carry on. You have to get used to this kind of performance pressure.

During the run of one of my shows that had a particularly classy set (in performance, not rehearsal), three shelves of a glass bookcase toppled to the floor, shattering in cascading waves as they came down. Fortunately, no one was injured, lines were quickly ad-libbed, and the quick-thinking young man who was playing the Valet came in to clean up. The cast of professional actors carried on. In another production (again, in performance), one of the leading actors not only missed an entrance, he missed an entire scene. The actors had to improvise and fill in the dialogue to get in the important information that was supposed to be revealed in the scene, and the show went on.

Rehearsal Costumes and Props

In most professional situations, major props (such as drinking glasses, dishes, towels, etc.) will be provided for rehearsal. These will probably not be the actual props to be used in the show, but will give actors an idea what they will be dealing with. Professional actors will be aware of ALL the props they need for the show, and will often use or bring in personal belongings they can use (such as eyeglasses, purses, or pipes).

If the prop is not something that people might have with them (or is something special that is being found or built), the actor may tactfully request that a reasonable facsimile be brought in for rehearsal work. (Make this request through your stage manager.) It's important to have at least *something* to simulate every single prop or removable costume piece (hats, gloves, scarves) you need to use in the show. Warning: Do not use any personal item of value that could be broken or lost, and never leave your own things in the rehearsal hall.

Costumes will not be available in early rehearsal; however, professional actors often wear specific things of their own to help themselves work, including shoes, vests, and long skirts. Women can wear their own high heels, and often the costume department will be able to provide long rehearsal skirts. If you know you will be wearing a hat and gloves (both men and women), it is wise to ask the Stage Manager if the costume department can provide rehearsal pieces. Again, these will not be the actual costumes, but will give you something to work with until you get into dress rehearsal.

Rehearsal may be the time to determine what *reads*. This term usually refers to small props, costume pieces, or bits of business. If it "reads," it means that it looks like what it is supposed to be, or that it can be seen from the audience. Depending on the size of your rehearsal hall, you may ask the director, if you are not sure, "Is this going to read?" If you are rehearsing in a small space you will probably want to wait until you get into the theatre to determine what reads.

Let's say, for example, that your character is referred to as always wearing a bow in her hair. You have dark brunette hair, and the costume department provides you with a black hair bow to match your black dress. Because the bow reference is so important, you may ask the director, regarding the black bow, "Does this bow read?" meaning, "Does it show in my hair—can you see it from the house?"

Rehearsing the Set: Practical, Non-Working, False, and Cued

Earlier we mentioned the fact that in professional theatre the actors don't actually get on the real set until a few days (at most) before the first performance. So we get used to using our rehearsal space as though it is the real set, and we get used to clarifying exactly what's going to happen when we do get on the set. The above terms are explained here so that you know what type of questions to ask about the kinds of challenges your real set might present.

The term *practical* can refer to props or the set. Practical means that the prop or set piece is actually working, and that it will be *used as a working piece* in the show. For example, if you have real running water in the sink on set, the sink is practical. If you have a real lamp, which is switched on by an actor and its bulb goes on, it's practical.

Non-working refers to a piece of the set that is there but doesn't work. For example, if the sink is in place in the kitchen but no water comes from the faucet when it is turned on, it's non-working. Obviously there are lots of things on the set that are not real and don't work, but the term only applies to things used in the action of the play. If that kitchen sink is never used, it doesn't matter whether it works or not. On the other hand, if somebody goes to the sink to wash his hands, it's important to know whether there will be running water coming out of the spout or whether the action will be mimed.

False refers to a set piece that is not only non-working, it's not real. Let's say there are cupboards in that kitchen. If they're just painted on and don't open, they're false.

Cued relates directly to lights and sound. It refers to an action that is mimed on stage but actually cues the stage lights or sound tape. Let's say the actor enters and turns on a light. The light switch is in place on the wall, but it's not practical, so the actor must place her hand on the switch, turn it up (or pretend to), and wait for the lights to come on from the light booth.

What's the point of all this? You should always ask in rehearsals pertinent questions regarding your set- and prop-related actions. The answers will tell you what's expected of you, such as your entrance: will you be ringing the bell yourself, or will that be cued? Are you expected to knock on the door itself, will you be knocking two pieces of wood together, or will the backstage crew be making the sound? When you turn on the light, will it come on itself, or do you need to hold your hand there for a second until the stage lights come up, or both?

Here's a short scene to demonstrate what might happen. Actor rings bell but nobody's home. Enters and turns on light. Crosses to living room and looks in cabinet, takes out music box. Crosses to table and turns on lamp. Opens music box and it plays a tune. Hears a crash outside. Quickly closes music box and exits through kitchen window.

Here's how this scene might actually work. Actor rings bell (outside bell is practical, so the actor must ring it). Enters and turns on light (light is non-working, so actor must physically move the wall switch, but leave hand on it until the lights come up). Goes to living room and looks in cabinet (only one cabinet door is practical, the other is false), takes music box from cabinet. Crosses to table and turns on lamp (lamp is practical, actor must turn it on to get light). Opens music box (music box is cued, sound comes from theatre speakers, not from the box). Hears a crash outside, quickly closes music box (must be expertly timed so that hand stays on the box until the sound stops), and exits through the window (only one of the windows is practical, the rest are non-working).

The more you know about the set and props, the more confident you will be when you get into final dress rehearsal. It is always wise to ask what to expect and what is expected of you, so you won't be surprised with responsibilities later on.

Getting Off Book

At a certain point in run-throughs, you will be requested to be *off book*. If you're smart, you will have used previous rehearsals to leave the book behind long before the off-book date (keeping it tucked in your pocket for quick reference). It is not wise to use the book all through rehearsals, and then to expect yourself suddenly to be off book, no matter how much time you have spent memorizing. Get off book in rehearsals, as soon as possible once the blocking is set and you feel confident that you know the words. You should, however, always go back and 1) mark blocking and business changes in your script and 2) check your lines for accuracy.

If you have not been given an off-book date, you should ask about it. A note to directors: Actors need an off-book date; there are always some people who only produce on a deadline. Needless to say, the date in question should be well in advance of opening.

During rehearsals, the stage manager will usually be "on the book," meaning he or she is following the lines and blocking. As soon as you feel sure of your lines, you may let the stage manager know that you will be trying to get through without the book, so that someone will be "on book" for you. You can do this gradually, scene by scene. Try without book those scenes you feel sure you know— carry your book if you're shaky. The person on book may or may not be the stage manager (he or she often is watching for a million things besides the lines), so an ASM or someone on crew may be the person on book for you.

As you are working, if you get lost or "go up," you will say "Line" or "Line, please," and you will be helped. Please do not say "Don't tell me, don't tell me, I *know* this!" or "What the heck am I supposed to say next?" or "I know it's me, but *what?*" The person on book will probably realize that you don't know the line and give it to you, but it's always clearer if you simply say "Line." In many professional situations, the stage manager (or whoever is on book) will NOT cue you unless you say "Line," but not necessarily because you haven't used the proper vocabulary.

I once worked with a seasoned actress named Frances Helm. During a dress rehearsal, in a particularly emotional scene, there was a long pause, and then the stage manager threw her the line. She stopped, came out of character, looked up to the stage manager, and icily retorted, "I KNOW the line, darling, I was ACTING."

Note Sessions

Once you get into run-throughs, notes are given at the very end of the play, rather than during the rehearsal or after individual scenes. Note sessions are tough. Everyone is tired, they want to go home. But it's sometimes the most important part of rehearsal, so pay attention and keep quiet during the session. The director has kept quiet during the entire run-through; this is the only time you will get his or her valuable input. All notes are important, and many notes pertain to the entire cast and/or production. If the note does not directly relate to you or your scene or character, that does not give you license to goof off, talk, or tune out. A friend recently related to me that some youthful performers in a show she was doing did not feel it was necessary to stay for "notes." It must be said: the rehearsal's not over until the final note is given.

Some actors write their notes in the script, which is fine if there's room. Some write them down in a separate notebook. One director I worked with asked that actors *listen* to the notes and understand them, rather than meticulously writing down and forgetting them.

There is *some* give-and-take in note sessions between the actors and the director. It's OK to ask a question or two in order to clarify the note. But this is not the time to get into an argument or even have a long conversation with the director. And get out of the habit of reacting defensively every time you get a note. Notes are construed as "criticism," and many amateur actors respond with "I *did* that, didn't I?" or "But you told me two weeks ago . . ." Just take the note and incorporate it into your performance next time.

Everyone in the cast is required to be at note sessions, and the director needs to get through all his or her notes. If you really have a problem, discuss it separately with the director, or in the next working session. Don't use the note sessions to take up everyone else's valuable time.

TECHNICAL AND DRESS REHEARSALS

Technical (tech) rehearsals are the longest and most difficult in the entire rehearsal process. The purpose is to coordinate all the technical aspects of the show with the acting. By now you will be in the theatre. Tech rehearsals may be *stop-and-go* or *cue-to-cue*. Stop-and-go means you will be running the entire show, stopping to work light and sound cues, entrances and exits, costume and set changes, etc., and then going on with the scene. A cue-to-cue rehearsal will skip most of the acting, going from the line cues at which technical things happen, work the technical thing, skip the scene, and go to the next line cue that involves a technical change. Cue-to-cue rehearsals are somewhat shorter than stop-and-go, and there are times when the rehearsal will begin as a stop-and-go, and as the director finds time is running short, may finish the rehearsal as a cue-to-cue.

Early tech rehearsals are usually done without costumes, primarily because they take so long. You may think that tech rehearsals in professional theatres surely could not be so endless, because all the tech people are pros. Even when this is the case, these rehearsals are arduous. In Equity theatres there are usually two or more days in which the actors may be called for ten hours of a twelve-hour day. That's a long rehearsal.

Once the technical aspects are in place, there will be a tech-dress rehearsal, meaning of course, that you will wear your costumes.

Dress Parade

Sometime before the first dress rehearsal there may be a *dress parade*. This is just what it sounds like. The actors dress up in their costumes and "parade" on stage, in front of the director, costume designer, lighting designer, and others who need to see how the costumes look. This is not a rehearsal; no lines will be said or scenes worked. You will change into your costume and will probably be asked to go onto the stage with others who are in the same scene, so that the designer and director can see how the clothes coordinate. If you have more than one costume, you will change immediately and "parade" as requested, either alone or with others in the next scene.

Makeup and wigs are not usually required for dress parade; however, if you feel that your wig considerably changes the way the costume looks, it may be wise to wear it. For example, a blonde in a light peach dress may look washed out. Once she gets into the brunette wig the look will be right.

Dress and Tech-Dress Rehearsals

There may be one or more *dress rehearsals* in which you will finally be wearing your costumes. Don't be surprised if your costumes are not completed, don't fit exactly right, or if certain costume pieces are missing. Wear what the costume department has for you, and if you're missing a piece that is part of the action of the play, use the rehearsal piece.

In Equity productions, *dressing room assignments* are usually made just before the first dress rehearsal. The stage manager will place your name on your assigned dressing room door or on the mirror in front of where you will sit. In some theatres, actors arrive very early in order to get the most desirable place in the dressing room if specific places are not assigned. (You can ask your stage manager if dressing room assignments will be made.)

It's always a good idea to be early for dress rehearsals anyway, so that you can organize all your costumes and makeup, and write a list of things you've forgotten. If you have been requested to bring your own socks, stockings, shoes, special underwear (such as strapless bras, foundation garments, dance belts, shorts, etc.), you must have them with you at the first dress rehearsal. In addition, you might as well bring your makeup, rollers, and everything else you need for the show at this time, including tissues.

Early dress rehearsals may or may not be technical rehearsals. But often after the technical rehearsals, you will go straight into *tech-dress*. This is a rehearsal with costumes, lights, and sound. It's wise to ask if makeup will be required for these rehearsals. If you have special character hair or makeup (wig, mustache, false nose), it's a good idea to practice with it, even if nobody else is wearing makeup. In some cases you may also choose to wear just the special piece (like a wig) without full makeup.

A dress rehearsal with all costumes and makeup is called a *full dress*. Yes, with tech, it's called *full-tech-dress*. The last dress rehearsal before you go into performance or previews is usually called *final dress*. Most often the final dress is a full-tech-dress, but maybe not. Perhaps the crew is not called for the day of your final rehearsal, but the director wants to see the costumes anyway. In that case you may have a final dress without the tech.

Half-Hour, the Calls, and Sign-In

Once dress rehearsals begin you are expected to remain in the dressing room or backstage until your entrance. In professional theatre, calling the half-hour is standard from dress rehearsals on. You should be informed at what time the half-hour will be called. Sometimes the rehearsal call will be the half-hour ("rehearsal begins at 7:30, which is half-hour"). In other situations, you may do a working or tech rehearsal for a couple of hours, take a lunch or dinner break, and after your return the half-hour will be called before you begin the dress rehearsal.

The half-hour is the time you will be expected to be at the theatre in the dressing room or backstage preparing for the show. Half-hour literally means you have thirty minutes until curtain. The stage manager or ASM will "make the calls," and it is imperative that you be present backstage for the half-hour, even if your first appearance on stage is not until Act 2. In professional theatre the calls are not casual and they are not approximate, they are: half-hour, fifteen minutes, five minutes, and places.

Most professional theatres also have a sign-in sheet, which is posted on a bulletin board backstage. You are expected to write your initials in the appropriate date and time box related to each specific performance. There is a separate sign-in for matinee and evening shows. Always sign in when you first arrive at the theatre; it's an important way for the stage manager to check who is there and who is not. Never sign in for anyone else, and never ask anyone to sign in for you.

Curtain Call

There is a superstition among directors in professional theatre that it's bad luck to stage the curtain call until the final full dress rehearsal. This makes it a bit difficult on directors who have great ideas about choreographing the curtain call. But actors usually have no difficulty remembering the blocking for their bows, and most curtain calls are not set until the last minute. When you finally get to staging the curtain call, you must pay attention and move quickly. It's usually late in the evening, everyone is tired, and the director still has notes to give. Get it right.

Traditionally, the bows are staged in reverse order of the size of the role, with the smaller roles bowing first. The chorus or walk-ons (often in groups), are followed by the cameo roles and supporting roles (often in twos), then the leads. The person with the most important role (not necessarily the most lines), bows last. If there is a star in your production, either a national or local one, they might bow last even though they are not playing the biggest or even the most important part.

There is absolutely no discussion with the director about who bows when. Because the curtain call is not staged until the last minute, the director must have given it some thought before the actual staging, so he has his reasons for the order. Don't be upset about when or with whom you will take your bow—if you do a great job and the audience loves you, they will applaud their approval wherever you appear in the curtain call.

Recently there was a great deal of controversy surrounding a management decision that the actor playing the villain in a Broadway revival of *Oh, Kay!* *not* be included in the curtain call. This is a serious breach of theatrical tradition. All actors deserve to be in the curtain call.

INITIAL PERFORMANCES

Invited Dress and Previews

In many theatres there is an invited audience for the final dress rehearsal, in which case it's called an *invited dress*. It usually occurs the night before your scheduled first preview or opening night. Invited people may be friends of the director or producer, board of directors members, cast members of other shows in town, or sometimes even friends of the cast. When you're in full costume and you see an audience, it's hard (but important) to keep in mind that the *invited dress is a rehearsal*. Use it as a rehearsal, and for heaven's sake don't have your friends come backstage afterwards. There will most likely be notes, and this is not the time for general celebration and self-congratulation.

Invited dress rehearsals are great—they give you a chance to perform in front of an audience and get some reaction, which is especially critical in comedies and musicals. But there is a catch: you might get "spoiled." Often the audience is composed of people or professionals who are directly connected to the theatre. They are probably going to love you no matter what you do, and they especially love theatrical bits, shtick, characters, and business. I've done comedies in which the audience at the invited dress roared with laughter; through the entire run of the show there was never such a great response. If you get a fabulous response from your invited dress audience, take it with a grain of salt.

Many theatres have previews before the opening night. There is no difference between a preview and a performance, except that the ticket price is sometimes a little lower, the show may still be working out some problems, and the critics are not (usually) invited. Previews are not rehearsals, and the actors are expected to give the very best performance possible. Previews are often scheduled for technically difficult shows and comedies. Some technical things may go wrong and the audience might laugh in the wrong places, but the actors are expected to go on just as though it were a performance.

Directors often give notes after previews. If you have a director who does, be grateful. Once the show opens, the director usually disappears, so take advantage of the time he or she is around to help you make your performance better.

Opening Night

There's another saying in professional theatre: "Bad dress rehearsal, good opening," and vice versa. If you're dress rehearsal was dreadful, don't get too crazy—things will probably go all right opening night. There's an electricity in the air on opening night, which happens at no other time in the theatre. It's exciting. There is also chaos, panic, tempers, and problems. Take it easy.

Opening night is the time that all your discipline, hard work, and control are put to the test. The more time you have spent memorizing lines and doing your homework, the more you have prepared in rehearsal, and the more you have used dress rehearsals to practice with your stuff, the better your performance will be. Use your relaxation exercises to control nerves and butterflies and deal calmly and quietly with last-minute problems.

Stage fright is par for the course. A standard opening night scenario: With a growing sense of panic, the actor whispers, "What's my first line?" You may feel that you cannot remember a single thing, much less the first line. It will come back to you—the important thing to concentrate on is self-confidence. My feeling about opening nights is that if you can just get through it without making major mistakes, you're in great shape.

Critics

David Mamet calls them "crickets." Your sense of panic is not helped by the fact that the critics are invited to the opening. It may help you to know that critics show up at various times—from previews to the last performance. Don't worry about them. You shouldn't even know they are there. Good directors and stage managers will not announce the VIPs who are in the audience, and it is best for actors not to know and not to ask. What, you say? I want to know if there's a critic so I can give my best performance. Well, you should always be giving your best performance, whether or not someone special is in the house.

Who to Invite and When

You will probably want all your friends and family to see you perform. That's natural. But before you go extending invitations to the world, you may wish to consider the following advice.

First, *never* invite anyone to attend your rehearsals, no matter how many people are in the cast. Rehearsals are *closed* (meaning only cast and crew allowed), and it is totally inappropriate for anyone else to be present. This includes your best friend, your little sister, and your cousin from Davenport. If you are allowed to have people at the invited dress, think twice. (Cast members are often NOT permitted to invite anyone to this rehearsal, so it may be a moot point.) The advantage of the invited dress is that it's free, so if you have friends who cannot afford the tickets, it is a nice gesture to invite them. Or maybe your Aunt Millie is in town for just a couple of days and will otherwise not be able to see the performance. That's special, so it's OK. Otherwise, it is not a good idea to ask people to the invited dress. Let the management take care of the audience for this performance, and you worry about more important things, such as your performance.

Some actors think it is important for voice coaches, dance teachers, or other professionals whose opinion they respect to attend an invited dress or a preview. That way they can get as many outside opinions as possible so they can "improve" their performance before opening night. This is very dangerous. What if everyone started getting notes from all their friends, and went to the director with a list of requested changes just before opening night? It would be a mess. Use the previews to work with an audience and your fellow actors. Period.

Opening night is very special, and for that reason actors may wish to invite friends and family. A word of warning: the opening night performance will not be your best. I guarantee it.

There is often an opening night party after the opening show, so if you wish to invite your parents or spouse to the party they should be at the opening performance. (Sometimes, too, guests at these parties are limited—don't invite more people than allowed.) Hopefully, your parents or spouse or best friend will be coming back to see another performance anyway. As for inviting all your personal and professional friends, relatives, neighbors, classmates, teachers, and coaches, it is best to invite them another time. *When* you invite others will depend somewhat on how long your run is—if it's only four shows, and you think they may be sold out, you'll have to arrange for the tickets early. I wouldn't recommend the second performance either (there's often a "second night" letdown), and anytime after that is anybody's guess. As a general rule, later performances are better than earlier ones.

PROFESSIONAL GIVE-AND-TAKE IN REHEARSALS

Different Strokes for Different Folks

Every actor and director has a different way of working; to every artist different things are important. You may have some idea of how the director works and what he or she "wants" by the speeches and notes given. It's very important for the actor to respect what the director is trying to do, and to work with him or her to achieve the desired result. Professional actors who are not familiar with the director's style will ask pertinent questions in order to understand exactly what is meant.

For example, the director may ask the actor for "more energy." Some people might know exactly what how to translate that. Others may say "Exactly how do you mean? More volume, more physical movement, what?" It's critical for you to understand what your director is trying to achieve. On the other hand, don't be argumentative, aggressive, or demanding; directors are doing their job as best they know how—the last thing in the world you want to do is alienate them.

Other actors have different ways of working too. At any given time they may be concentrating on one of a number of elements that go into the entire process. If you are working with someone whose approach or method is very different from your own, respect his or her need to work it out. For example, some actors feel that discussion is vital to the work and want plenty of it before or during rehearsal. You may feel like this is a waste of your time. However, if the director decides that it's a good idea, get involved with it—you might just learn something new about your character or action.

Conversely, maybe you're working with a director who seems to be only concerned with style and technique, but you have always felt that the emotional or psychological aspects of the character are most important. It is OK to try to use the director to get as much emotional information as you can, but don't monopolize rehearsal time with these personal needs. Your director is concerned with other aspects of this production, and if you listen you might just learn something new about style and technique.

Do your own homework. Study your own character and accent and blocking and emotions at home ON YOUR OWN. The rehearsal is no place to try to dominate everyone else so that you can figure out what the heck you're doing. I don't care if you are playing the lead. You must find a happy balance between getting the information you need from the director, but not using all the precious rehearsal time to do so. In some cases, if requested, the director will take the time to sit down and work individually with an actor who really needs personal discussion or work rehearsals.

Who's On Top?

There is definitely a certain "pecking order" in theatre. You won't find it listed in any book, and it's never discussed, but you should be aware of it. The people who are playing the leads have more responsibility, and therefore are given more of the director's time and energy. The people who are "professional" (Equity members or others who make a living acting) will be deferred to more than those who are not. The people who are older and have more credits will be given more respect than the younger ones. The people who are friends of the director may be given more leeway than those who just met him. You might as well be aware of these politics. If you're a spear carrier you're not going to get as much attention and you can't demand as much time as the person who is playing Medea.

In addition, when you're in rehearsal, you'll have to "suss out" when it would be OK for you to stop and take up time, or when it would be better for you to go home and consider how it might be handled, or if it's even worth mentioning. Let's say, for example, you think someone is upstaging you. If you're an intern and she is an Equity actor, the director may side with her, and you may have to just be upstaged, even if you feel it's not right.

This does not mean that you take direction from everyone who is more experienced than you are. In fact, don't. Take direction from the director. But you will have to learn how to deal tactfully with these kinds of situations. Your awareness of your position will greatly help your performance as well as your "public relations" with rest of the cast.

One additional note: Older or more experienced actors may try to be "helpful" to someone who is less experienced. If this help becomes direction, which may conflict with the director's, then it is important to do one or all of the following: 1) mention this new suggestion to the director and request that you'd like to try it; 2) explain to the adviser that you have been directed to do otherwise and suggest that it be discussed with the director; 3) ignore it (often not a good idea).

On the other hand, if you get a tip, it wouldn't hurt you to check it out. Perhaps the suggestion is a piece of business—you might try it, the director might love it. Or maybe you are using an accent and mispronouncing some words. Your fellow professional actors are not trying to criticize you, they are trying to help. You owe it to yourself to at least consider what they say before you discard it.

Stars and Temperament

What's a Star? In the profession, the term is used frequently and loosely. All things being relative, a star may be defined as: 1) a universally recognized international celebrity, like Cher or Michael J. Fox, or a medium-recognition professional who has appeared on national TV, a soap or series; or 2) a regionally or locally well-known actor or personality; or 3) the person who has the most longevity in a rep company or community theatre, i.e., a "director's pet" or an "audience favorite"; or 4) the person or persons who have the leading roles.

If you're working with a star, either a nationally recognized one or a local one, good luck. Some people consider themselves stars, whether or not they really are, no matter what the size of their role.

On the other hand, some people really are stars, and will certainly receive preferential treatment. A star doesn't have to be someone who makes a living in the theatre; it could be someone who is a local personality and whose name and involvement could bring commercial success. Whatever the case, the star is at the top.

The director will probably do everything is his or her power to make the star comfortable, including changing someone else's performance to make the star the center of attention. In the old days, stars would get paranoid if someone else on stage MOVED when they were speaking. Other actors were literally required to freeze, so as not to steal focus.

Contrary to stories you may have heard, there is absolutely no place for temperament from anyone in the theatre at any time. You may not believe this, because you've seen it from your "star," your leading man/lady, or even the seniors in your school. No matter how badly someone behaves, that's no indication that it is proper, or that you will be "allowed to" someday. Many stars, including some of the biggest names in the business, are delightful to work with and the most professional people around.

When dealing with your fellow actors, learn how to use tact and diplomacy. Even if you remember their blocking and they don't, it's not a good idea to say to them, "Hey, aren't you supposed to be over there?" It's much better to stop, if necessary, and say to the stage manager or director, "I'm confused, if I make my cross on the next line we'll run into each other." Don't boss people around on stage. Don't give them their lines. Let the director and the stage manager do their jobs and you stick to yours.

Ensemble Acting

Before the Age of Paranoia, there was such a thing as *ensemble acting*, in which everyone in the cast worked toward a common goal—in the words of the Actors' Equity Association motto, "All for one and one for all." In true ensemble, there are no stars, there is no temperament, there is just a bunch of good people giving and sharing with each other. The result is phenomenal. Ensemble groups give the impression that they really know and love each other and what they're doing, that the play is the star, and that it's all happening for the first time ever.

There have been many attempts to create ensembles in this country, and some, such as the Group Theatre of the 1930s, have worked successfully for a number of years. But generally, our attempts at ensemble fail miserably, even in resident and repertory theatre. Though I am no Anglophile, I do believe that British tradition fosters and achieves ensemble acting much more often than is found in American companies. Is it because of the American dream—that we are all trying so very hard to be the star? Or is it because we lack the kind of training, dedication, and respect for the craft that you often see in British companies? Whatever the reason, it is a shame, because our plays and our productions suffer as a result.

I once did a Joe Orton play called *What the Butler Saw*. It was a crazy, zany show, and a wonderful, caring, sharing, giving, fun company. Between the matinee and evening performances, everyone in the cast had dinner together and discussed stuff that wasn't working. Somebody would throw out an idea, and the actor would try it. Actors would toss around new thoughts they had for shtick or business that might make the show even funnier. This was all within the confines of "keeping the show as directed." Nothing was ever said by way of criticism, all the discussion revolved on brainstorming to make the show livelier and better. It was the most creative experience I've had in the theatre and one of the most fun.

If you want to try to work toward an ensemble in your play, share with your fellow actors. Ensemble acting is "pure," because actors are not afraid to give. Acting is twofold: it involves ACTION and REACTION. You can make or break someone else's focus or laugh by your reaction (or lack of it). But if you steal focus or don't react, does that make you better? Does it make the play better? If you are willing to give to your fellow cast members, and if you are interested in serving the play rather than yourself, then you personally will be working toward the ideal. Who knows? If everyone in the cast did it, you'd have a true ensemble.

3

Theatre Personnel and Crew: Helping Them Help You

Many amateur actors have the notion that crew people are not terribly important, that they are there to serve the actors, that they are somehow secondary to the production. Please try not to make this mistake. People on crews are experts in their own fields, craftspeople in their own right, and not the actors' servants. Actors often think that because they are the ones on stage, they are taking all the risk "out front," and nobody else could possibly matter. "It's my neck out there," is the general attitude. This kind of thinking can ruin not only relationships, it can ruin a production.

I once asked a crew member, "What's the worst thing about your job?" and the response was "Being taken for granted—actors don't know what we do." Learn to know the people on the crew (or better yet, work on a crew yourself), trust them to do their job, realize that they are terribly overworked, do as much as you can to cover yourself, and recognize that crew people are just as critical to the production as actors.

The following is a list of the designers and crew people with whom the actor will probably come into contact during rehearsals and the run of the show. It is by no means an exhaustive list. In a large professional production there may be a hundred people on various crews. But in most theatrical situations, large and small, there are certain people who will be working on crews. The actor should be familiar with them—their titles, what they do, and how to work with them, including:

- Stage Management
- Designers
- Construction, Light, and Sound Crews
- Maintenance Crews

- Rehearsal and Running Crews, and
- Theatre Personnel

Stage management is in charge of running the show from the first rehearsal until the final performance. Designers are not technically "crew" people, they are artists who conceive the ideas for their specific areas (which are then executed by the crew people in each department). Construction crews build the sets; costume crews produce the costumes; light crews place and focus lighting equipment; and sound crews research and make the master tape. Note: In a Broadway show, national tour, or other large production, crew personnel may be members of the stagehands' union, the International Alliance of Theatrical and Stage Employees (IATSE).

Rehearsal crews provide props and costume pieces for rehearsals, and are often on the running crew as well. The running crew (also called stage crew) includes the backstage people at every performance who do stage and prop pre-sets and changes, make light and sound cues, assist backstage with costumes and quick changes, and essentially perform all that is necessary for the show to run. Maintenance crews ensure that costumes, hair/wigs, and props stay in good working order and are repaired or replaced as necessary.

Theatre personnel includes people "up front" in the box office and house, as well as the folks who handle publicity and programs, sales and subscriptions, accounting and theatre management. (Note: On Broadway there is a union for box office personnel and ushers, and another one for theatre publicists.)

WORKING WITH STAGE MANAGEMENT

You've already met the **Stage Manager** and **Assistant Stage Manager** in rehearsals, and a discussion of what they do and how professionals work with them may be found in the previous chapter on rehearsals.

It is critical to remember that a suggestion or directive from the stage manager must be followed, otherwise who would maintain discipline for the director? Who would be in charge when the director isn't there? Under Equity contract, a stage manager's minimum wage is higher than an actor's, because he or she has greater responsibility. There is no necessity to be chummy with your stage management personnel; however, it is essential for you to respect and help them. Be on time for every rehearsal and half-hour call, notify them if you have a conflict or problem, observe the disciplinary guidelines of rehearsal and performance, and use them as your communication line to the crews.

Professional stage managers are members of Actors' Equity Association. In addition to running the show, they also "run interference" between cast members who are having problems. If there is a conflict among two or more members of the cast, the stage manager will try to iron it out. It's also the stage manager's job to see that the show stays exactly as directed, so it is entirely appropriate for the stage manager to give notes to actors who are going off track. If there is a problem or complaint regarding management, the stage manager is the liaison between the company and management. Actors may go to the stage manager, who will rectify the problem or contact the appropriate person to do so.

In professional productions, the Equity cast members nominate and elect a **Deputy**, who acts as spokesperson for the company. Any problems or complaints regarding the theatre (unacceptable or unsafe conditions, housing, paychecks, etc.) may be communicated to the Deputy, who then works with the stage manager, company manager, or producer to iron out the difficulty.

WORKING WITH COSTUMES

Who's Who in the Costume Department

Costume Designer—This is the person responsible for the entire look of all the costumes. He or she designs or finds all the clothes for all the actors. Designers often have Assistant Designers who work closely with them.

If the budget allows for complete costume creation, the designer does *renderings* of the costumes he or she has in mind for each character in each scene. The costume designer then consults with the director (and other necessary people, including stars) to make sure the ideas are going to work. Once the renderings are approved, the costumes are then *built* by the costume department. (In theatre parlance, when a costume is sewn from scratch, it is "built.")

The costume designer will probably attend one or more rehearsals, and if he or she has done renderings, you may be shown the sketches either at rehearsal or during one of your costume fittings. (Renderings are only done for originally designed costumes.)

If the play is a period piece such as a Shakespeare or Molière, the costumes may be built, rented, or pulled from storage. For more modern or contemporary plays, the designer may find or borrow clothes. Costumes are often a combination of found, built, borrowed, and in-stock garments. Whatever the case, the costume designer has the ultimate say in who wears what.

Costumer—In a large production with a large budget, the costume designer works with a costumer, who assists in executing the designer's ideas. In a production requiring that a lot of costumes be built, the costumer oversees the costume crew, which includes expert cutters and seamstresses. (The costumer usually is an expert seamstress.) The costumer may also be pulling things from storage or running out and finding costumes that may appropriately suit the designer's ideas.

If the costumes are to be built, the costumer will sometimes make *mock-ups*, which are exactly what they sound like: the pattern is used, but a cheap version of the real costume is basted together with muslin or other inexpensive material. This allows the designer and costumer to check that the costume will fit properly before the real material (which can be very expensive) is cut.

Wardrobe Supervisor—The wardrobe supervisor, sometimes also called wardrobe mistress (though nowadays it may be a man or woman), is responsible for maintaining all the costumes from dress rehearsal through the run of the show. This includes any reinforcement, mending, and cleaning as required.

Dresser—The dresser is the person who helps actors get into their costumes (if this is difficult) and make quick changes. Stars used to employ their own dressers; however, these days a dresser is provided only if a major star requests one, or where required in the production for difficult or quick changes.

Wig and Makeup Designers and Maintenance Crew—If the show requires elaborate and difficult wigs and makeup, there may be a professional expert who designs the hair/wigs and makeup. Once the look is designed, a professional hair/makeup maintenance person may be available (or may come in from time to time) to maintain the hair/wigs and check the actor's makeup to be sure it has retained the designer's look.

Fittings

You will be scheduled for costume fittings as the rehearsals progress. In Equity productions, the costume fittings are considered part of the overall rehearsal time; however, they are never scheduled to conflict with your actual rehearsal. Needless to say, it's important to be on time for your costume fitting. If it is scheduled close to your rehearsal call time, it's up to you to let the costume department know when you have to go.

At your first fitting you will be measured from top to bottom. It may be wise to wear snug-fitting clothing or a leotard underneath your baggy clothes. It's important for the costume department to have accurate and complete measurements, so try to cooperate when you're being measured. (No, they will not take your word for it, be prepared for the tape measure, and accept that it's going to be done.)

Though some people (particularly women) are uptight about their measurements, the costume department often has no sensitivity to this. In one production, measurements were taken at the first reading with the crew milling around the actors in the rehearsal room. Costume crew people pulled the actors a couple of feet away from the rest of the cast and the one doing the measuring dictated the numbers aloud to another who was writing them down. Not much privacy there. Another theatre posted the measurements on the costume department wall. Good grief! Keep in mind that measurements are just numbers and try not to be embarrassed.

You'll be called for costume fittings throughout rehearsals. Please remember that it's important to spend time in the costume department (as much as they can allow) to get things right. Don't wait until dress rehearsal to discover that your first act skirt is miles too short, or that the suit they want you in for Act 3 looks great, but you can't do that pratfall in it. During your fitting, go through in your mind all the major actions you do in the scene in which you will be wearing that costume, and remind the costume people about any potential problems that may arise.

Undergarments

If you are being fitted for a period costume, or if your costume requires a special look, you will probably wear special undergarments. This would include bras (strapless, backless, padded, or push-up), corsets, girdles, garter belts with stockings, dance belts, etc. Please note that it is not "ridiculous" for the costume designer to request that you wear appropriate undergarments for their costumes—the style of clothing and the look was very often dependent on what was underneath.

You may hear the designer or costumer use the term *silhouette*, which refers to the specific period "look" you create on stage. Up close you may feel that you look silly, but from the audience you have the perfect silhouette for the period and style of the play.

Sometimes the costume department will ask the actor to bring in and wear a personal undergarment if he or she has it; if you are providing one of these items, always bring it to your costume fitting and put it on before you dress. The proper undergarments will really make a difference in the fit, the length, and the overall effect of your costume.

Break-Away Costumes

If a costume gets torn or ripped off on stage (this happens a lot in comedy and farce), it's designed to be *break-away*, which means that the seams are done with Velcro® so it can rip off easily. Costumes involved in unusually quick changes may also be break-away. If one or more of your costumes is so designed, you can help the costume department by dressing very carefully in these clothes to make sure they don't look shoddy when you first go on stage; additionally, you should always do an inspection after you wear them to ensure that the seams that are not break-away are not breaking away and that the Velcro® is still properly in place on the break-away seams.

Quick Changes and Dressers

Historically, actors used to provide their own costumes for all productions. Leading actors were expected to hire their own dressers, who traveled with them and helped them get into their costumes (in addition to performing numerous other odd jobs, such as general go-fer and secretary). This was the subject of a very successful play called *The Dresser.*

Today, because the theatre usually provides the costumes, and because (at least in most contemporary plays) the actors can dress themselves, the role of full-time dresser is rare. However, in some instances, a costume or other crew person may be assigned to help actors dress, especially into fragile period costumes. In addition, a dresser will usually be standing by to aid with quick changes backstage. If you are lucky enough to have a dresser, allow the dresser to dictate exactly how the change will be done. Professional dressers "choreograph" all quick changes, so that the actor and the dresser know exactly who executes which part of the change and when. The changes are done exactly the same way each time. Nervous actors should be cautious not to try to help too much—they only get in the way. In the Off-Broadway production and national tours of *Greater Tuna*, the dressers joined the curtain call—they were that important to the show (two actors played twenty-plus characters).

Wearing Your Own Clothes

If the play is contemporary, you may be asked what clothes you have that may be appropriate for the show. Actors are often requested to wear their own shoes, no matter what the period. In Equity productions the actors must be reimbursed by management for wearing their own clothes—it's called costume rental. However, in many community and summer stock companies, it's not unusual for the director to request that you provide your own contemporary apparel. (There may be no costume department, much less a budget.)

If this is the case, only offer clothing that you wouldn't mind wearing every night for the run of the show. Keep in mind that what you wear could potentially be damaged or completely wrecked. And don't bring in anything that you really don't *want* to wear—the designer may fall in love with the one outfit that you really abhor.

Your Own Taste

It is OK to discuss your preferences and tastes with the costume designer—your proclivity for wearing solid colors instead of prints, for example, or your preference for a two-piece outfit instead of a dress. Usually they will try to be accommodating when they are looking for clothes for you. If you have very definite, strong feelings about certain styles or colors, it can't hurt to let them know up front, but the final decision is up to the designer.

I've often found it easier to bring and wear my own clothes for contemporary shows than to let the costume department try to find something that I like, that fits well, and that reflects my taste. Don't forget, they often have a budget of two dollars, and even though they will try to get the best for you, that kind of money just doesn't go far.

Repair and Costume Maintenance

During the run of the show, take care of your costumes. Treat them just as if they were your own favorite clothes. Hang them up properly, and check hems, seams, buttons, and zippers after each performance. Of course, it is the costume department's responsibility to keep the costumes in good repair; however, it's up to you to let them know (or take the costume to the wardrobe mistress) if it needs repair. Most professional actors are as helpful and cooperative with the costume department as possible. I have often re-sewn my own hems, reinforced loose buttons, and done other minor jobs to help out an overworked department.

In professional theatres, a repair list may be posted on the dressing room or bulletin board: you are asked to fill in your character's name, the article of clothing, and what's wrong with it. After you have listed the repair, remember to check before the next performance that the costume is back in your dressing room and is fixed.

Check your costumes after every performance, and if you notice a seam or button getting shaky or loose, have it repaired or reinforced *before* it rips or comes off. You are the one who will be embarrassed on stage if it does. I always have a needle and thread at my dressing room table—at times I've made last-minute repairs immediately before going on.

Laundry and Dry-Cleaning

In professional theatre, washable items are washed twice weekly and dry-cleaning is done once a week. You may want to check with your costume department as to what their policy is for washing and cleaning. In many community and school productions actors are expected to maintain their own costumes. That's fine, as long as it gets done. Take your washables home and wash and iron them as needed.

Needless to say, men's white shirts need to be washed and ironed fairly frequently, as do tights and other articles that (depending on the action of the play) get dirty on stage. Other articles may need daily maintenance. I once had to wear a slip in a scene which always got the leading man's makeup all over it (don't ask!). This I washed out myself after every performance and ironed before every show.

Regarding dry-cleaning, be cautious and use your own judgment. Dry-cleaning can be very damaging, particularly to old clothes. In one period production, I was wearing an authentic 1930s floor-length gown, which was already coming apart at the seams when it was acquired. I requested that the costume department NOT dry clean this dress—it was a dark color that didn't show dirt (it didn't get dirty anyway), and I didn't want to deal with coming in for a Tuesday performance and finding my costume in shreds.

Often if I'm wearing my own clothes for a play, I will request that these items *not* be washed or cleaned by the costume department—I will take care of them after the run. It's easy for personal items to get tossed in hot water with a bunch of other things and come out less than perfect afterward, which is OK for the stage but not for personal wearing. Also, you may know and trust your own dry-cleaner a lot more than the theatre's. Protect yourself by doing as much of your own costume maintenance as you can.

Altering Costumes

It is never appropriate for an actor to alter any part of a costume to suit personal preference. Do not change the hemline or the fit of your costume in any way, or add any accessory, unless you have the express permission of the designer. Even if you are using your own clothing, you must wear exactly the items (including shoes, hats, scarves, etc.) designated by the designer.

Wigs and Hair

If the role or the show requires a specific look, there may be a hair/wig designer, as well as a maintenance person. The designer styles the wigs or cuts and styles the actors' hair; the maintenance person places wigs and styles hair for each performance. This is truly a luxury—many theatres cannot afford a separate wig/hair person. Sometimes the wig and hair designer will also do the maintenance; sometimes the designer will come in once and instruct the actors in how to do their own hair/wigs; sometimes a costume person will be in charge of hair and wigs; and more often, the actors will be left to their own devices with their own hairpieces.

If you are lucky enough to have a wig and hair person, you will have regularly scheduled appointments for wig fittings, styling, hair coloring, and/or cuts. Be on time. Bring your own supplies, if requested, such as the wig or hairpiece (if you're using your own), bobby pins, wig caps, glue, etc.

Accept the fact that period hair styles look ridiculous to us. Don't try to re-style or change the look of the wig (or your own hair) to make it more contemporary. Both men and women: if your own hair has been cut, colored, and/or styled for the show, you must not change it during the entire run. If it needs a trim, shaping, or touch-up, the designer or maintenance person should take care of it.

Do as much as you can yourself to maintain your own wigs. I've often re-set a wig every night after a performance, and brushed and styled it personally before every show. You may let the wig/hair or costume department know that you plan to take care of your own wigs or hairpieces.

In one professional show I was doing, I came into the theatre one night and discovered that my wig was very damp—it felt wet on my head, and no longer held the set. Someone in the department had decided that it needed to be washed and re-styled, but unfortunately there wasn't quite enough time for it to dry. I had to wear it, but it felt like a wet hat; from then on I took care of my own wig.

Checking Your Costumes and Hairpieces

Before a performance it is your job to check that all your costumes are in your dressing room and ready to go. It's easy for the costume department to accidentally forget to return costumes to the dressing room after they've been cleaned or repaired, and even though the costumes are supposed to be there, it is absolutely essential for you to check them well in advance of getting dressed. This includes costumes, props, shoes, and wigs. If costumes are pre-set backstage for a quick change, always check to make sure they are there before the performance. This is easy to do because you will also be checking your backstage props.

Overall, yes, it is the costume department's responsibility to build, find, sew, maintain, and clean all the clothes and shoes for the show. But don't forget, *you* have to wear them.

WORKING WITH PROPS

Who's Who in the Prop Department

If there are special requirements for the "look" of a show, if unique props need to be built, and if budget allows, there may be a **Property Designer**. He or she creates an overall effect with props, and selects or makes the props that are correct and functional for the production and the period of the play.

The **Property Master** is the person who organizes all the props, makes sure the actors have props they need, pre-sets the stage, and pre-sets the prop tables. Because props include all the "movables" on all the sets and all the things carried on by actors, the prop master has an enormous job—there may be hundreds of props in a single show. In many productions there is only one person who acts as both prop designer and prop master.

Using Your Own Props

If you have appropriate personal props such as eyeglasses, cigarette holders or cases, pipes, canes, etc., you may wish to offer their use for the show. It is advisable to bring in only things that are expendable. Letting the production "borrow" valuable personal items may be asking for trouble.

Prop Tables and Their Use

There are usually several places where props may be kept for the show: offstage right, offstage left, backstage near the dressing room, and, of course, in the dressing room. Be sure you know the organization of your props and where you can check and find them before every performance.

The property tables should never be used for anything other than props. Don't put your coffee cups, water glasses, sodas, scripts, or other personal items on the prop tables. The prop tables hold all the props for all the actors—there isn't enough space for personal stuff and it gets cluttered and confusing. Similarly, never remove a prop that is not yours. It will be very upsetting to the other actors to discover props missing.

Checking Your Own Props

The prop master has an impossible job. In one production of *How The Other Half Loves*, I personally had twenty-two props for one dinner scene. Though the prop master is responsible for pre-setting all props it is the actors' job to check them. I worked in one company in which the stage manager requested that the actors go on stage before every show (at the half-hour, just prior to the house being opened), to check their own on-stage and backstage props.

The kind of pre-show check you do may depend on the kind of prop you have and whether it's practical or non-working. For example, if there's a guitar pre-set on stage, and you have to play it during the show, it will make a difference if the music is coming from the guitar or from a sound tape. If the guitar is practical (sound comes from the instrument), you must not only make sure it's there, you must check the strings and tune it.

If there's a practical prop you must use on stage, it is wise to have a backup plan in case the prop doesn't work. For example, let's say you're in a murder mystery set in the 1940s. You have to light a cigarette with an on-stage period "conversation piece" prop lighter.

Your backup plan is: 1) ask props to have boxed matches on the set near the lighter, and 2) carry book matches (not a Bic lighter). If you have to shoot a gun on stage, make sure there is a backup plan if it fails. Often these days gun shots are done backstage anyway because of the danger of prop guns and blanks. Whatever the case, insist on a backup plan because there is just no way you can "cover" or fake it if the gun doesn't go off.

WORKING WITH LIGHTS AND SOUND

Who's Who in Lights and Sound

The **Lighting Designer** prepares a lighting plot, which lists every lighting instrument used in the show, and when and how they change. Light crews will set the instruments and gels, and the show is run by the **Master Electrician.** (Often one person runs lights and sound.)

The **Sound Designer** creates a sound plot listing all the noises needed for the show and how they will be executed—by backstage crew, by the actors, or on tape. In plays, the sound plot may also include taped music: pre-show, act break, "under-scene" music, intermission, curtain call, and post-curtain. A master tape with all the sound cues as well as music is created by the sound crew or an independent production company. Another sound (crew) person runs the show.

Working with Lights and Sound

Actors don't usually even meet the light or sound crews until tech rehearsals, when nerves are on edge. Be cool. You should have used early rehearsals to find out as much as possible about how the lights and sound will be working.

Learn how to find your light. This is one of the things that's done in tech rehearsals. Don't be surprised if, when you look at the lights shining on you from above, they are glowing amber and lavender. Every professional actor knows that these color gels are most flattering to skin tones.

When you turn on a light switch on stage that is not practical, stage lights will be brought up. Even if a lamp or light is practical, area lights may be brought in when the light is turned on, so you will probably be asked to leave your hand on the switch for a few seconds while stage lights are coming up. Get in the habit of doing this. Nothing looks sillier than the actor who rushes in, flips up the switch, walks away, and several seconds later the lights come up.

The same is true with sound. If you're turning on a radio or putting a record on a stereo, leave your hand on the instrument until the sound comes up. This may be even longer than it is for light—sound often seems to "fade in." If you're answering a telephone, get in the habit of picking up the phone *between* rings. It's nearly impossible for the sound person to time cutting the sound to your pick-up. (Have you ever heard a sound tape "squeal" when it's cut off mid-ring?)

If you are expected to make off-stage noises (such as background for a party, a scream, or off-stage dialogue), you must be in place backstage at the right time. This should be considered just as important as your on-stage role; if you miss a backstage sound cue, it's just as bad as missing an on-stage cue.

You may be requested to say the cue lines (where lights or sound changes happen) a little louder than normal, so that the stage manager or light/sound person can hear them clearly. Never argue with this logic. First of all, if the line isn't heard, the technical cue won't take place, which could effectively stop the action of the play. Second, and perhaps more important, if the stage manager can't hear you, can the audience?

WORKING WITH SETS

Who's Who in Sets

The **Set Designer** is the artist who conceives and creates the total look of the set (or sets), which includes all rooms, walls, furniture, colors, floors, fabrics, etc. Actors meet the set designer and see the model set in an early rehearsal.

There are numerous people who execute the set. The construction crews build the basic set, construct the flats, stairs, levels, and sometimes even furniture. A **Master Carpenter** may be in charge of set construction and moving the set into the theatre. **Scenic Artists** may be responsible for painting or creating special finishes on walls, floors, or background. **Set Dressers** may be credited with drapes, curtains or wall hangings, unique furniture or props, photos or paintings, and/or all the other things one might find in a home or an exterior setting.

Working with the Set

You should take the time to study the model set and ask questions about it. Consider space relationships, furniture placement, platform levels, and stairs. The more you can learn about your surroundings, the fewer surprises there will be when you do get on the finished set. It's a good idea for actors to make a small drawing of the floor plan on paper and carry it with the script. This gives you something to refer to when you're at home going over blocking. During rehearsal, the model set may be left on exhibit in the rehearsal room. Smart actors refer to it often, especially during blocking rehearsals.

Actors sometimes feel completely at odds with the set—and it shows. Actors often forget that the set is supposed to be their home—and it shows. They leave the set entirely to the crew—and it shows.

One of the reasons you should familiarize yourself with the model set is so that it isn't completely alien to you at the first rehearsal in the theatre. You have had several weeks to learn your lines and discover your relationships with other characters in the play. You will have only several hours to become familiar with the set. That's why you should have a very clear picture of the set in your mind and as definite an idea as possible of what your stage surroundings will be.

Professional actors take the earliest opportunity to get on the set—even going in during construction (with an OK from the stage manager) to look at it and walk around if possible. Once the set is finished, you'll find the pros up there a half hour before rehearsal, just walking around, checking out the spatial relationships, soaking up the atmosphere. At early dress rehearsals, with an OK from the director, I always try to watch at least one or two scenes (which I am not in, of course) from the house. You will get a good idea of what the audience is seeing, and how the set looks and feels from their perspective.

As was discussed in the section on props, the stage manager will often allow the actors on stage before the actual performance to check props. This also allows the actor time to feel at home on stage for a few minutes before the performance. If this opportunity is available, and if you have an OK from the stage manager, by all means walk around the set and check your props before every performance. Being allowed on the set will usually happen from one hour to one-half hour before a performance. After that the house will be open and actors will be forbidden on stage. Try to get to the theatre early to perform this little ritual.

Common Sense with the Set

There are always people who abuse the stage set, even in professional productions. The following advice may seem obvious, but since these common mistakes happen so often, they bear repeating.

If your set is built of flats, don't plan to lean on a wall—it won't support you. If your set is built of flats, don't knock loudly on a door. The door may be solid, but the flats all around it will jiggle and sway. (Often a makeshift "door knock board" will be provided. You knock on a piece of board on the floor, or knock two pieces of wood together.) Be very careful if your character goes out slamming the door. Unless the door is completely offstage, the entire set will practically fall down if you put your weight into the door slam. Actors sometimes have to come up with more inventive ways to express their anger on exit lines.

If you are working with a cyclorama, be aware that backstage movements anywhere near the *cyc* (pronounced SIKE) will create a ripple effect to the audience—it looks like the sky is shaking. Generally, it is impossible for actors to make a cross behind the cyc because they will be seen, but cycs are very touchy, and even a tiny movement anywhere near them will create havoc.

The same types of rules and common sense apply to set furniture. Don't put your full weight on a little makeshift table attached to a set wall. In fact, don't put any weight on it. Be conscious of the fragility of some stage furniture. Often, period pieces are rented or rickety antiques, and you simply cannot use them with the same comfort as your own durable home furnishings.

In short, don't break anything on stage, and don't do anything that would destroy the audience's "willful suspension of disbelief." They should feel that you are in a solidly constructed house with walls made of real plaster and wood. Actors sometimes use the excuse that their character simply *has* to do an action, and the set is not as important as their feelings. Let me tell you something. An actor who goes storming around breaking furniture and slamming out the door, leaving the set in shambles and shaking behind him, looks pretty silly, no matter how "strong" he thinks his performance is.

WORKING WITH THE TECHNICAL DIRECTOR AND RUNNING CREW

Who's Who on the Tech Crew

The **Technical Director** (TD) is in charge of the technical aspects of the show and usually works directly with stage management. The tech director makes sure that all the technical aspects of the show (from lights to sound, stage changes to revolving sets) are in working order and functioning as the designers and director want them to.

The **Running Crew** includes all the people who work backstage during each performance. Running crew people will probably be familiar faces, but possibly not. For example, let's say at the first rehearsal you were introduced to a prop designer who then went off to create special pieces for the show; a rehearsal prop person provided things to work with during rehearsals; when the show went into production, there was another person running props.

Running crews will probably include: stagehands who change sets, a prop master, a master electrician who runs the light board, a master sound person who runs the sound (often one person runs lights and sound), a wardrobe mistress/master, a hair/makeup maintenance person, and dressers who help with quick changes. Actors should know who these people are and what they do because they will be seeing them backstage at every performance.

Complaints

Professional actors who have a problem with any aspect of the show involving the crew never go directly to the crew person. The stage manager is the one to talk to regarding props that aren't there, lights that go out before the scene ends, misplaced furniture, sound problems, or quick change mess-ups.

Actors as Crew

It is not unusual, in a professional or non-professional production, for actors to be requested to help with set, prop, and costume changes. I have worked in shows in which there was no crew to make set changes because there were no intermissions and no blackouts. In the Off-Broadway production of *Vanities*, for example, the set pieces were minimal, and all changes were done by myself and the other two actresses in the show. Sometimes actors are requested to move small pieces of furniture during a quick scene change—a perfectly acceptable request. Or you may be requested to bring on or clear a prop or costume piece for yourself or another actor, particularly during a blackout or short scene change. This makes sense. How silly it would be to have a crew person fumbling around in the dark with the actors who have to do that anyway.

Actors may also be requested to help other actors with quick changes backstage. In the production of *History of the American Film* at Hartford Stage, there were twelve of us all quick-changing at the same time in a tiny backstage area. Even if crew had been available to do it, there wasn't time or room. (As one actor wryly commented, "This production is brought to you by a grant from Velcro.")

You may have gathered by now that there's nothing wrong with actors being asked to help out with set, prop, or costume changes, if the actors are available (and if it does not conflict with union crew jurisdictional rules). Do everything you can to cooperate in these matters—without jeopardizing your own performance, of course. The request is usually made in order to provide a smoother-running show with a minimum of effort.

WORKING WITH THEATRE PUBLICITY

Who's Who in Publicity

Publicity departments are behind-the-scenes people who usually work day and night to get newspaper, radio, and TV coverage for the show and the actors. The person responsible for getting material to the press and other media is the **Press Agent** or **Publicity and Public Relations (PR) Director**. This person is probably also responsible for advertising: from placing show advertisements to distributing flyers and posters to selling program ad space. The publicity department (particularly if there is no advertising) may be responsible for the success of the entire run. If the public doesn't know about the show, if the critics don't come, if there are no photos and no reviews, who will come to see the show?

Bios

Even before rehearsals begin, actors may be requested to write and hand in a *bio*. Short for "biography," this is a brief prose summary of the actor's experience, to be printed in the program. Actors may also be requested to provide one or more photos that will be used for the program and/or other publicity.

Bios should preferably be typed and limited to the number of words the theatre specifies. If the theatre doesn't specify, you should *ask*. You might write 150 words, and all they have space for is twenty-five! The bio is a short résumé in essay form, which includes your theatre, film, and TV credits. If you are a beginner with limited experience, list your school plays, recitals, and other stage performances, academic activities, and honors—things you think the audience might like to know about you as a person.

Before you turn it in, check your bio for spelling of names, play titles, and characters, and have it ready on time as requested. Don't expect the publicity department to edit your bio for you. They won't know what's important to you and may well cut out your favorite credit or line. Put your name at the top and provide a current telephone number (not part of the bio) at the bottom so they can check with you if necessary. Bios should always start with your professional

name, followed by your character's name in parentheses. If you don't
follow this format, the publicity department will just have to reword
the first line.

A personal note to actors about bios: try to keep them as
professional as possible. If you have few credits, this is not the place
to be cute and say things like ". . . he hasn't appeared in any films
you would recognize and hasn't won any awards . . ." (from an actual
bio in a professional program). It's also not the place to lie. Don't
make up fabulous credits for your bio; somebody out there will surely
know the truth. Though it has been done, I don't recommend using
your bio space to preach or give your life's philosophy either. (In one
show I did, a major star requested, and the theatre printed, the
"Desiderata" instead of a bio.)

I don't mind a final line that includes something personal, such
as "she is happily married to actor Jeffrey Jones, and they have three
lovely children," or "In his spare time, George enjoys race-car
driving and hang-gliding." Personally, however, I think it's going a
bit far to end with something like, "I want to thank my mother and
father for their everlasting support, my teacher Mrs. Pincushion for
her terrific coaching, and my dog Jumbo." While it is certainly
thoughtful to give credit to deserving family and friends, it is of
absolutely no interest to 99% of the audience. Thanks may be ex-
tended when you win your Tony.

Photos: Pre-Production and Production Shots

The publicity department is often in charge of photos. *Pre-
production photos* will usually be set up and taken during rehearsals.
Costumes are not finished, frequently the show is not even blocked,
and usually the set is still a figment of the designer's imagination.
Often only the people in leading roles will be asked to participate in
pre-production shots.

If you are one of the lucky ones, realize that these photo sessions
are "sketchy"—they are often just tight shots of two or three actors,
with the barest suggestion of costume and set. Actors will be
expected to do their own makeup and hair, and may really be
"winging it." If you're asked to participate in pre-production shots,
try to wear something that suggests the period of the play and your

character. Even if you are told "these are just rehearsal shots," the finished product will look so much better if you are dressed appropriately than if you're in jeans and a T-shirt. Good photographers try to stage pre-production shots very close-up so the setting and costumes aren't really seen, but you can't count on that. These photos do provide something for the newspapers to use along with a feature or article *before* the show opens, so do your part in making them look as professional as possible.

Production photos are taken after the show has opened, when all the costumes, wigs and makeup, and sets are finished. They may be scheduled to be taken during or after a dress rehearsal, or after a preview or performance. If the photos are taken *during* a dress rehearsal or preview, actors should be notified that someone will be taking photos while they are performing.

Photo sessions scheduled *after* a performance should run smoothly and quickly. The publicity department and/or director should have posted a list of the specific shots they want, in what order, and who is involved. In Equity productions, only a certain amount of time is allowed for photos without paying overtime. Often production shots are taken after a show, and in reverse order, so that the final act scenes will be taken first (because these are the clothes you are in). And, yes, you will be expected to change into all your costumes in reverse order for the photos.

Make your changes as quickly as possible, and when you are ready, go immediately backstage to await your next photo. Try to be disciplined and orderly during photo calls. The more the actors cooperate, the quicker and smoother the process will be.

Keep in mind that pictures are an important part of the production, both for publicity and for the "historical record." You may want copies of some of the production shots; normally you may look at the contact sheets and order the pictures you want for a per-photo fee. Production shots are usually reproduced in 8 X 10 black and white.

WORKING WITH THE BUSINESS
AND BOX OFFICES

Business and House Managers

Theatres usually have a **Business Manager**, who is in charge of accounting (making sure you get paid), subscription and group sales (Theatre Development), and all other things having to do with money coming in and going out. If you have a problem with your check, you will generally be talking to the business manager.

The **House Manager** is charge of the ushers, program dispersals, and audience seating. Many theatres have a policy of offering free tickets to people who volunteer to usher; if you have friends who wish to see the show this way, you can put them in touch with the House Manager.

Box Office and Comps

The **Box Office Manager** is in charge of tickets and seating arrangements. Actors may get to know the box office people quite well, because they will be calling them or stopping by to reserve tickets for their family and friends. In many regional and stock theatres, checks are picked up at the box office, and mail is held there for actors. Needless to say, it never hurts to have a good relationship with the box office people.

Most theatres allow actors a specified number of complimentary tickets (*comps*) per production. A typical allotment is two comps for the run. (Your stage manager should know how many your theatre allows.) While it is not appropriate to exceed the specified amount, sometimes if a show is not sold out, actors may obtain comps at the last minute for friends or family by a simple request to the box office. However, don't abuse the privilege.

On the other hand, if the show is not selling so well, the stage manager or box office may offer unlimited comps for those performances that are practically empty. It's a good idea to keep in touch with the box office to determine if and when you may be allowed additional free tickets.

4

The Ten Commandments of Theatre

I.   The director is God. Thou shalt not take notes from friends nor family, coaches nor critics.

II.   Thou shalt not take the name of the producer thy angel in vain, for he shall sign thy checks.

III.   Remember thou keep holy the half-hour; keep in mind that an actor is never on time, an actor is alwaysearly.

IV.   Honor thy author and thy composer, for in the beginning were the words and the notes.

V.   Thou shalt not kill laughs nor step on lines; still, thou shalt pick up thy cues.

VI.   Thou shalt not adulterate thy performance, for thy stage manager is always watching.

VII.   Thou shalt not steal scenes nor focus nor props.

VIII.   Thou shalt not bear false witness in thy bio nor résumé; indeed, thou shalt be truthful in thy entire performance.

IX.   Thou shalt not covet thy neighbor's lines; for truly, there are no small parts, only small actors.

X.   Thou shalt not covet thy neighbor's good fortune; for in fact, all actors must pay their dues.

THIS ABOVE ALL:
THE SHOW MUST GO ON

The Ten Commandments of Theatre provide sound advice for actors in auditions, rehearsals, and performance. Though each one stands alone and is fairly self-explanatory, I should elaborate a little to illustrate these ten important points. (Note: The use of the "Ten Commandments" is not intended to be sacrilegious in any way; rather the "commandment" analogy reinforces the importance of these guidelines in an easy-to-remember format.)

I. THE DIRECTOR IS GOD. THOU SHALT NOT TAKE NOTES FROM FRIENDS NOR FAMILY, COACHES NOR CRITICS

Of course, nobody is God except God. But in theatre, there has to be one person within the process who has the final say in how the production looks, what the actors are doing, and the overall style and development of the play. Without a director, there would be chaos —a bunch of egomaniacal actors all trying to be stars.

Directors work in all sorts of different ways. Some are totally "pre-prepared" with blocking, scene composition, character development, and line readings before rehearsals start. In rehearsals for *Barefoot in the Park*, the director loved to demonstrate exactly how he wanted me to play Corie, to the extent that one of my compatriots commented that the director really seemed to want to play my role. In another situation, for a comedy of manners, the director was so specific about technique and style that he would get up on stage and demonstrate characters' moves and gestures.

Other directors come into rehearsals with very few preconceived notions of how the thing will actually evolve; they are totally relaxed and seem to have a very laissez-faire attitude about what their actors do. One of my directors liked to sit in the back of the theatre drinking wine and shouting directives at us. He would say to us at the end of the day, "OK, you guys, I want you to come into rehearsal tomorrow with something entirely different." That was the case for every single rehearsal.

I have worked with directors who love to sit around and discuss intention and motivation, and others who get the play on its feet and work and work and work it. Sometimes hours are spent breaking down and working on each scene practically line-by-line; other times, after the blocking is done, run-throughs start and continue right through to production.

The point I'm making is that it doesn't matter how your director works. What's important is that you TRUST THE DIRECTOR, and that you are willing to accept what he or she suggests. This doesn't mean you can't discuss certain elements of your blocking and character with the director, particularly the points with which you strongly disagree.

But an actor who is constantly saying "I can't move there, I just don't FEEL it," or "I think that's so WRONG for my character," gives the director nothing but grief. In the final analysis, you are better off if you have the attitude that you will sincerely and genuinely try what the director wants because: 1) it might just work, and 2) even if it doesn't, you will certainly have a better relationship with the director.

I've seen actors sabotage their own performances because they "didn't like the director," or "didn't feel the director was prepared," or "didn't feel the director knew anything." Who are actors to decide this? The director was hired because he or she has a directing background. The director is the only person in the theatre who can see objectively what the actors are doing. If you disagree with this, witness the number of productions that fail because one of the actors (usually a star) is also the director. Unless you are Laurence Olivier, you probably are not capable of acting and directing yourself simultaneously. Even actors who have had experience as directors cannot usually direct themselves successfully on stage.

Some actors come into rehearsal with very strong, definite ideas of how their scenes should be blocked and how their characters should be played. These inflexible people are simply not willing (or able) to change any part of their performance from the first reading to the final show. This attitude always creates problems, because the director now has to compromise to get the actor to try it a different way. Because the actor doesn't really *want* to do it another way, the attempt always seems to fail—it rings false. (Of course, they are out to prove to the director that it won't work.) Sadly, the actor's performance suffers, because it looks like some things are clearly motivated and working (their own ideas), and others are always awkward (the director's input).

I am not suggesting that actors become "doormats," but if they are not willing to work in a cooperative effort, they disrupt rehearsals and undermine the director's authority. All sorts of problems are created for others in the cast—the "squeaky wheel" takes up all the rehearsal time, and the director devotes all his or her energy to problem-solving rather than helping to create an artistic experience with a working ensemble. Actors who cannot or will not take direction should think seriously about an alternative career; there are certainly plenty of other creative outlets in which people can work more independently.

The attitude that "The Director is God," doesn't give directors license to abuse or mistreat actors, or to be tyrannical, dictatorial, or nasty. The finest directors in theatre usually have the attitude that "we are all in the same boat," and their approach is kind, sensitive, and loving toward their cast.

Actors on a High Wire; The Director is the Net

Here's an analogy: the actors are up there on a high wire— taking chances, going as far as they can, risking their emotional lives, letting it all hang out—and the director is the net. Good actors are willing to take risks, do all sorts of different things, try all sorts of creative approaches to a scene. A good director will keep them on track, and the actor can feel free to take chances because there will always be someone there to "catch them."

I once congratulated a director on his recently won award, and he said, "Thanks, I cast good actors." You have to believe, up front, that the director is brilliant, creative, and intelligent. After all, he or she chose you to be in the show. Believe from the first reading that the director likes you, feels that you were the very best person for the part, and really wants to work with you to get your best performance. There is no director in the world who would cast an actor for any other reason. By all means, do your preparation, do your homework, be creative, have fun, take chances, come in with strong ideas—and in the end, be willing to let the director do his or her job.

Getting Notes from Others

There is nothing more frustrating to a director than to have actors change their blocking or performance because someone else told them to. Since rehearsals are closed, notes from outsiders usually start with the invited dress. An actor gets together with people after the performance and makes changes based on their advice and ideas.

In other cases, actors will work separately with coaches on scenes, and come in with entirely different work based on what some outsider has decided is best. Once you are in production, everything that happens in rehearsal should be considered sacrosanct. You should not work with outside people on the material you are doing in production. It will only become confusing. This applies to acting as well as singing coaches. Your coach is not your director. Your director, for the duration of the rehearsal and performance, is your coach.

Changing a performance because of what a critic says is worst of all. For this reason, many seasoned professionals do not even read reviews. (There is more discussion about this in the section on theatrical superstitions in Chapter 7.) Suffice it to say critics are terribly subjective, can be extremely cruel, and are often wrong. Don't change one iota of your performance because of what you read in a review.

II. THOU SHALT NOT TAKE THE NAME OF THE PRODUCER THY ANGEL IN VAIN, FOR HE SHALL SIGN THY CHECKS

A lot of people who have the money to invest (or lose) in a theatrical venture don't know diddly-squat about theatre. Anybody who sinks money into a theatrical production probably has a few loose marbles anyway. That doesn't mean they should bear the brunt of actors' complaints or be the subject of company jokes. Producers do a lot of hard work for the theatre, and they deserve respect and consideration.

Actors often forget that if it weren't for the producer, there would be no production at all. Producers supply the bucks. It is not

the producer's job to know the artistic elements of the theatre—
those are left to the artistic and creative staff, which includes the
directors, designers, et al. That is not to say there aren't a lot of very
savvy producers out there—there are. Many of them, however, are
not themselves directors or actors, and do not have the same artistic
background as those who are involved with the creative aspects of
production.

Most producers are in the business of theatre because they love
it. They are willing to gamble a lot of money (their own and others')
because they believe that good theatre should be done and seen.
They are willing to trust their directors to provide the finest possible
shows for audiences. They are often willing to lose their shirts when
a new, controversial production is done, because they believe in it.

Other VIPs in Theatre Production

Along with the producers, there is a whole raft of other people
who make theatres work. These folks include the patrons and
sponsors who donate money, a board of directors who make decisions, a ladies' guild that helps provide meals and lodging, and other
influential townsfolk who offer support, from advertising to printing,
from construction materials to furniture, from benefits to opening
night parties. The producer and artistic director work closely with
these people because they need and depend on their financial and
volunteer help. A theatre does not exist in a vacuum—it can only
happen with the help of the community.

Production Functions

Actors should be aware of the functions that some of these groups
provide, and should have "an attitude of gratitude."

Opening Night/Closing Night Parties—Often the producer,
along with some other group of volunteers such as the ladies' guild,
provides an opening night party for the cast. This should not be
regarded as a free-for-all. The board of directors and other influential
folks attend the party after the performance, so actors should not get
drunk and carry on. If the actors are smart, they will try to meet some
of the people who may be there. One of the reasons these people get

involved in theatre is the opportunity to meet and chat with the actors.

Post-Show Discussions—In numerous regional theatres, there is often at least one post-show discussion provided for audience members who wish to discuss the show in more detail with the actors. This may be for adults after an evening show, or for students after a matinee. In professional productions, the actor's attendance at these discussions is entirely optional—the actor is requested, not required to attend. In every post-show discussion I've attended, all the cast members were there. It's a good idea. Again, it shows respect and support for the community people and students who are interested in the workings of the theatre. P.S. The artistic director is often there too.

Meals and Housing—In professional productions, if there is only a certain amount of time between shows (a matinee and evening performance, or two evening performances), the theatre is required to provide a hot meal for the actors. Often this meal is provided by a ladies' guild or some other volunteer group. Attendance is optional, but most cast members usually partake because there isn't time to go out; also, it's free. If actors do take advantage of this meal, it's a good idea to recognize who has done the cooking and thank them for the hard work.

In some regional theatres, housing in hotels or motels is in short supply or impossible to obtain. Sometimes members of theatrical support groups volunteer a room or rooms in their home to accommodate the actors. Even though there may be a charge for these housing arrangements, it is a special service provided on a volunteer basis, and actors would do well to respect the privilege of living in someone else's home.

Your Checks

I'll never forget after one particularly hilarious and fun rehearsal of a professional production, one of the Equity actors broke away and said, "Well, I have to go pick up my check." To which a fellow professional responded, "You mean some of you guys are getting PAID for this?" Acting can be a lot of fun, and getting paid for doing it is the frosting on the cake. You should know, however, that the pay, even in Equity productions, is often notoriously low, and that it's very difficult for actors actually to get cast in enough shows throughout a year to support themselves.

If you are lucky enough to be getting paid, your salary should be considered completely confidential. It is not to be discussed with anyone but your agent. Ever. It is particularly risky to discuss salary BEFORE the show goes into rehearsal. Keep it to yourself.

In many regional and stock theatres, the professional actors are paid the same amount no matter what the size of the role (see Glossary: *Favored Nations* clause). Similarly, some theatres are notorious for paying minimum and advertise the fact, so company members assume they are all getting the same salary. Never assume. Because there are so many variables, salary should be considered private business.

In school and community theatres, of course, there are no checks. But even though you are doing a play for the credit and/or the love of it you should still behave like a professional. Perhaps you're not getting paid. But if your attitude is "Hey, you're not my boss, you don't sign my checks," then maybe you belong somewhere else where you do have a boss and do get paid. Plenty of people would love to be acting in any theatrical production. If you really don't want to be there, let someone else do it.

III. REMEMBER THOU KEEP HOLY THE HALF-HOUR; KEEP IN MIND THAT AN ACTOR IS NEVER ON TIME, AN ACTOR IS ALWAYS EARLY

Most professional actors come into the theatre well before the half-hour. Many of them arrive as early as two hours before the performance. This has nothing to do with getting ready on time—it has to do with soaking up the atmosphere, getting into character, having time to chat informally with other cast members, going over the script, making sure costumes and props are all in order, checking the stage, etc., etc., etc.

I did a production of *The Great Sebastians* starring two great pros of the theatre, Eileen Herlie (Gertrude in Laurence Olivier's *Hamlet*, "All My Children") and Werner Klemperer (Colonel Klink in

"Hogan's Heroes," Tony nominee for *Cabaret*). Both came into the theatre at least an hour and a half before performance. Each would sit quietly in his or her private dressing room, usually mulling over the script. It was not unusual to hear either calling out, "Listen, Ducky Cakes . . ." (they had pet names for each other), "Listen, Ducky Cakes, what about trying this on that line . . .?" Then one would drop into the other's dressing room for a little discussion. This went on for the twelve weeks of the run. Right up until closing night they were each consulting the script, getting new ideas, sharing them, and going out there with something fresh.

Speaking of being early, it is always wise for the actor to check with wig/hair people, makeup artists, and dressers to be sure what time they may need your head, face, or body. The fact that in professional productions, actors are not REQUIRED to be in the theatre *before* the half-hour may be beside the point. It may simply be impossible for the wig person to handle six ladies within thirty minutes. If you want help with your wig, hair, makeup, or costumes, it may be necessary for you to come in early.

Respect for Others

In addition to getting to the theatre early, there are certain procedures an actor is expected to follow, as well as some common sense behavior required for the backstage and dressing room areas.

There is a certain atmosphere that settles backstage once the half-hour is called; in professional theatre it's almost a reverential quiet. Vocal warm-ups are kept to a minimum in areas where others can't hear; hilarity in the green room settles down to quiet chatting; any extraneous music (either from an individual's radio or the sound system) will be shut off. Whatever the actor's particular way of getting into character and getting energized, after the half-hour is called, the ambience that prevails is silent concentration.

IV. HONOR THY AUTHOR AND THY COMPOSER, FOR IN THE BEGINNING WERE THE WORDS AND THE NOTES

This guideline seems so simplistic, it is hard to believe it actually needs discussion. But it does, apparently over and over again. It is the actor's job to memorize the script as it is written. It is the actor's job to go over the script after it is *believed* to be memorized, to learn it again. It is absolutely wrong for actors to change the words. Paraphrasing is totally unacceptable. It is wrong for singers to change the notes. Period.

I once worked with an actor (who shall remain nameless in more ways than one), who almost never gave a correct cue. Even his *errors* changed from performance to performance, so that the rest of the cast could never tell what the cue line would be. Closing night after the final show, sitting around over cocktails and having our "truth" session, the actor blithely remarked, "Well, I always think if you get the general idea of the line, it's OK." Wrong.

Playwrights spend their professional lives writing, rearranging, correcting, and editing their scripts to say exactly what they want to say. They are wordsmiths who use thesauruses and dictionaries and references—they STUDY and pick and choose each and every single word that goes into a final script. Before that script gets published, it often goes through readings and workshops and all sorts of discussions and conferences and processes, which result in rewrites and final editing. Who do actors think they are to change the written words?

Actors who paraphrase are creeps. They violate the script and its author; they hurt the director and the play; they insult their fellow actors. How can a director tell what a character is supposed to be like when he is not hearing the right words? How can other actors respond correctly when they're not getting the right cues? (Actors *always* know when someone is giving an incorrect cue line.)

In comedy, it is very dangerous and critically damaging not to memorize precisely. There is a very important rhythm to a comedy script, which involves both the character's individual pace and the timing of dialogue. The slightest change can destroy the rhythm, which will then wreck the laugh. I guarantee it.

There is another serious problem that is very common: people think it's OK to add little "realities," such as "Well," or "Umm," or "Oh," or "You know," to the front of a line, or throw it in the middle of a speech somewhere. Maybe these little additions are supposed to make the speech more common, so the character speaks just like a "real person" (the actor). Or maybe it's done unconsciously—the actor never memorized the line properly in the first place. Perhaps a little addition or expansion got added at rehearsal and was kept in because it "felt right."

Whatever the cause, the result is sloppy acting. If the author wanted your character to say "Well," or "Umm," or "Oh," or "You know," he would have written those words out for you. It doesn't add anything to your character to add words—it detracts from your acting and from the play. Example: In a recent production I was in, the line that one actress was supposed to say as written was "We're just talking." It came out "Oh, well, we're just talking about it." You might be thinking, well, that's not so bad, I mean, it's not critical, it's not a laugh line or anything. OK, get this: what if everybody in the play changed every line just that much? You would end up with a different play.

Author Harvey Fierstein, who wrote *Torch Song Trilogy*, among other notable scripts, is credited with one of my favorites. When an actor stopped rehearsal and whined, "But my character would NEVER say that!", Harvey replied, "Listen, I WROTE your character, and believe me, he says that. You figure out how to make it work." As an author, Harvey has every right to speak for every writer of every script. It's the actor's job to say the lines as written, and determine why the author chose those particular words in that particular order for the character to use. If more actors would respect what the author has written, instead of constantly fighting a script, they would get a better idea of what type of character the author intended.

Musicals

With the same painstaking work and research that authors write words, composers write notes. Every single note is important. It's one thing for a vocalist to have a distinct "sound"; it's entirely another to be sliding up and down the scale doing all sorts of musical high jinks instead of the notes as written. Singers who do well-known musicals run a terrific risk when they do this sort of thing. First, there are always people in the audience who know the music, and they will *know* when the notes are wrong. Second, music is written in a particular *style*, and adding notes or changing rhythms to "contemporize" songs will seriously destroy the overall style of the music. Unless a musical director or arranger requests and encourages this sort of thing, it's always best to sing the songs as they were meant to be sung.

V. THOU SHALT NOT KILL LAUGHS NOR STEP ON LINES; STILL, THOU SHALT PICK UP THY CUES

Comedy is the most fun, difficult work in the business. A famous comedian, on his deathbed, was sympathetically asked, "Is it hard?" to which he croaked, "Dying is easy—comedy is hard."

Some people believe that you either have a talent for comedy or you don't; that it is not something that can be taught. That may be true; on the other hand, there are some technical guidelines that all actors should be aware of. You never know when you might be called on to do some comedy. Look at Leslie Nielsen. He spent the first thirty years of his career playing the heavies in "serious drama," but his career really skyrocketed with the hilarious work he did in *Naked Gun*.

General Rules of Comedy

1. **Learn your lines and deliver them as written.** Nothing will screw up comedy more than paraphrasing or adding "junk" to the script. To work, comedy must be "clean."
2. **Learn to recognize lines that are "set-ups" and deliver them loud and clear.** Your lines may not be funny, but if they are the set-ups and they are muddy or indistinct, the punch lines will not register. Comedy is rarely done alone on stage—unless you're a stand-up, which is a completely different animal. Almost all comedy is dependent on at least two actors working together. If you have the set-up and someone else has the punch line, the laughter you get is shared. If your set-up isn't right and the punch line bombs, you killed

the laugh. Never think you are getting the upper hand by destroying the laugh—you're hurting yourself, hurting the other actors, hurting the play, and hurting the audience.

3. **Be aware of timing.** Comic timing is largely a matter of pace.

4. **Learn how to develop characters** and find the fun in them. Actors rarely take the time to find the uniqueness, the quirkiness in characters, but in comedies it's most often right there in the author's words. If you search and can't find the unusual, try to develop a "handle" on your character—some unique trait or specific physical or vocal mannerism that sets your character apart. Character work is essential to comedy.

5. Once you've mastered the technical things like timing and character development, **learn how to play the truth in comedy.** This is the only thing that will make comedy genuinely funny. I recall at one first read-through, the very savvy director said, "Ladies and gentlemen, this is Neil Simon, we don't have to *be* funny." The implication was that if we just played the characters and the truth, the show would be funny. And it was.

6. **Faster, louder, funnier.** This expression is a common backstage mantra when the show isn't working. If the audience is not responding and funny stuff is withering on the vine, you'll hear the professionals softly repeating: "faster, louder, funnier."

Faster implies picking up both cues and pace, two different things. *Pace* is your own character's delivery, and you would be surprised how fast you pick it up and can still be heard and understood. This doesn't mean just rattling like a Gatling gun. You still have to know what you're saying, just say it faster. One director I worked with was fond of saying, when things weren't working, "PUPY" (rhymes with Snoopy), meaning Pick Up Your Pace. (No, it's not an exact acronym, but it's easy to remember.)

The other element of "faster" is picking up your cues. You may have heard the familiar expression, "The pauses between lines were so long there were trucks driving through them." (An expression that probably developed from theatres situated on highways.) Long beats between another character's lines and your lines will surely kill laughs. Picking up cues is done by starting to speak AS SOON AS another actor finishes speaking. You don't need to step on the ends of their lines, but neither do you need to pause, at all.

One reason audiences don't laugh is that they are usually miles ahead; if the delivery is too slow, the audience knows the punch line before the actor says it. They don't laugh because they have anticipated the joke. An important operative word when playing comedy is BRIGHT. Keep it up, keep it bright, keep it sparkling.

Louder means just that: talk louder. If the comedy isn't working, sometimes it's simply because the audience can't hear the set-up or the punch line. And there is no excuse for that.

All professionals know that if you go faster and louder, the play will be funnier. You don't have to struggle at *being* funnier. On the other hand, if you're playing your comedy as though it were a tragedy, that won't work either. Examine your own conscience. Are you simply being too serious, too heavy? Comedy is also supposed to be LIGHT. Keep it light.

7. **Learn to play the house.** Perhaps the most difficult and advanced part of playing comedy is learning how to incorporate the audience into your performance, in theatre terms, "playing the house." Here are some tips.

Once something funny is working, *do it exactly the same way* every time. Don't muck around with success. When there is a laugh, the next line should be delivered *just after the laugh peaks*. Start your line before all the laughter has died down. You must necessarily speak a little louder to be heard, but this is an important element of keeping up the pace.

Don't count on laughs—every audience is different. You must constantly be on your toes to come in with your line, even if the line before has always gotten a huge laugh. This may be the time it doesn't work. If you're playing to a small house that is not very responsive, don't get angry if you don't get the kind of explosive reaction you're used to. A quiet house does not mean the show is not working. It simply means the audience is not reacting as vocally as some other audiences. Nothing will destroy a comedy performance faster than an angry actor.

Yes, as the old actor said, "It's hard." If you're working with a "tough house," if you're "dying out there," try to imagine that all the critics, your family and friends, the director and producers, and important agents and talent scouts are in the house—that may help you change your attitude. Try to have fun and make the most of every single performance.

VI. THOU SHALT NOT ADULTERATE THY PERFORMANCE, FOR THY STAGE MANAGER IS ALWAYS WATCHING

It doesn't matter whether the stage manager is watching, or whether the director is in the house, or whether there are critics or coaches or family or friends in the audience—professional actors simply do not mess around with their performances once the show is up.

Exactly what does this mean? Aren't good actors supposed to "keep it fresh" and new and different every night? How do you keep your performance the same without turning into a robot? Aren't you supposed to "play the house"? What if another actor forgets a line or misses a cue, or what if the furniture breaks or part of the set comes crashing down?

Not "adulterating" a performance means keeping it ESSEN-TIALLY the same as it was directed. This leaves good actors leeway for expansion, finding new things, keeping it fresh and improving the performance throughout the run without adulterating it by changing lines, changing blocking, cracking up, trying to crack other actors up, adding cheap laughs, or otherwise generally screwing around. It is sometimes difficult for actors to understand this concept, so I'll give some specifics and examples.

1. **Do not change the blocking.** Nothing is more distracting to other actors than finding someone on stage in a different place every night. Often actors who feel that they are being upstaged will sneak upstage just a little at each performance until the blocking is actually changed. Or they just arbitrarily decide that they want to move at another time or to another place. Once you're in performance this is just not done. Upstaging and awkward blocking must be worked out in rehearsal. By the time you're in production it's too late.

In some shows, particularly farces, blocking may be choreographed down to the split second—the slightest change will not only destroy the comedy, it could be physically dangerous to others. Don't do it.

Warning: All stage fights and physical business are carefully and exactly choreographed so that actors won't be hurt. The original staging must always be followed. In professional theatre, if an actor subjects another actor to physical harm or danger on stage, that person may be brought up on charges through Equity and/or possibly be involved in a lawsuit.

2. **Do not change the lines,** and don't let the lines get "accidentally" altered along the way. Refer to your script frequently *after* you are in production, and make sure you are saying the correct words and giving the right cues. If a laugh line isn't working, don't use that as an excuse to get "creative" and rewrite the line. This is also very disturbing to other actors who never know what's going to come out of your mouth.

3. **Do not change business, bits, or shtick.** In professional productions, business, bits, and shtick are just as choreographed as the blocking. Whether it's working or not, it's not up to you to cut it, change it, or expand on it without the express consent of the director and/or stage manager. Some things are terribly clever without getting huge reactions or laughs. Some bits or business are written into the script, and the plot or another scene depends on them. It's not up to you to change them arbitrarily. And don't start adding junk that wasn't there in rehearsal. It was your job to be inventive then; don't start having fun at the expense of your fellow performers and the show once you're in performance.

4. **Never play down to an audience.** If you feel they are not getting it and that makes you want to spell it out, they will detect your patronizing, condescending attitude. Never try to get an audience to react by using shtick, bits, takes, or other cheap stuff that hasn't been rehearsed into the show. It's not fair to your fellow players or the audience, and it's not funny.

Never compensate for a lack of response in the audience by trying to crack up your fellow actors. This is the absolute lowest form of non-professionalism, an insult to your fellow actors as well as the audience. No matter how small the size of the audience, no matter what their age range or group affiliation, they are entitled to your best show.

5. **Avoid the temptation to add "improvements."** When a show is working, and an audience loves a particular character, scene, or bits, the actor's ego often takes over and the performance gets so over-blown it's no longer recognizable. Even though you are having fun and creating laughter (or tears), there is still a decorum in all fine performance, which requires a certain amount of restraint. This is true as much for contemporary reviews as period farce and style pieces. This is not contradictory to playing the house—bear in mind the old adage from vaudeville, "Leave 'em laughing." If you go too far, the audience will just get bored, and you will become a cartoon caricature, which may be funny but ultimately detracts from the truth of the story, the character, and the play.

6. **Always give your best performance.** When a show's been running for a while, and the cast gets tired and bored, the actor may be accused of "phoning it in." Don't ever phone in your performance. Always warm up, exercise, and energize prior to each and every show you do. Remember, you never know who might be in the audience that particular performance. It could be the big break of your life, so give it your best.

VII. THOU SHALT NOT STEAL SCENES NOR FOCUS NOR PROPS

Everybody knows what upstaging is, and almost everybody does it. It drives professional actors crazy.

When you are in a shared scene with someone, place yourself on a direct line with them, as we discussed in the section on blocking. How are you going to do this without taking a tape measure to rehearsal? You will improve by just being aware of it. If you feel that you are being upstaged or are upstaging someone else in the blocking rehearsals, ask the director if this is the case. In performance, the blocking may vary by a few inches, so always come down to your fellow performer and adjust yourself by those few inches so that you are on the same line with him or her.

When I was a newcomer to the theatre, after having done several Equity shows, one seasoned professional made a point of letting me know that I was unconsciously upstaging him in rehearsal by placing his two hands on my shoulders and moving me downstage a few inches to his level. It was embarrassing to me, but from then on I was very conscious of it. You should be constantly on the alert to avoid this common error.

Stealing focus can be done (and has been) in many ways: moving around, fooling around with costumes or props, looking elsewhere, or simply not being involved in the scene. I have never quite understood the logic of stealing focus: what's the point of calling attention to yourself at the expense of the play? What does it accomplish if the audience notices you but misses important dialogue? Amateurs who steal focus have terrific inferiority complexes—they think they always have to be the center of attention, and they don't have enough confidence in their ability to hold an audience when they do have the focus.

Granted, it's tempting to try to steal focus when you have a small role and you want to stand out. Don't. You may not stand out at all, but you may be doing everything you're supposed to be doing for that particular play in that particular role. Have confidence in your ability and your professionalism that a small role (even if you don't get noticed) will lead to a larger one in which you will.

It goes without saying that if you're not supposed to upstage anyone or steal focus, that whole scene-stealing is the greatest crime of all. Of course. This is when the focus-stealing goes on and on, and the audience is completely distracted from the business at hand by the thief. However, scene-stealing sometimes just "happens," and it's not always bad.

There are times when the author writes in a character (often a cameo role) who is just supposed to be funny and outrageous, and if you get a good actor in that role, he is naturally going to "steal" the scene. What can you do? Let him—it's intentional. In other situations, the director may feel that a scene isn't strong enough to stand on its own, and he/she will give an actor bits, shtick, or business that will steal the scene. Again, this is intentional. If you really feel that it's distracting to the scene (because you're the lead, acting your heart out up there and nobody is watching or listening), you can do one of two things. One, talk to the director to try to get the stuff cut or trimmed; or two, give focus to the business and react to it. You may just create a shared stolen scene.

If you're working with a star, either a national or local one, bear in mind that you may be upstaged a great deal of the time. Stars are notorious for upstaging others, and some directors will try to stroke the star's ego by always giving them focus, even when it's not appropriate. If you are stuck with a "little" star (one who can't stand not being the center of attention), make the best of it. It's useless to fight it. Some stars will get terribly upset if anyone has focus except themselves.

Most stars are very easy to work with and unlikely to upstage anyone. Some seasoned professionals actually take some perverse pleasure in upstaging themselves and playing a good deal of the show with their back to the audience.

Regarding stealing props: most actors would never consider actually *stealing* props but think nothing of helping themselves to the potato chips set out for the cocktail party scene in Act Two. Though there will probably always be the stereotypical "starving actor," prop food should not be eaten except on stage.

VIII. THOU SHALT NOT BEAR FALSE WITNESS IN THY BIO NOR RESUME; INDEED, THOU SHALT BE TRUTHFUL IN THY ENTIRE PERFORMANCE

If you're not familiar with the traditional ten commandments, maybe you don't know that "bearing false witness" means lying. We've already talked about this in the section on bios, and we'll discuss résumés in the chapter on becoming a professional.

Acting is a business; you wouldn't lie on a business résumé, and you shouldn't do it on an acting résumé or in a bio. Somebody will always call you on it. Which is not to say that you should belittle your own credits—if you were in a movie as an extra, that is a legitimate job, and it is not necessary to say "I was ONLY an extra." On the other hand, don't make yourself a principal player. If you were in the chorus of a musical, that's a good credit. Most casting people and agents know how talented chorus people are and how hard they work. But when it comes to your résumé or bio, don't list yourself as the lead.

Even though there are thousands of actors doing thousands of productions throughout the country over the years, the theatre community is basically a small world. You never know when the very person you're trying to impress might just have been intimately connected with a production that you're lying about. You might even get called on the carpet about it; more often, you simply won't ever get called at all.

Actors spend all of their professional lives learning how to give a truthful performance. Jimmy Cagney is credited with saying about performing: "Get out there, plant your feet, and tell the truth." This is often easier said than done, particularly if you're playing a challenging character outside of your range, or you're in a play that requires a special style.

Actors are inundated with technical problems—costumes, lights, blocking, accents, choreography, etc. Often they come into rehearsal with a nice sense of the truth and then lose it along the way because they are concentrating so hard on all the technical stuff. While you are learning your lines, try always to come back to what you are really saying, what the other characters are saying, and how to find the most real way of playing it.

Learn how to relax on stage, while at the same time keeping your own concentration and energy up. Study the MASTERTRACK for Actors (Chapter 6). Keep confidence in your own ability and choices, and learn how to make the direction your own. Don't fight the material, work with it. Don't fight your fellow performers, learn how to compromise. The more productions you do, the more easily you will be able to find and play the truth in each character and play.

I had an almost scary experience once. I was playing Bobbie Michelle in Neil Simon's *Last of the Red Hot Lovers*. Bobbie is a sweet, mixed-up, empty-headed, pot-smoking young woman who always gets into trouble with men. A woman I met after the performance said, "I wish you could talk to my daughter, you and she seem to have the same problems. She is very mixed up, she gets into all kinds of trouble with men, and I know she smokes pot." Interesting. At the time, I was a very ambitious, hard-working young actress who had never smoked pot. I took it as a compliment—this woman thought I *was* Bobbie Michelle.

IX. THOU SHALT NOT COVET THY NEIGHBOR'S LINES; FOR TRULY, THERE ARE NO SMALL PARTS, ONLY SMALL ACTORS

According to Webster's dictionary, "covet" means to "ardently desire something another person has." I worked with an actor once who actually counted the number of lines he had in a script. (I'm talking over a hundred.) At the time I thought it was ridiculous—I still do. I've seen actors with ten lines steal the show.

Not coveting your neighbor's lines encompasses lots of things—you shouldn't covet their roles or billing either. Most actors who audition want the lead, but there's only one lead. Directors need good people in supporting roles too. And in little roles. Many who auditioned for the lead will end up in the chorus. It's asking a lot to say "don't covet that role that you were dying to get when you first auditioned." Once you're in rehearsal, however, you just gotta let it go.

For one thing, you must trust that the director knew what he or she was doing to give you the role you have. You are probably much better suited to it than the one you thought you wanted. For another thing, if you're given a walk-on or put in the chorus, you simply must be grateful to have the experience to be performing. You will get something out of every single show you do.

Two of the toughest jobs in theatre are understudy and stand-by. The difference between the two is that an *understudy* is cast in the show and appears on stage in a smaller role, then goes into the larger role if the actor cannot appear. A *stand-by* doesn't appear on stage, simply waits in the wings in case the performer breaks a leg (literally). It's tough for these folks not to covet the other person's role—they are prepared to do it and it might just be their big chance. If you are ever in this position, remember the following. You will get a lot of experience from memorizing the lines, being at rehearsal, working on the character, watching and learning from a more seasoned performer, and doing understudy/stand-by rehearsals. You will get the credit as an understudy or a stand-by. Not to mention that there's always the tiny possibility that you will go on. A lot of superstars got their first big break as understudies. A young, unknown Shirley

MacLaine, for example, walked away with rave reviews when she went on for an indisposed star in *Pajama Game.*

The old adage "There are no small parts, only small actors" was not written to be a consolation prize for spear carriers. People who have been in the business for years will swear to the absolute truth of it. If you study and do a lot of plays, you will discover that the leading roles carry forward the action and are on stage a lot of the time and have most of the lines. But they certainly are not the ones who get the most attention all the time. Frequently, the supporting roles are far more interesting, fun, or dramatic. And just as often a tiny little cameo role will blow the audience away. Look at Bronson Pinchot in *Beverly Hills Cop.* That was a dinky little part (which led to costarring in TV's "Perfect Strangers"). Every single actor in the play is essential to that play. Otherwise, in this age of tight budgets, the role would be cut. Make the most of your role, no matter how small. Only small actors think less of themselves if they have a little role.

X. THOU SHALT NOT COVET THY NEIGHBOR'S GOOD FORTUNE; FOR IN FACT, ALL ACTORS MUST PAY THEIR DUES

It's tough not to compare your personal situation with others. Actors are constantly measuring their own success against their competitor's, and burying their envy by saying things like, "Oh, well, she's a friend of the director, that's how she got cast," or "If my parents contributed the kind of money that his do, I'd be playing the lead too." Nothing in theatre seems to be "fair." Somebody gets a role because they look the part, not because they have one iota of talent. Somebody else gets cast because they went to school with the director. You might as well get used to it, because nothing in life is fair either.

Something to remember here is: be nice to everybody. The person playing the smallest walk-on might be doing the lead in the next play. As much as you must have respect for yourself and your role if you are doing a small one, watch out for your own ego if you're playing a lead.

Some actors seem to be born with a silver spoon in the mouth—they go to all the right schools, make all the right connections, and next thing you know they're doing a soap, they have their own series, or they're a movie star. This is *sometimes* the case. More frequently, actors have really paid their dues, meaning they had years of struggle before they became an "overnight sensation." They did showcases and shows on the road, they played the little roles, they took the stand-by and understudy jobs, and when they couldn't get arrested, they waited tables or drove taxis or typed.

A lot of young people who come into acting really don't WANT to become actors—they really want to be stars. Ask yourself: Am I willing to pay my dues to become an actor? Do I want to act more than anything else, even if that means that (maybe) I won't be a big star? Am I willing to study and learn the craft to become a real professional?

THIS ABOVE ALL: THE SHOW MUST GO ON

This universal maxim is so familiar that it has crossed over from theatre into our general vocabulary. Because it's true. Nothing should keep you from your appointed performance.

I have gone on stage with laryngitis, bronchitis, flu, colds, backaches, headaches, and a number of other maladies including a sprained ankle and a broken toe, but I'm not trying to brag. So have millions of other actors for thousands of years since theatre began. Sickness should never keep you from a show. I worked on "Another World" with veteran Bob Hastings, the day after his mother had died. He was hurting, but he was working. (In fact, a death in the family is just about the only legitimate excuse to miss a show.) Many Equity contracts do not require hiring of understudies, so even professional actors get used to the reality that the show cannot proceed without them.

Along the same lines, professional actors do not leave a show once rehearsal has started. While there are exceptions (including union rules that allow Equity members to be released from a contract to take a better-paying professional job), the usual attitude is that you are committed to this show, and you will do it. Recently I heard of a community theatre actress who "bowed out" of an important leading role in a show one week prior to opening, because she "just couldn't take it and besides, she was having problems with her boyfriend." Please don't do this. Part of the professional attitude is learning to sacrifice your personal life to fulfill your artistic commitment.

5

Voice and Verse, Period and Style

VOCAL DEVELOPMENT AND STANDARD AMERICAN SPEECH

Just like musicians, actors need to learn proper technique and should practice with their instrument daily. It may take years of initial development as well as consistently applied discipline to keep the instrument working properly.

Singers must study with their voice teachers and coaches on a regular basis. (The distinction between a teacher and a coach is this: the teacher works on technique and tone production, while the coach helps select and rehearse specific material for auditions and shows.) Professional actors (even those who are not singers and dancers) religiously take singing and voice lessons, dance and exercise classes. They know how important it is to have a voice and body that can withstand the use and abuse that are required of stage as well as musical performers.

The Voice

In vocal development studies, actors learn how to breathe properly (from the diaphragm), how to place the voice, how to utilize a wide pitch range for various characters, and how to project without straining. There are many disciplines of vocal training; one widely-used approach is the Kristen Linklater method. Whatever system is studied, it should be practiced and applied consistently until it is second nature. Of course, singers must learn to breathe properly in order to produce the notes, but they should also study vocal production as it relates specifically to speaking.

Why Bother?

A lot of young actors, encouraged by the example of movie and TV stars, seem to think that voice work is a waste of time. They see superstars who do not appear to have studied at all, and who use essentially the same persona and voice for every role, and assume that it's not really that important.

Granted, it's possible to become a star without any kind of vocal training, without having to change your voice or do any serious developmental work. But somewhere along the line it's going to catch up with you. Sooner or later, as a big star, you're going to be tempted or cajoled into doing a classic play or film and you're going to be embarrassed.

Witness: Dustin Hoffman in *The Merchant of Venice* (most critics and professionals agreed he was OK, but not great), Barbra Streisand in *Yentl* (she still sounded like Fanny Brice in *Funny Girl*), film stars Michelle Pfeiffer and Jeff Goldblum in the Central Park *Twelfth Night* (both roasted by critics), Al Pacino as Paul Revere in the flop film *Revolution* (tormented in reviews with his Brooklynese "Da British are comin', da British are comin'").

Now consider Meryl Streep. With a strong background in theatre, she parlayed her ability to do a wide variety of accents and characters into a number of Oscar-winning roles. And Mel Gibson brought tremendous range to his film portrayal of *Hamlet*. Who would have imagined this Mad Max of *Road Warrior* fame would be given the opportunity to do Shakespeare? But when it came, he was ready.

Accents and Regionalisms

Any kind of regionalism, accent, or speech defect is considered a problem for a serious actor, so you're going to have to get rid of it. Needless to say, if you have a speech defect you should work with a speech therapist, but don't be discouraged. Many of our finest actors and newscasters developed their resonant speaking voices and excellent diction as a result of having to overcome a speech defect. We have also discussed the accent problems of people whose parents' first language is other than English, as well as the vocal characteristics of certain racial groups and the problematic speech patterns peculiar to some geographical areas.

Some of you from the Midwest or the Western states are probably saying, "Well, I don't have to worry about that." Don't be too sure. Almost every area in our great country fosters bad habits and vocal problems. For example, the Midwestern nasality is legend, and it seems the larger the metropolitan area (Minneapolis, Chicago), the worse it is. And there's definitely a "Valley inflection" in California natives. There are even minor regional infractions, which I call *suburbanisms*—regional mispronunciations or distortions of words, which stick out like a sore thumb.

Standard American Speech

All aspiring actors should develop Standard American Speech. This is defined as "accent-less" American; you can hear it by tuning in your national radio and TV news. Most national spokespersons use Standard American so they can be understood clearly by the greatest number of people in our country. Standard American is free of accents, regionalisms, and suburbanisms and is also pleasant to listen to.

Listen to newscasters and radio announcers. Tape them. Tape yourself and compare. Work with someone who can teach you Standard American. I once did a play with a young woman who told me, at the end of the run, that she was from the South. When I mentioned that I hadn't noticed a trace of an accent, she said, "That's because I worked steadily with a coach every week for FIVE YEARS—she drummed it out of me."

If you really want to be a professional who is capable of doing different periods, styles, and characters in all media (theatre, television, and film), you must work on your voice. First get rid of the accent, regionalisms, and suburbanisms. Take courses in vocal development to learn proper placement and breathing. Work with voice coaches and attend classes devoted to Standard American Speech.

VERSE PERFORMANCE

The area of verse performance is largely ignored in all except a handful of professional schools, which is curious because it is so critical for an actor's work in classical theatre. Many experienced actors couldn't even recognize verse if they saw it. Numerous professional directors and producers believe that "all good actors," regardless of their training or background, can do Shakespeare or the classics. As a result some of the most beautiful poetry ever written gets mutilated and interpolated into American prose slang. In the chapter on auditions, we discussed the probability that you will be requested to do a verse piece in a general monologue. Professional actors know what verse is, how to recognize it, how to scan it, and how to do it.

Many of Shakespeare's plays are written entirely in verse; most of his others combine verse with prose. Most classics (from Greek and Roman to French and Italian) were written in verse in their original language, so the translations are in verse. Even large sections of the best-selling King James version of the Bible are written in verse.

Why is Verse Important?

It is important to know verse for many reasons. First, there is the responsibility to the author. If the play's original form is verse, then the performers of that play need to know it. Second, there is the responsibility to the form itself—verse is not only a play, it's a work of poetry. Actors as interpreters must be aware of the inherent musical rhythms in the work, and they must respect the meter and beat.

If these aesthetic reasons aren't enough to convince you, fear is always a good motivator: critics know verse. No matter what a critic's credentials or reputation, he or she generally is knowledgeable about and able to critique a play for its literary value. Most critics do know classical literature, and they base their reviews on the writing as well as the production. Critics always try to read a copy of the particular play they are seeing, and by the very nature of the job, most critics have seen several previous productions of a classical play. They are going to compare.

If you as an actor don't know what verse is or how to approach it, your interpretation will probably be wrong. Why? Because authors who write in verse are very aware of where the accents are and purposely place words to coincide with the stressed syllables. If you approach a piece of verse just as if it were prose, you may not even make sense, much less have any idea of the basic inherent rhythm that verse requires.

Iambic What?

The verse found in most classical plays is "iambic pentameter," which simply means each verse line is composed of five iambs. An iamb is a metrical beat (called a "foot") consisting of an unstressed syllable followed by a stressed syllable. Pentameter (from the Greek *pente*, meaning "five") refers to the five beats or feet. Since an iamb is composed of two beats, unstressed followed by stressed, iambic pentameter is verse that usually has ten basic syllables in a regular order of unstressed, stressed.

Iambic pentameter is usually marked with a little upside down half circle for the unstressed syllables, and what looks like an apostrophe for the stressed, for example:

‿ ╱ ‿ ╱ ‿ ╱ ‿ ╱ ‿ ╱
Oh spite! O hell! I see you all are bent

‿ ╱ ‿ ╱ ‿ ╱ ‿ ╱ ‿ ╱
To set against me for your merriment:

‿ ╱ ‿ ╱ ‿ ╱ ‿ ╱ ‿ ╱
If you were civil and knew courtesy,

‿ ╱ ‿ ╱ ‿ ╱ ‿ ╱ ‿ ╱
You would not do me thus much injury.

‿ ╱ ‿ ╱ ‿ ╱ ‿ ╱ ‿ ╱
Can you not hate me, as I know you do,

‿ ╱ ‿ ╱ ‿ ╱ ‿ ╱ ‿ ╱
But you must join in souls to mock me too?

∪ ╱ ∪ ╱ ∪ ╱ ∪ ╱ ∪ ╱
If you were men, as men you are in show,

∪ ╱ ∪ ╱∪ ╱∪ ╱∪ ╱
You would not use a gentle lady so;

∪ ╱ ∪ ╱ ∪ ╱∪ ╱ ∪ ╱
To vow, and swear, and superpraise my parts,

∪ ╱∪ ╱ ∪ ╱ ∪ ╱ ∪ ╱
When I am sure you hate me with your hearts.

Helena, A *Midsummer Night's Dream*

Though some experienced actors might disagree with such an extremely regular interpretation of the speech, for our purposes this is a good illustration of regular verse. A *Midsummer Night's Dream* is also a perfect example of a play written in a combination of prose and verse. The upper class folks, including Helena (example above), and the elegant fairies speak in verse, while the lower-class "Players" (the commoners) speak in prose. How can you recognize lines that are verse as opposed to prose lines? Sometimes you can tell by looking at the line. Verse lines stop at the end of the line of iambic pentameter, while prose lines go on to the margin of the column or page. You can clearly see the difference by looking at this prose paragraph (the one you are reading) and how it contrasts with Helena's speech in verse above. Other times you must scan the lines to determine whether they are verse. You will see that there is a regular pattern to poetry.

Determining where the stressed and unstressed syllables are is called *scanning* the verse, or *scansion*. As with all creative forms, iambic pentameter has its regular "feet" and normal lines (as illustrated in Helena's speech), but then there may be all sorts of variations on the theme. If the verse line is fairly straightforward with no variations, it is called a "regular" line. A line may be considered to be regular even if it has the common variation known as a *feminine ending*. This is simply an additional unstressed syllable at the end of the verse line. For example, Viola in *Twelfth Night* says:

∪ ╱ ∪ ╱ ∪ ╱ ∪ ╱ ∪ ╱∪
I left no ring with her. What means this lady?

The last syllable (the eleventh) is obviously not stressed. It's a feminine ending. Scanning will also give you clues to how to pronounce certain words. For example, scan the last line from Juliet's speech to Romeo in II:2:

Which the dark night hath so discovered.

The word "discovered" is intended to be said in four syllables. Not exactly contemporary American, you might think. No, but if you want to do verse properly, you should add that last syllable. You don't necessarily need to *punch* it, but you should be aware of it—it makes the poetry work. This issue is one that often confuses young actors— when do you pronounce the "ed" endings, and when do you ignore them? The answer is to be found in scanning the verse.

You may have noticed that this example line of Juliet's doesn't exactly scan as a "regular" line. If you're scanning (or trying to scan) the verse, and it doesn't make sense to interpret the line as regular, it may be because the line *isn't* regular. If a line contains irregular feet, in which the stresses are reversed or identical, or feet that have more than two syllables, the line is considered "irregular." Scholars have devised names for these irregular feet:

Trochaic	= ╱∪	(stressed, unstressed)
Anapestic	= ∪∪ ╱	(two unstressed, one stressed)
Dactylic	= ╱∪ ∪	(one stressed, two unstressed)
Spondee	= ╱ ╱	(two stressed)
Pyrrhic	= ∪ ∪	(two unstressed)
Dipodic	= ╱ ∪ ∪ ∪	(one stressed, three unstressed)
OR	= ∪ ∪ ∪ ╱	(three unstressed, one stressed)

Here is an example of each of these types:

╱ ∪ ╱ ∪ ╱ ∪ ╱ ∪ ╱∪
Trochaic: Cursed the heart that had the heart to do it
              (all trochaic)   Anne, *Richard III*

Anapestic: It is too hard a knot for me to ŭntie.
              (last two words)   Viola, *Twelfth Night*

Dactylic: Thus have I politicly begun my reign
              (First foot)   Petruchio, *The Taming of the Shrew*

Spondee: Two households, both alike in dignity
              (first two syllables)   Chorus, *Romeo and Juliet*

Pyhrric: Which the dark night hath so discovered
              (first and last feet)   Juliet, *Romeo and Juliet*

Dipodic: Unless I spake, or looked, or touched, or carved
              to thee.
              (first four syllables)   Adriana, *The Comedy of Errors*

You may have gathered by now that doing verse can be rather complex. True, but it can also be fun. Sometimes you add syllables to make the verse work; sometimes you subtract them. Sometimes the foot is not irregular at all but was intended by the author to be said in two syllables. When you slide two syllables together to make one, that's called *elision*. For example:

Either heav'n with lightning strike the murderer dead
                                          Anne, *Richard III*

If you count the syllables in this line, there are thirteen. However, Shakespeare obviously intended the actor to elide the word heaven into one syllable (clue: the apostrophe). Next we checked our version of a First Folio, and found the word "murth'rer." In addition to learning that the "th" substitutes for our "d," we can also conclude that Shakespeare intended this word to be elided into two syllables. If you scan this line, you will find that the first foot is

Voice and Verse, Period and Style ▷ 151

anapestic (either heav'n), and the rest is regular if you do the two elisions. This line correctly scanned looks like this:

$$\breve{\cup}\,\breve{\cup}\quad/\quad\cup\quad/\,\cup\quad/\quad\cup\quad/\,\cup\quad/$$
Either heav'n with lightning strike the murd'rer dead

After you have exhausted all the possible ways to scan a line, determining the various irregular feet and applying elision where appropriate, you may find that some lines, no matter how you try to work the syllables around, simply have twelve beats. Scholars even have a name for this phenomenon: a six-foot line is called an *Alexandrine*. This is a rare bird, however, and most of the time iambic pentameter follows a fairly regular pattern of ten beats. It's up to the actor to determine how to do it.

Once you have properly scanned the verse, you begin to determine your interpretation, using both the poetic stresses and your own good judgment. The words should always make sense. When working on verse, it's important to avoid a singsong effect. In Shakespeare's plays and in good translations of other authors' works, this is not a problem because the poetry is peppered with irregularities. To help eliminate a nursery-rhyme monotony, follow this cardinal rule of verse interpretation: do not stop or pause at the end of the verse line. Stop only at a period or semicolon, and only do that if it's a very long sentence; this is when you may also take a breath. Not only will the verse be smoother, but you'll soon realize how critical proper breathing is. You may be doing as many as ten verse lines without taking a breath.

What about dialogue? Now we're getting tricky. But no trickier than Mr. Shakespeare himself. In verse plays, the dialogue is also in verse, even though two actors may be sharing one line of iambic pentameter. For example, from *Richard III*:

Anne: Name him.
Richard: Plantagenet.
Anne: Why, that was he.

Notice how this dialogue exchange is printed; together these three lines form one single line of verse. If you are dealing with verse dialogue, both you and your partner must work closely with the director to ensure that these combined verse lines are scanned and interpreted properly.

Editions

Here is a true story. A neophyte actor rushes into the Drama Book Shop in New York , holds up a copy of a familiar Shakespeare play and asks, "Do you have a different translation of this?" Shakespeare is sometimes difficult to interpret, nevertheless, he did write in English. What the actor meant was a different edition.

You must have a good edition of Shakespeare or the particular verse play or piece you're working on. Good editions are not only the most faithful replicas of Shakespeare's words, they provide clues to the verse structure. There are as many variations on Shakespeare's actual text as there are translations of French farces and Greek tragedies.

Some Shakespearean editors were excellent indeed, and some were dreadful. Early editors, hoping to improve on the original, changed words, rewrote scenes, and often even tacked different endings onto Shakespeare's plays. Most of these early editions were printed prior to the author's worldwide recognition as the greatest writer in the English language. Today, editors painstakingly work to reproduce the original text faithfully. As a friend of mine once remarked, "They don't call him Shakespeare for nothing."

Scholars of Shakespeare usually work from a First Folio edition. Check the "About the Editors" section of your edition for the sources used. Actors may obtain their own copy of a First Folio. One particularly faithful reproduction is an oversized hardcover book called *The Norton Facsimile* (though less expensive copies are also available). In a good edition you will find that the words most closely match the First Folio, and the verse is printed in iambic pentameter.

It is sometimes difficult for beginners to recognize good verse translations of foreign language (Greek, French, Italian) plays. Of course, if you are actually doing a play, you will be working with the edition or translation that the director has selected. But if you are looking for a verse monologue, you may find that you have several choices. How can you decide what's best? This is a highly specialized area, because the translator must accurately reproduce the words that the original author intended, in the style and vernacular intended, and in good English verse. If you aren't sure where to look, ask a librarian, coach, director, or teacher who is familiar with verse plays and various available translations.

Character Clues

The study of verse also gives you clues to the character you are playing. As mentioned earlier, in *A Midsummer Night's Dream*, people of the upper class and the elegant fairies speak in verse, while the commoners speak prose. Further distinctions of character may be found in the *type* of verse itself; in *Twelfth Night*, for example, the poetry ranges from lyric to high declamation. Other clues may be found in the *irregularities* of the verse. In Shakespeare's *Richard III* the title character's speeches are filled with strange rhythms and odd stresses. Most scholars agree that this highly irregular verse was intended by the author as an accurate reflection of the crippled, hunchbacked character. John Barton, in his excellent book *Playing Shakespeare*, believes that irregularities of verse also provide contrast and emphasis within regular verse; that "Shakespeare gets his dramatic effects by the way he rings the changes on it." Mr. Barton also stresses the importance of finding a balance between the two traditions of heightened language (poetry) and naturalistic acting (realism).

The study of verse scanning is limitless. To confuse the matter further, it is sometimes arbitrary. Actors and directors who specialize in verse plays may disagree about how a particular line scans. (Shakespeare didn't write in the accents, so it is entirely up to the actors and directors to figure out the best way to do them.) This fact should not prevent you from studying verse—you can't have an argument unless you know what you're talking about. If you *choose* to depart from the verse at a particular time, at least you can defend your choice intelligently.

If your school or background has not provided you with the training and tools you need to scan verse, take a class or course in verse interpretation and get some constructive practice with it. As *New York Times* critic J.R. Bruckner states, "It is the gift of good poetry that, as one's understanding of it deepens, the verse teaches one how to speak it.

USING THE BODY

Taking classes and exercising should be part of every actor's routine. Dancers take classes and/or work out daily, developing their skills in all dance disciplines, including ballet, jazz, tap, and modern dance. But even if you're not a "triple threat" performer (one who can sing, dance, and act), you should be in good physical shape, for several reasons.

• **Stamina**—It takes a terrific amount of sheer stamina to do a leading role in any type of drama or comedy, as well as to remain resistant to colds, flu, and respiratory and vocal problems.
• **Physical Strength and Flexibility**—Many roles are physically and vocally demanding—from classical tragedies to modern farce, from contemporary comedy to old-fashioned melodrama. In addition, many roles call for physically challenging feats such as hand-to-hand combat and sword fights or split-second timed comedy bits and business. A slight slap on the face (even if it's choreographed or "faked") can hurt you if you're not in shape.
• **Vocal Production**—Because the body is the resonator for the voice, if the body is weak the voice will be small and tinny. A strong body will help you breathe properly, which is critical in musicals and classical works. Exercise also reduces stress and eliminates tension from the voice.
• **Physical Variety**—Only actors who are aware of their own bodies and who practice various postures, ways of walking, and physical mannerisms have the flexibility to create other characters through radical physical transformations. Awareness and exercise help the actor to "become" someone else, both vocally and physically.

There are three great ways of staying in shape that are available to everyone: dance classes, exercise classes, and sports and games. It's important to know your own body and what you need. It may be good for you to balance an aerobics class to build stamina, for example, with a yoga class for relaxation.

Actors who are specializing in a particular type of theatre may wish to become proficient in a movement or sport required in that area. For example, there is a lot of swordplay in Shakespeare, so those interested in classical theatre should study fencing. Actors who specialize in comedy and farce may benefit from learning tumbling. Almost all actors should study mime.

There are also numerous types of classes in stage movement available at colleges and theatre schools. One highly recommended study of movement designed specifically for performers is the Laban method, described in Rudolf Laban's book *The Mastery of Movement*. Studying a method in this detail will help performers develop a wide variety of physical traits and types of movement for developing characters and style.

The Alexander Technique, though not expressly a movement technique, is a valuable tool for achieving balanced posture and relaxation on stage. Developed by Matthias Alexander in the late 1800s, the Technique was originally devised to address the problems of performing artists, specifically actors and musicians. Its value is now so widely recognized that the Technique has been incorporated into the curriculum of numerous professional schools and is also available through private instructors and Alexander Centers.

PERIOD PLAYS AND RESEARCH

For some reason it is excruciatingly difficult for American actors to do plays that are set in a different period and therefore require a different style. By "different," I mean any style that varies from the excessively naturalistic, overly relaxed, stumbling and bumbling way that we usually behave and act. Perhaps this is the influence of our training, which encourages young actors to think that anything that "isn't real isn't right." Unfortunately, that kind of attitude sometimes leads to the mistaken assumption that plays written in a different period or style should be stylistically transformed to conform to contemporary movement and behavior, rather than the other way around.

Most actors would agree that, if you're dressed in a full-length gown or a high-collared suit, you're doing a "period play." Because the language is so formal, and because of the restrictions of the costumes, one would think that people must have walked, stood, moved, and gestured differently from contemporary Americans. Instead, you find American actors walking and moving just as they do in contemporary life—it may seem very natural to them, but it looks ridiculous in a period play.

Actors who are resistant to learning and doing various periods and styles are not only doing a disservice to the playwright, the director, their fellow actors, and the audience, they are losing out for themselves. One of the greatest joys of acting is to transform yourself through your character and the play into another time and place, to play a character who is *not* just like you. It opens the mind to the possibility that there were people who behaved in very different ways from ourselves but nevertheless were very real. It also allows the actors to transport themselves to a totally new context, a foreign country, an unusual lifestyle, a different social class.

Actors are often "dying" to get into a play, and then they are so reluctant to take direction regarding the period and style that the director wishes he had never cast them. I often wonder why actors are so determined to play their own play, so stubborn are they to direction, so convinced that only their own interpretation is correct. Actors who know they are controlled by this kind of ego would do better to investigate other areas in which they will have more independence and control. In the theatrical environment we must always be open to learning new things and willing to work together with the director as well as the company.

Theatrical Periods

A "period play" is defined as any play set in a different time period from contemporary time. It is important to note that period may be derived from two sources: 1) when the play was actually written, and 2) the timeframe in which the author intended the play to be set. For example, Shakespeare's works are often assumed to be set in Elizabethan England, and since that was when they were written, it is generally acceptable to present them within that timeframe. However, many of his plays are actually based on ancient stories or legends, and numerous innovative productions have utilized more primitive settings.

Notable periods in theatre usually include the following broad categories:

Greek and Roman	(c. 525 to 400 B.C.)
Medieval	(c. 500 to 1500)
Shakespearean, Elizabethan, and Jacobean	(c. 1560 to 1625)
Commedia Dell'Arte and French	(c. 1575 to 1675)
Restoration	(c. 1660 to 1690)
18th-19th Century European and American	(c. 1770 to 1850)
Modern	(c. 1850 to 1950)
Post-Modern and Absurdist	(c. 1950 to 1970)
Contemporary	(c. 1970 to present)

No one would argue that the first five or six categories require very specific knowledge of the period and study of style for performance. Though certainly more recent, the Modern category also implies "period"; notable authors of this era include George Bernard Shaw, Noel Coward, Oscar Wilde, Eugene O'Neill, Henrik Ibsen, and Anton Chekov, to name just a few.

The closer we get to our own time, the less likely we are to study the period. Most of us will plunge in without thinking or caring about period in a play by Tennessee Williams, Arthur Miller, or William Inge. And yet those plays require as much work as a classical piece to deliver a strong sense of the period and place.

Many plays set in a twenty-year period previous to our own we consider "contemporary," and usually the director will use trendy new costumes and high-tech sets to update them. However, a play that was written in the 1960s or 1970s may also be done in "period." If so, it's important to research that historical time just as if it were thousands of years ago. We simply must do our homework.

Researching the Period

Entire courses are devoted to the study of period and the various specific styles that are appropriate for each. It behooves actors who are serious about their craft to take these courses and study in detail every important period in theatrical history. You will learn not only the basics of style, but the *reasons* for the postures and mannerisms, costumes and props, makeup and wigs. A strong background will also

give the actor an intelligent approach to the character and relationships, so that the director has that much more to work with.

If there is sufficient time, actors can take the opportunity to do
independent research on the period, the author, and the play, in
other words: read, read, read. Read as much outside source material
as possible before going into rehearsal. There are many source books,
including autobiographies and biographies of the author; other
books, articles, or reviews about the play; books or articles about the
character; and popular novels or magazines of the time. Reading a
biography of Shakespeare, for example, will help the actor transport
himself into Elizabethan England and better understand the author's
background and references. Many authors write from their own
personal experience—you will find a great deal of autobiographical
detail in the works of Eugene O'Neill, Arthur Miller, and Tennessee
Williams.

Let's say you're doing *Hay Fever* by Noel Coward. You can read
The Life of Noel Coward by Leslie Cole. You will discover that in *Hay
Fever*, Mr. Coward based his eccentric family on that of a leading
actress and personal friend, Laurette Taylor. Then you can read a biography called *Laurette*, written by Ms. Taylor's daughter Marguerite
Courtney. If you're fascinated by now, you can read Mr. Coward's
own autobiographical diaries, *Present Indicative* and *Future Indefinite*.
You may even be able to find an audio recording of Mr. Coward (as
an actor) in performance.

Another terrific way to research the period, provided it is recent
enough, is to watch movies set in the same timeframe as the play. If
your play is set in the 1930s, '40s or '50s, you'll find that the style
of acting and language will help you get a bead on how people behaved in those days. Be careful though: if you're doing a Greek play,
it's probably not going to help you to watch a 1940s movie version
of it. That's going to confuse you with two periods (Greek and '40s).
I also do not necessarily recommend watching a movie of your
particular play. It's an easy way to get yourself up to performance
level, but it could mislead you into an imitative performance, one
that might be at odds with what your director wants.

Some plays performed in the early part of this century (particularly those starring leading actors of the time), which were not made
into films or recorded on video tape, may have been preserved on

audio records or tapes. Check out a good library, which might have copies of these classics. Again, I do not necessarily recommend listening to your particular play. The most important element in doing this kind of research is simply to read information or watch the film and "absorb" the period. Let all your research work sink in by osmosis, and after you have read the information or watched the movie, forget it.

Don't come into rehearsal with expectations of changing the script based on your research. You can't do it. For one thing, you must work with what you have, as in "the *play's* the thing." A movie version of a play often bears little or no resemblance to the original stage play. In addition, your research may show you that the play bears little or no resemblance to what actually happened. Authors often distort or concentrate the facts in order to create a good drama. Don't ever forget: you must play the play, not the research.

All your research should be done BEFORE you go into rehearsal and should not take away time from your memorization or rehearsal homework. If you need all your spare time to memorize the lines of the play, don't do ANY research. (There is nothing more frustrating than an actor who knows every minuscule detail of his character's life but doesn't know his lines.) Once you are in rehearsal, ALL your time should be devoted to specific work on the lines of the play, your characterization, business, and blocking.

Researching the period thoroughly will also give you a sense of the style of your piece.

Types of Plays

In order to understand style, we should first define the basic types of plays, as the entire approach and interpretation of the play will naturally be strongly influenced by the kind of material you are presenting. Types of plays include:

Tragedy—A serious work in which the hero strives to overcome great obstacles but does not succeed; traditional tragedy involves the death of the hero.

Comedy—A humorous work in which the hero succeeds in overcoming obstacles and provides laughter along the way.

High comedy or "Comedy of Manners" is a work that draws

characters from the upper strata of society; much of the humor is dependent on verbal wit.

Low comedy or "farce" is a work that depends on physical action, ludicrous situations, and unexpected happenings.

Drama—A play that is serious but does not result in the death of the hero.

Melodrama—A serious play in which there is a maximum of physical action, suspense, and overt conflict, usually with a happy ending.

Satire—A comedy of social criticism, which holds up to ridicule human foibles and absurdities of behavior.

Just to be confusing, contemporary plays may now be described as "Satirical Tragedy," "Tragi-Comedy," "Comedy Drama," etc. (There seem to be almost as many descriptive denominations as there are plays.) Though the above are general categories, most plays can be classified as being *predominantly* one of these five. Directors and actors should always keep in mind the type of play they are working on. While there may be many moments of comedy in good tragedy, or moments of melodrama in drama, the approach should generally be consistent with the type of play being done. For example, when playing a high comedy, actors and directors should be careful not to lapse into farce; when doing melodrama, don't let it become parody. I was personally involved in a dreadful misinterpretation of play type when I was working with a "terribly serious" group of regional the-atre actors—a silly little contemporary satire suddenly evolved into high tragedy. (P.S. The critics hated it too.)

TYPES OF STYLE

Style can be defined as the manner or fashion of presentation. It is an expression of:

1. The *author's* personal way of translating life to the stage.
2. The *conventions* in use during the historical period of the play.
3. The *director's* determination of how best to project the play's meaning.

There are two basic types of style, period and theatrical. In *period* *style*, the fashion of the day is translated into the theatrical fabric of the production. (Examples: Restoration, 19th Century, Elizabethan, etc.) As mentioned previously, to get a grasp of period styles, actors should study theatrical history, particularly as it relates to the actor's work with costumes and props, postures and mannerisms of the period. Seminars and classes devoted specifically to period style are also beneficial.

Theatrical style comes from a particular view of the theatre and the nature of theatrical creation (examples: Naturalism, Expressionism, Symbolism). The three very broad categories of theatrical style are: 1) presentational; 2) representational (realism); and 3) post-realistic (revolts against realism).

At first glance, it would seem that choosing a style for a play is easy; however, in contemporary theatre practice you will find that often various elements of style are mixed. What's important to remember is that there are basic conscious choices in selecting style, and actors should have some idea of what the director envisions as the predominant style of the piece.

Presentational

In the presentational style of most classical theatre, the play was "presented" to the audience rather than disguised as life itself. The first theatrical productions were essentially presentational, and the style was accepted as theatrical norm until the nineteenth century. All the following categories are presentational:

Classical Greek and Roman drama
Oriental theatre
Medieval theatre
Shakespearean, Elizabethan, Jacobean, and Restoration
Commedia dell'arte, French (Molière), 18th century drama

Elements of the presentational style include:
- Actors play directly to the audience
- Conventions: asides, soliloquies, enlarged movement
- Poetic language

Representational (Realism)

With the advent of the scientific attitude in the nineteenth century, along with advances in lighting and stagecraft, the theatre began to strive for an illusion of real life on the stage. The presentation of a play as though it is real led to a new style called representational, or more commonly, *Realism*. The proscenium arch is thought of as a picture frame or "fourth wall," behind which all action is confined. Realism is an attempt to convey the illusion of reality through careful attention to detail and no direct contact with the audience. The actors presume not to know the audience is present, and the audience presumes to be watching real life.

The timeframe of the Realistic period is the Modern period, from about 1820 (when gas lighting became capable of producing effects of sunlight, moonlight, etc.) to about 1920, when elements of Post-Realism began to surface. The major playwrights of the movement include Ibsen (*Hedda Gabler*, *A Doll's House*) and Chekov (*The Cherry Orchard*, *The Seagull*).

Elements of Representational theatre or (Realism) include:
- Actors play to each other
- Conventions such as asides and soliloquies eliminated
- Everyday language

Realism carried to its farthest extreme developed into a style termed *Naturalism*—an attempt to give a complete photograph of reality or "slice of life" without eliminating or selecting details or structuring material into a complex plot. (Examples: the works of Zola, Gorki, O'Casey.)

In *Selective Realism*, scenery may be a combination of realistic and symbolic elements; for example, such a set might feature real windows and doors, along with a framework suggesting a roof. (Examples: *No Time for Sergeants*, *Billy Budd*.) *Suggestive Realism* uses fragments of realistic detail to suggest a whole. For example, a Gothic arch may suggest a whole cathedral, and with artistic lighting the rest is imagined. (Examples: *The Caine Mutiny Court-Martial*, *The Lark*.)

Post-Realistic Styles

The twentieth century has seen many efforts to free the theatre from the limitations of realism and restore greater scope to the playwright and director. These "revolts against realism" became very influential as a unique way for the author and director to express the inner meaning of the play. (From the 1950s to the 1970s Non-Realism became so popular that the movement was called "Experimental Theatre.")

Although our theatre today remains basically realistic, the trend away from realism is ongoing, and realistic elements are often juxtaposed with elements that are non-realistic or non-illusionistic. In *Acting with Style*, by John Harrop and Sabin R. Epstein, the authors state: "It may well be that eclecticism will be the style of the future—an overlay of styles that will require a discontinuous form of acting to match the fragmentary 'byte-sized' nature of a high-tech society."

Elements of the Post-Realistic Style as outlined in *Directing for the Theatre* by W. David Sievers (Wm. C. Brown Company) include:

- Combining presentational and realistic styles
- Breaking the fourth wall; speaking directly to the audience
- Poetic or formal language mixed with contemporary slang

Some of the most influential movements of the Post-Realistic style include:

Symbolism—The use of symbol to convey meaning or emotion. Also called the "new stagecraft" movement, symbolism attempts to synthesize all the arts in the theatre, including painting, music, lighting, and dance. Also called: Multi-Media theatre.

Neo-Romanticism—A return to the poetic form in costume drama, which permits a heightening of effect and language not possible in Realism. (Example: plays of Maxwell Anderson.)

Expressionism—Purposeful distortion of reality to express inner meaning or the impact of twentieth century mechanization and other sociological influences upon the individual. (Examples: *The Great God Brown*, *Serious Money*.)

Constructivism—Elimination of external surfaces in order to penetrate to the skeletal construction, showing ramps, levels, steps, and joists. (Example: Broadway set design of *Sweeney Todd*, which looked like a construction site.)

Surrealism or Subjective Realism—Influence of Freudian psychology in attempting to express man's inner unconscious life through dream symbols, psychological distortion, and "free association" of ideas. (Example: *Death of a Salesman*.)

Stylization—Enlarging a certain detail or series of details beyond natural proportions; the audience is aware of the way actions are done as well as what is done; often used for 17th-18th century artificial comedy. (Examples: *The Matchmaker, La Bête*.)

Theatricalism—Calling the audience's attention frankly to the fact that they are in a theatre rather than watching a slice of life. Deliberate breaking of the "fourth wall," use of imaginary props, or scenery shifted in view of the audience. (Examples: *The Skin of Our Teeth, Six Degrees of Separation*.)

Formalism—Return to permanent architectural settings based on classic or abstract forms; using "unit" sets and "space-staging." (Examples: Classic architectural set used for Broadway production of *Medea* starring Zoe Caldwell; space-staging in *Whose Life Is It Anyway?*.)

Epic Theatre—The "learning theatre," which rejects realism, empathy, and illusion in favor of teaching a socio-political thesis through the use of narration, projection, slogans, songs, and sometimes even direct contact with the audience; also called "Experiential" theatre. (Example: *Execution of Justice*.) Note: In England, this type of production is called "Agitprop" (Agitation and Propaganda).

Absurdism—(Theatre of the Absurd) Plays that seem to have no rational meaning; elements of surrealism and symbolism are utilized, along with absurdity and irrationality in order to suggest the meaninglessness of life and the difficulty of human communication. (Examples: *Who's Afraid of Virginia Woolf?, Waiting for Godot*.)

AN ACTOR'S WORK IN PERIOD AND STYLE

There is a great deal to learn regarding the various styles that have been prevalent through the years, and the myriad choices of stylistic elements that directors and designers may incorporate into a production. Actors should always be concerned with the overall period and style of the production, listening carefully to the director's and designers' stylistic choices.

Study the model set to see how the production is going to look. If the director chooses a very bare, minimalist set he or she may expect the acting style to embody a very stark approach to the material. Note carefully the various designers' (costumes, lights, music) concepts and how they plan to carry out the overall scheme. These design elements can give us clues to how the production is going to look and the ambience the director wishes to convey.

Working with Costumes, Makeup, and Props

It is important to understand period clothing and how it affected the way people walked, stood, posed, and even talked at the time. As mentioned in the chapter on rehearsals, you should work with mock period costumes and props in rehearsal. For women, long skirts and heels are a must; women should also practice with special undergarments (such as corsets) in later rehearsals, as these pieces restrict movement and affect posture. Men should get into the habit of wearing clothing that resembles the period costume and its constraints; for example, a dress shirt and slacks as opposed to jeans and a sweatshirt.

Work tirelessly with props both in rehearsal and at home. Use of period props should come so naturally that the audience really believes you handle these things easily and naturally every day (fans, snuff, cigarettes and lighters, canes, scrolls, swords, etc.).

When you go for costume fittings, walk around in your costume and get a feel for it. Try to remember how your costumes fits and moves when you are in rehearsal, and keep in mind its special construction when you are rehearsing. For example, how do you sit down if your dress has a bustle? How will a helmet affect your fighting stance?

Start practicing with your period makeup as far in advance as you can at home. Look at yourself in the mirror in full makeup and imagine what the audience is seeing. When you start dress rehearsals, get to the theatre early and use this time to practice with your makeup and costume. Study yourself in a full-length mirror to examine how the audience will perceive you.

One of the most crucial questions to keep in mind is: what were the behavioral confines of people of this class and period? What is the sociological setting, and would each of the characters be affected by it? The costumes may help actors gain a sense of the postures and physical movement, simply because of their construction or design. However, you cannot rely on the costumes to give you a sense of style.

For example, I was once in period play in which all the characters were pretentious, rich, upper crust British types. The time frame was 1930, and the costumes were gorgeous. During rehearsals I had been blocked to sit on a "window seat" in my floor-length red satin gown. Unfortunately, when we got to the set, the cute little cushioned seating area I had imagined turned out to be a six-inch painted wooden shelf. I kept the original blocking, but when my agent saw the show he remarked, "A woman of your class dressed as you were would NEVER have sat on that." From then on I was very careful about what I was doing in my classier period plays.

Economy of Movement

Sanford Meisner, teacher and director of the famed Neighborhood Playhouse in New York, is credited with saying "Don't just do something, stand there!" This is probably one of the cleverest and most perceptive pieces of advice ever written. It applies to the actor's work in general, but is especially applicable to the work in plays of period and style. I call this approach *Economy of Movement*: simply put, don't move when you don't have to.

One of the traps that amateur actors fall into is trying to do too much. They move on every line, they develop twitches and mannerisms for their characters, they fiddle with stuff, they overreact physically and facially to every line and bit of business. Experienced actors know that all this movement is extraneous and detrimental to good theatre. They know this because real people simply do not do it.

During blocking rehearsals, be careful that you move only when it makes sense for you to move and resist the urge to cross on every line. Busy blocking can almost always be traced back to blocking rehearsals, when actors cross too much because they are bored and feel like "doing something." (Some of this extraneous movement stems from an insecurity that if you're not moving, the audience won't be looking at you.) Most actors forget that blocking rehearsals take a long time, so they compensate by crossing here and there all over the stage. When they get into run-throughs and things are moving four to five times faster, there is usually way too much movement.

Economy of Movement involves learning how to use the movement on stage as though it were choreography—it is fluid, it is beautiful, it is perfectly timed. Trust yourself to remain perfectly still when you don't have the focus or when it isn't necessary to move. When actors choose to remain still, the audience will really notice them when they do speak or move. If you are doing a period play, which has a particular style, think of yourself and the rest of the cast as an ensemble of dancers. You will get a much stronger sense of the blocking as choreography and the quiet strength of stillness.

Economy of Movement also helps the audience understand the story of the play—the less movement there is, the more likely it is that the words and plot will be clearly understood. Acting does not have to mean getting on stage and moving around to get attention and generate artificial "action." And it does not mean that actors need to use their bodies and hands to "translate" every single word for the theatregoers. If actors really focus on the words and the story, it will be apparent that less movement is more effective.

Jason Robards, in reminiscing about Colleen Dewhurst, said, "As actors, we were always very kind to each other. The play's the thing. All we tried to do was get the best out of the play that we could. You put yourself into the service of the play and that of your character. And Colleen knew this. On stage, she remembered the old axiom: don't move when the other actor is talking. She kept in character and listened to him. It seems like a very simple rule, but it was the greatest help, and no one seems to know it anymore."

SHAKESPEARE'S ADVICE TO THE PLAYERS

No book for performers would be complete without the inclusion of

Shakespeare's Advice to the Players. This piece has become so popular that alone it is commonly referred to by the above title, and many actors regard it as the finest condensed advice ever written.

Note: It is in the same play that we also find the quotation, "The play's the thing." Though not part of this famous speech, the line is certainly paramount to theatrical work and should also be remembered along with the rest of this remarkable author's advice to actors.

Back to the point. The speech is found in *Hamlet*, (III:2) as he is instructing his hired "players" (actors) exactly how he expects them to perform. (To facilitate the explanation that follows, I have broken the speech out into eight numbered points.)

Shakespeare's Advice to the Players

1. Speak the speech, I pray you, as I pronounce it to you, trippingly on the tongue.
2. But if you mouth it, as many of your players do, I had as lief the town crier spoke my lines.
3. Nor do not saw the air too much with your hand, thus, but use all gently. For in the very torrent, tempest, and as I may say, whirlwind of passion, you must acquire and beget a temperance that may give it smoothness.
4. Oh, wig-pated fellow tear a passion to tatters, to very rage, to split the ears of the groundlings, who for the most part are capable of nothing but inexplicable dumb shows and noise. I would have such a fellow whipped for o'erdoing Termagant—it out-Herods Herod. Pray you, avoid it.
5. Be not too tame neither, but let your own discretion be your tutor.
6. Suit the action to the word, the word to the action, with this special observance, that you o'erstep not the modesty of nature. For anything so overdone is from the purpose of playing, whose end, both at the first and now, was and is to hold as 'twere the mirror up to Nature—to show Virtue her own feature, scorn her own image, and the very age and body of the time his form and pressure.
7. Now this overdone or come tardy off, though it make the unskillful laugh, cannot but make the judicious grieve, the

censure of the which one must in your allowance o'erweigh a whole theater of others.

8. Oh, there be players that I have seen play, and heard others praise—and that highly, not to speak it profanely—that neither having the accent of Christians nor the gait of Christian, pagan, nor man, have so strutted and bellowed that I have thought some of Nature's journeymen had made men, and not made them well, they imitated humanity so abominably.

Say What?

Students of theatre may wish to obtain their own copy of *Hamlet* and study this speech line by line, interpreting the more obscure references with the help of footnotes and a Shakespearean dictionary. I have taken the liberty of doing my own "translation," which is not a word-by-word explanation but rather a simple rewrite in more contemporary language. I hope the essential meaning of each bit of advice remains intact, as Shakespeare intended when he wrote it in 1603.

1. Pick up your pace and practice your vocal exercises.
2. If you want to mumble like Marlon Brando that's your business, but it's just as bad as shouting and screaming; you owe it to the audience to be heard and understood.
3. Use gestures carefully; even though you're really into the passion of the moment, too much flailing around becomes meaningless. Learn to move gracefully like a dancer and use economy of movement.
4. Don't overact—it isn't necessary. If you are too wrapped up in your own emotion, nobody will be able to understand your words. Never underestimate the intelligence of the audience.
5. On the other hand, don't underplay everything—your performance will be boring. Try to find a happy medium by using your own discretion and listening to your director.
6. Suit the action to the word and the word to the action, always keeping in mind that you're trying to look like a normal person doing plausible actions. The whole purpose of acting and theatre is to hold a mirror up to Nature. Search for the truth in your

performance and relax; trying too hard will only work against
you.

7. Stealing scenes and getting cheap laughs might amuse some
    people in the audience, but this behavior doesn't serve the play
    and will insult the intelligence of the audience, infuriate the
    director, and alienate your fellow actors.

8. If you don't look like a real person up there, you have no business
    on a stage anywhere. Keep your day job.

It is amazing to see how on-target Shakespeare's advice still is
today. He covers the territory from underacting to overacting, from
doing too much to not doing enough. One of the major points to be
derived from the speech, in Shakespeare's own words, is "acquire a
temperance." When studying style, bear in mind that along with the
conventions and artificial poses you may be doing, you should always
keep coming back to the truth of your character and the dramatic
situation. Acquiring a temperance will help you balance these two
elements.

Many actors spend their entire careers specializing in particular
periods and working in various theatrical styles. Facility of doing
style cannot be acquired in one class or a single production; it must
be practiced and experienced numerous times before it becomes
second nature. It doesn't happen overnight. But learning and using
style may be the deciding factor between an uninspired, uninformed
performance and one that is brilliant and sophisticated.

6

The MASTERTRACK
for Actors

The MASTERTRACK for actors is an easy-to-remember acronym—each letter in the word MASTERTRACK corresponds to a guideline. It's not an acting theory, but a methodology for work, a compilation of sound advice gleaned from the way professionals work. Not intended to contradict any other approach that actors have learned, the MASTERTRACK is rather designed to complement all theories and acting strategies. Just as the Ten Commandments provide the actor with guidelines for dealing successfully with *other people*, so the MASTERTRACK provides the actor with a structured method for approaching the *work*.

The MASTERTRACK is based on personal observation and on-the-job experience working with hundreds of professional actors in more than seventy-five professional productions over a period of twenty years. Performers who are truly professional consistently use these guidelines (in this form or another) throughout the creative process, particularly in rehearsals.

Many of these important points have already been explained in detail throughout the book. If a guideline has been discussed, the previous section will be referred to, and this chapter will contain a few summarizing "refresher" points.

THE MASTERTRACK FOR ACTORS

MEMORIZE Early and Exactly
ACTING is Action and Reaction
STUDY at Home
THINK

EXERCISE
READ for Comprehension
TRY New Things
RELAX
ANIMATE the Moment
CONFLICTS and CONTRASTS Create Good Drama
KEEP it Simple

MEMORIZE Early and Exactly

The vital messages about memorization have been covered in detail in Chapter 2 on rehearsals, in which several tips for easy memorization are outlined. And in Chapter 4, we stressed the importance of exactness of memorization.

• Begin memorization as soon as you are cast.
• You don't need the blocking to memorize.
• Use a tape recorder.
• Practice daily.
• Don't paraphrase, add, or delete words.

ACTING is Action and Reaction

Many young actors approach the play as though they are the only creatures on the stage. The work that results is one-dimensional, because the actor is doing only one-half of the job, the "acting" half. After some experience and confidence is gained, the actor begins to *listen* on stage and react to what is being said. Really listening, and reacting appropriately to what you're hearing, is the other half of acting: the "Reaction." Learning to listen and react marks the beginning phase of a more fully developed stage presence.

Solid memorization will help you enormously with this step. The more confident you feel about where your line comes and exactly what it is, the freer you will be to relax, listen to others, and enjoy what's happening on stage without being paranoid, thinking, "What's my next line?"

As we discussed in Chapter 4, comedy is sometimes totally dependent on reaction. Some lines will simply never work without a reaction; in addition, a laugh may be obtained from a marginally funny line by an appropriate reaction from another character.

Note: Don't fall into the amateurish trap of *over*-reacting to every single line you hear or bit you see on stage. Audiences will "get" subtle humor, but they will not laugh if the reaction is too broad. Also, sometimes it is perfectly legitimate *not* to react if your character wouldn't react to a given situation or line—as long as you can justify your position.

STUDY at Home

There is simply no substitute for doing your homework. Actors often mistakenly assume that, aside from memorization, nothing can be practiced alone or in another environment. They reason that too much is dependent on the other actors, the presence of the director, the theatrical environment, the stage, the costumes, the props, etc., etc., etc. Nothing could be further from the truth. Throughout the book we have discussed various ways in which actors should study at home, including:

- Reading and researching the play
- Memorization
- Writing and reviewing blocking
- Rehearsing blocking and business
- Working on character development and accent

THINK

In our pursuit of things creative and artistic, we have lost sight of a very necessary ingredient to every effective process: analytical thinking. Our educational systems, compared to the rest of the world, fall short in teaching children how to reason things out for themselves. An intelligent approach to the creative process will add immeasurably to our work.

Learn how to use your mental powers as well as your artistic abilities when approaching a play. Before you even begin to analyze your own character or relationships, look at the "Big Picture." What's the story? What's the plot? What's happening here? Who are these people and what do they want?

This will give you a much greater understanding of your own

character and relationships with others, because you'll figure out where you fit within the overall scheme. Most actors realize that these questions need to be answered, but they take valuable rehearsal time trying to "discuss" them out. It is often more productive to apply your mental abilities to these issues all by yourself—many answers will be provided through study of the script and your own logical reasoning powers. Applying a thought process to your work will help provide you with a more fully-rounded character and totally realized motivations. There may be one or two questions left un-answered—these are the points you may bring up in rehearsal.

I have always believed "it takes a very intelligent lady to play a dumb blonde." Award-winning actor Jack Lemmon says, "I've never met a dumb, good actor." Please don't make the mistake of assuming that because you are working in a creative environment you should "check your brains as you enter." Applying your intellectual and analytical skills to your work will bring much greater depth to your role and the play.

EXERCISE

We have discussed the importance of physical and vocal exercise in Chapter 5. An actor's weekly regimen should include:

- Voice and singing lessons
- Dance and exercise classes
- Sports, games, and special skills

A young musician with a violin case rushes up to a man on 57th Street in New York City and says frantically, "How do I get to Carnegie Hall?" The man looks down and responds, "Practice." Don't forget that exercise also includes daily practice. You may have studied Standard American Speech for several months, but without regular practice you may lose what you have learned. Formal classes are not necessary for practice: you can do your dance, stretching, and breathing exercises at home every day.

Another important aspect of exercising is to keep your machine "well-oiled." Successful professional actors often do showcases or take jobs as "extras" in film or TV just to be in the working environment and to keep their skills up. There is no substitute for being in a play, but classes and scene work may also be helpful, and ultimately anything that gets you together with other actors is beneficial.

Actors who are serious about developing their overall talents spend much of their time working on *something*. Audition for everything you are remotely right for. Get tickets and go to every theatrical production in your area. You will learn something from every play, even if that particular production is not especially good. Get yourself a new script (from the library, bookstore, or book club) every week and read it. Watch plays that have been videotaped for TV on your public television station, or rent movies that are based on plays. Search for, memorize, block, and perfect your monologues. Even when you are not performing, there are many areas in which you can exercise your skills and keep in shape.

READ for Comprehension

I must have said this a thousand times to hundreds of students, and I've also said it before in this book: Read for Comprehension. Comprehension means "understanding." Before you decide on any "acting values," read the play for the story, what it means. The operative word here is WHAT.

As we mentioned in the chapter on rehearsals, most amateurs look only at their own lines and they instantly begin to decide, "HOW shall I do this line, HOW shall I say this word?" You cannot begin to answer the HOW until you know the WHAT.

Reading for comprehension answers this question: WHAT AM I SAYING? I'm not talking about sub-text or deep analysis here but simply the basic sense of the line. If you don't have the sense of what you're saying, even though your interpretation is terribly "dramatic" and you may even FEEL it, it will be wrong and your work will only scratch the surface.

You must engage your brain when reading the script. You must read the entire script and reason out what other characters are saying, what the entire play is saying. You must go back and reread the play after you have begun to memorize so that with every detail you fill in, you don't develop "tunnel vision" and forget the overall picture.

When you are working on your character development and re-lationships, you will probably have several questions. Make a list, then go back and reread the script. The answers will usually be found somewhere within the lines. Many actors spend a great deal of time "fleshing-out" their characters and background *without* consulting the script, and the result is almost always off-track.

Here's an example: Joan was trying to fill in the background of her character's life, and concluded that the woman had a history of fertility problems, which led to the inability to bear children. As a result, her character developed a special attachment to a young woman in the play as a substitute daughter. The night before the closing performance, Joan exclaimed, "My gosh, I *do* have children. I just realized it when I said the line about the recipe being from my daughter-in-law." We had been working on this play for fully eight weeks. Granted, there is no other reference anywhere in this play to this character's children, but Joan had been saying this line from the very beginning of rehearsals. Her interpretation of the line might have been wonderful, but did she know what she was saying? (If she'd thought about it, it would have been apparent that she must have had at least one son.)

TRY New Things

Most actors could approach their work in a much more creative manner. Some people prepare like crazy for an audition, get cast, and never do another exciting thing again. Directors like to work with people who know how to trust their own instincts and try different things. The ability and willingness to do this requires a great deal of courage on the part of the actor. What if it doesn't work? What if everyone doesn't laugh? What if the director thinks it stinks? But the creative process is all about getting ideas and trying as many of them as possible to see which works best. You may have ten or twelve ideas, and the director may only like one or two—but those one or two are brilliant and all yours.

Trying new things does not apply just to bits and business, it applies to the totality of the work. It may be a "handle" on a character or an accent. It may be a different approach to a particular scene. It may be simply a willingness to "go too far" with a section, to "stretch the boundaries" in order to find the balance.

Actors who keep in physical shape and who exercise their mental capabilities will find themselves more open to inventive and creative work. If you are in shape and relaxed, great ideas will come to you "out of the blue." These moments don't really come out of the blue, they come to people who do their homework, think, and are on the alert for new possibilities.

Trying new things also involves trusting your instincts and your character to do creative work in the rehearsal process. If you are secure in your memorization and relaxed, wildly exciting and fun things might develop.

RELAX

Relaxation is critical to good performance. The following techniques have been discussed as ways to aid relaxation in rehearsal and performance:

- Alexander Technique
- Deep breathing
- Exercise

Relaxation is also key to the creative process. Without an attitude of ease and comfort, the mind and body will not function to their fullest capacity. As noted previously, any type of alcohol or drugs will have a detrimental if not disastrous effect on performance as well as personality and general well-being.

Through concentration, deep breathing, and exercise, actors can develop their own techniques for relaxation. We have listed some of them in the chapter on auditions, because auditioning is typically the most nervewracking of theatrical experiences. Relaxation does not mean being "laid back" or having no life. Creative relaxation is energized—the performer is operating at a peak level, free of tension.

Relaxation will also aid actors in developing the feeling of being one with the work and the character. We have alluded to the phenomenon of being "in the zone," a term from the sports world. Athletes in the zone are unaware of their surroundings; the mind is effortlessly concentrated and the body seems to work automatically. Winners have attested to being "in the zone" while breaking world records. For the actor, this phenomenon can happen when the character begins to take over and the actor is open and relaxed to whatever might happen. It is not a feeling of being "out of control"; rather it is a sense that the play really is happening for the first time, and the character really is present in every moment.

Actors who are in the zone find that their characters do things that are not necessarily planned and as a result are creatively brilliant. A director asked me where I came up with an idea that he particularly liked, and I had to respond, "I don't know. I guess it came from the character." In performance, an actor in the zone feels in total coordination with the rest of the cast, completely at one with the audience, the character just "happens," and the play seems to play itself. Being in the zone will occur more and more frequently as you develop your relaxation technique.

ANIMATE the Moment

This is synonymous with "Play the Moment." Animation involves bringing life to your performance. Anyone who saw the recent Tony-winning Broadway triumph *Lettice and Lovage* will recall Maggie Smith's vivid performance and her eccentric character's fervent belief in the philosophy: "Energize, Enliven, Enlighten."

A very common hurdle in performance is getting through the first act, because Act One usually establishes characters and relationships by means of that traditionally dirty word: exposition. Once the second act starts, the actors are warmed up and working at performance level, but by that time half the audience may have left. It is critical to energize and enliven every moment the actor is on stage—from the very first entrance.

It must be taken for granted that the author chose certain characters to be in a scene. Even if you are not the center of attention, it's still important for you to be there. It's up to you to determine how best to animate your particular moment, even if you have only one line.

This brings to mind another well-worn story about an amateur who was asked to appear for the first time in a community theatre production. He was terrified, but the director assured him that he only had one line. As soon an off-stage explosion was heard, the actor was to say, "Hark, I hear the cannon roar." He practiced the line faithfully throughout the day for many weeks. When they finally got to opening night, the explosion went off and the startled actor exclaimed, "What the hell was that?"

Playing the moment involves being in the now. Do not play the ending of the scene in the middle of the scene. Don't play the end of the play at the beginning of the play. If you're in a tragedy, for example, don't give a "tragic" performance from the moment you step on stage to the final curtain. This defeats the purpose of a play —you're *telegraphing* the ending and people might just as well go home after the first scene. In our discussion of types of plays, we talked about the importance of keeping in mind the basic type of play you are doing, i.e., comedy, tragedy, satire, melodrama, etc. But that does not mean that you should take a Johnny-one-note approach to the whole play.

You need to look at every single line as separate and distinct from the one above it and the one below it. Learn how to be "in the now" and in the moment, and learn how to play the contrasts and the opposites.

CONFLICTS and CONTRASTS Create Good Drama

Most good plays are replete with conflicts and contrasts. Conflict is the essence of drama—without it, there's no story. The dictionary defines conflict as "a struggle, a clashing of views or statements." So right away, most actors assume that the fight scenes are the conflict. True, but incomplete.

Theatrical conflict is implied or inherent in numerous areas *besides* the fights and arguments. It's up to the actor to study the character and relationships and look for the conflict. For example, another character might just rub you the wrong way, or may be out of place in your world. It's possible your character has underlying reasons for not liking another character, even though the two of you do not share a fight scene. There may be implied conflict through what others in the play say about you and another character, even though there is no direct confrontation. Your character may be in tremendous conflict with himself or her*self*. Delve into your play and your character, and find the numerous ways that conflict may be generated.

American actors are usually very nice. They want to be perceived as "likeable, sweet, pleasant, polite, and personable." In other words, bland. Very few interesting characters on stage are bland. They are full of fire and fun, idiosyncrasy and idiocy, arrogance and eccentricity. We need to search to bring out the more "unpleasant" aspects of our characters, because these traits make them not only more human but infinitely more interesting. It is not necessary to play the epitome of evil. In fact, most characters who appear to be really rotten turn out to be pussycats in the end. But it is necessary to look for the dark side of your character, which will give you more clues to the potential conflicts, as well as making your character more complex.

Contrast means "a striking difference." Contrast in drama is created by not only the dissimilarities between characters, but by the striking differences of emotion generated by individual characters from one moment to the next. Using contrast effectively is some-times referred to as "playing the opposites." Too many actors analyze their "beats," and decide that they have just one attitude or ap-proach for a whole scene or section. Other actors spend a lot of time and argument trying to come up with reasonable "transitions." Unfortunately, these techniques can destroy the author's finest work by deleting the dramatic contrast.

Good authors know that real people can jump from one emotion to the next in a split second, and they provide this contrast in order to present the greatest emotional impact; e.g., a comedy moment within a dramatic scene. These contrasts and opposites are purposely written into the material, and good actors need only look for and play them. Tony-Award winning author Neil Simon uses contrast to great effect in his Pulitzer Prize-winning play *Lost in Yonkers*. The actors run the gamut from hilarious comedy to extraordinarily moving drama within each scene, and the audience is with them every step of the way.

Contrast is rampant in real life. If you don't believe me, attend a funeral or wake, where you will often find people laughing hysterically in the midst of their tears. It is entirely possible and indeed common for human beings to make emotional transitions from laughter to tears, from anger to remorse, from screaming to sympathizing, from the heights of happiness to the depths of despair within seconds. These contrasts will help you find a great deal more variety in your character work and your entire performance.

KEEP it Simple

In whatever circumstances you find yourself, no matter how embroiled you get in the politics of the theatrical environment or the intricacies of establishing exactly what you're doing on stage, it's important to keep a perspective. Your job is to know your lines and blocking, be heard and understood by the audience, and help them have a good time and get involved with a good story so they can laugh a little and perhaps cry a little.

Keep it simple, or in the words of an oft-repeated bit of advice frequently quoted by professionals: "Go out there and say your words and don't bump into the furniture." As actors, we tend to get so involved with the minutiae of each production element that it's easy for us to forget what the heck we are supposed to be doing out there.

Prepare for each performance by reestablishing your "truth" in the work. Consult your script to fill in the little details about your character and the play. Use your intelligence to continue to puzzle out your relationships with other characters. Once you have found your reality in the script and in all your previous work, keep coming back to it.

Part of your preparation before going on stage should entail eliminating all distractions and getting yourself centered. Energize yourself, so that you are warmed up and excited about every performance, no matter how many times you have done it or no matter how bad the reviews. Try to keep a positive attitude about your work, your fellow actors, and the audience.

On stage, concentrate on the moment. Think. Listen. React. Be present. You will find yourself truly in the moment, playing each line for all it's worth, full of life and vitality.

7

Backstage Procedure and Theatrical Superstitions

BACKSTAGE AND THE GREEN ROOM

"Backstage" is a general term that actually refers to one of two areas behind the scenes: 1) the immediate off-stage area, also called "the wings," and 2) all the areas and rooms not "on stage" used by the actors and crew, including the dressing rooms and common rooms. When they're not in their dressing rooms, actors usually congregate in the "Green Room."

The green room supposedly got its name from Elizabethan times when actors were generally considered a "bad lot" of uneducated, crude ruffians. (Hence the sign "No Theatricals"—rooming houses would not even rent to actors.) Of course, at the time the actors were all men. Because of their lousy reputations, getting a fine lady of the aristocracy to go out with them was next to impossible, so actors commonly "dated" prostitutes. The signal dress color for prostitutes was green, and the room where these ladies waited for their actor friends came to be called the green room.

Today the green room is the place you may eat, smoke (if fire law permits), and chat with other actors and the crew. It's not unusual to find stage management and/or crew in the green room because they sometimes have nowhere else to hang out. Green room rules vary from theatre to theatre; generally, only actors and crew people are allowed in this backstage room before the curtain. After the curtain, the green room *may* be the designated room to meet your family and friends.

Even though the atmosphere in the green room is generally relaxed, consideration should be given to others. Very loud talking and hilarity will not only disturb others waiting in the green room but will carry to the dressing rooms. If you take something to eat into the green room, clean up after yourself and dispose of your trash; when coffee mugs and drinking glasses are provided, wash your own out after the show. Keep the green room neat and liveable—it should not be up to the crew to clean up after you.

THE DRESSING ROOM

You should be in the dressing room or backstage area prior to the half-hour, having signed in when you arrived. In professional theatres, dressing room assignments are made by the stage manager, usually before the first full dress rehearsal. If assignments are not made in your theatre, it would make sense to get to the theatre early for the first full dress to claim your favorite space.

The Calls

The stage manager or ASM will come around and "give the calls," meaning, of course, that he or she goes to each dressing room and announces: "half-hour," "fifteen minutes," "five minutes," and "places." Most conscientious stage managers make a point of finding each actor, wherever he may be, to ensure that every individual knows what the call is. If your backstage area is large and you are allowed to go into classrooms or other spaces to warm up, make sure the stage manager knows where to find you.

The actor should respond to each call with a "Thank you," a courteous acknowledgement that you have heard the call. While it is very important to let the stage manager know that the call has "registered," any other response besides "Thank you" is not appropriate. I have actually heard, "That's easy for you to say," "You're joking!" "Oh, God, I'll never be ready," and other (worse) expletives. Imagine yourself as the stage manager—making the calls is part of the job, and most stage managers try to bring an aura of polite civilization to the theatrical experience. It can't be very pleasant for the stage manager to hear a smart remark from every cast member every time a call is made.

"Places, please." Once you hear this call you must be ready to go promptly to the immediate backstage wings if you appear at or near the top of the show. I once worked with an apprentice who was appearing in her first leading role in an Equity company. Though she was in the curtain-up scene, she was never ready for "places," and would spend another five minutes finishing her makeup, dressing, and frantically grabbing props. Don't let this happen to you, and don't assume that "the curtain will go up late as usual anyway." Get yourself into the dressing room that much earlier so you can be ready for your "places" call.

Note: It is generally not appropriate for the actors to go up to the immediate backstage *prior* to the places call. The stage manager may not be finished preparing the stage; also, he or she won't know where to find you to make sure you know that the curtain is going up.

The Squawk Box

The intercom that goes from the stage area to the backstage is informally called the "squawk box." These intercoms are placed strategically backstage in all the dressing rooms and usually in the green room. If the intercom is turned on prior to the show and there is music or extraneous noise (lights check or other conversation), the volume may usually be adjusted so that you don't hear it. Just be sure to turn it back up when the show starts so you won't miss your entrance. In some professional theatres the calls are made over the intercom, and if this is the case the volume should never be turned down. (There is obviously no need for actors to respond to calls made in such a fashion.)

During the show it is imperative for actors to wait in a room with an intercom so they can follow the show's progress. The squawk box is there so you can hear what's going on in the play and to ensure that you don't miss an entrance. When you are backstage waiting for a cue, always keep one ear plugged into the "box." Keep your conversations low-key, and don't be afraid to interrupt someone in order to find your place.

If you have long stretches of time between on-stage appearances, don't do anything requiring such great concentration that you might miss a cue—for example, don't study or try to finish a terrific thriller, don't write your autobiography or thesis. Actors understandably like to do something during great gaps, but the best activities are mindless busywork such as crocheting and knitting, or short-attention projects like crosswords and puzzles, or reading a newspaper or magazine.

Quiet and Consideration

Do your more strenuous physical and vocal warm-ups at home before arriving at the theatre so that you won't disturb others. If you need to do a small amount of vocalization or exercise just before going on, try to do it out of the dressing room and away from others.

As we discussed in Chapter 4, actors' radios, tapes, and TVs in the dressing room must be turned off after the half-hour is called. In one summer stock company, taped classical music was played backstage prior to the performance. A very distinguished veteran actor politely requested that the stage manager turn off the music after the half-hour had been called so that we could have quiet in the dressing rooms. He was perfectly within his rights to do so.

As in the green room, dressing room conversation should be kept relatively controlled. Try to be aware of the special rituals and needs of others—if you are sensitive, you can tell which people don't mind chatting and which others prefer silent concentration.

Dressing Room Spaces and Privacy

There are as many different dressing room set-ups as there are theatres. I've worked in all sorts—from a third-floor walk-up closet, to a spacious carpeted suite complete with private bath, to one single co-ed (and not very large) dressing room for the entire cast.

Whatever your situation, it is always appropriate to expect some privacy in your own dressing room space or area. If men and women are sharing the same dressing room, there should be a sheet or screen dividing the sexes. If there isn't, you are perfectly within your rights to request one. (You can work around awkward dressing-room situations where there is little privacy by dressing at home, or using a restroom to change.)

Actors and dancers are noted for being somewhat blasé about undressing and showing their bodies; those who have experience are often fairly casual about changing in front of others. If you feel that your sense of modesty is being put to the test, it is perfectly reasonable to make your own changing arrangements so you don't have to compromise your principles.

Along these same lines, dressing room doors are often open, and actors sometimes move freely about from one to another. However, a certain amount of respect for another's space or privacy is always in order. If you must visit another dressing room, finish your business and be gone. If you have a favorite friend in another dressing room, arrange to meet him or her in the green room so you won't disturb other actors. If you wish to speak to or visit someone in another dressing room and you find that the door is closed, it is common courtesy to knock and wait for an OK before entering. (Most stage managers will do the same when they are making the calls).

Valuables and Security

In professional theatres, valuables are collected by the stage manager at the half-hour and locked up in a briefcase, lockbox, or safe during the performance. "Valuables" include wallets, billfolds, and/or cash, and any jewelry (either of monetary or sentimental value, including watches, wedding rings, etc.). The stage manager in some theatres may provide an individual manila envelope to each actor in which to put valuables; the marked envelopes are then collected at the half-hour. If your theatre has a policy of collecting valuables, always make use of it. If there isn't such a policy, you might want to suggest one, which is easy enough to implement. The backstage area of the theatre is notorious for its lack of security, and things can easily be taken.

If you are using your own costumes or props in a show, protect yourself from thievery by taking things home, locking them up, or at least hiding them from open view. This includes your jewelry, eyeglasses, cigarette cases, scarves, gloves, shoes, belts, etc. I worked in one theatre that provided lockers in which we could place the more valuable things left overnight. In another case, I bundled up my costumes and zipped a garment bag around them before leaving for the evening. Many actors wisely cover their makeup area with a towel—it would be quite costly to have to replace all your theatre supplies.

Costumes and Props

Always check your costumes and personal props as well as on-stage props before the performance. If you want to walk around the stage, do so prior to half-hour at the time appointed by the stage manager.

There is generally a spirit of helpful cooperation among actors regarding getting into tricky costumes. It is not unusual for another cast member to ask your help with fastening back hooks, lacing up corsets, attaching jewelry, tying four-in-hands, etc. If a dresser is not available, help others in your immediate dressing room get themselves into their costumes, and they will do the same for you.

Needless to say, if another actor has a quick change in the dressing room, you should be aware of it and either get out of the way or facilitate the change. Sometimes actors have just enough time to get back to the dressing room (as opposed to changing in the immediate backstage area), make the change, and get back on. This is not the time to have a conversation with them. Quick changes, whether you are helping or not, should take place in total silence and concentration. Actors who have quick changes in the dressing room area may request that the stage manager assign someone to help them, or may personally ask a reliable friend to help them make the change for every performance. This "buddy system" should always be prearranged and consistent. If you leave it up to whoever might be available, you may find yourself in an empty dressing room in dire need of help.

Never "borrow" a costume piece or prop from another actor's table. If yours is missing, you must find or replace it through the costume or prop department. When actors are wearing or using identical things, the costume department should label them with the actor's or character's name. (If your things are not labeled, write your name on a piece of masking tape and stick it inside your costume, prop, or shoes.)

Eyelash Etiquette and Other Makeup Tips

Because of the rather freewheeling attitude around the theatre, actors get the impression that anything in anyone's room is fair game and whatever they need they can borrow from another actor. This should never be the case. Before the first dress rehearsal gather all your supplies, buy what you don't have, and arrive at the theatre with all the makeup and supplies you need for your performance. This may include: tissues, greasepaint or base, mascara, eyeliner, brow pencils, shading pencils, false eyelashes and glue, rouge and contour shadow, lip liner, lipstick, and translucent powder, plus all the brushes, sponges, and applicators that go with these things. Don't forget hair: rollers and pins, curling irons, mousse, gel, spray, wigs and mustaches, wig caps, bobby pins, clippies, glue, spirit gum and remover; and nails—polish, polish remover, cotton balls, and "quick dry."

It is very annoying for actors who come in well-prepared with all their stuff (which they have paid for), to have everyone in the cast descending on their one box of tissues or bottle of glue remover. During the dress rehearsal make another list of additional things you need; if you have forgotten something essential you may borrow it for one performance only, then get your own.

Your makeup should be suited to the size of theatre you are performing in and to the lighting. If you are acting in a large auditorium with stage lighting, the makeup generally needs to be heavier and more pronounced. If you are working on a small stage, you can usually get by with street (or just a little heavier) makeup.

The phrase "Eyelash Etiquette" was coined by a young actress in a summer stock company, who asked the other women in the cast whether or not they were wearing false eyelashes, and remarked, "I don't want to breach the Eyelash Etiquette." Though the term is not formal, it is appropriate for women to discuss among themselves and to reach a consensus as to whether or not false eyelashes will be worn. The decision will depend on the size of the house and the lighting, but if there is any question, check with the leading lady. "Etiquette" would require others to do what she's doing (and if she's not, you don't). Of course, there are always exceptions: some characters would wear heavier makeup than others, so the use of eyelashes might be justified even if other women are not wearing them.

For practical reasons it's not a bad idea to check with fellow cast members about their plans regarding other false hairpieces, including wigs and facial hair. If only one woman in a show is wearing a wig, it may stick out like a sore thumb. If one of the men is growing his own mustache and beard and another is wearing a false one, the false one should be very good or it will compare unfavorably. (Many of these decisions should be discussed the first day of rehearsal!) Regarding men's makeup, if the theatre is small, men may not need it at all. Find out what other people are planning to do with regard to makeup and hair so that you don't look ridiculous and out of place.

Eating and Smoking in the Dressing Room

Eating in the dressing room should be limited to coffee, tea, or soda and small candies or snacks. If you've been so busy that you have to bring a sandwich or dinner to the theatre, take it to the green room. Though it may be considered quite a feat, it is not a pleasant sight to watch an actor gobble up a whole meal while talking and applying makeup at the same time. If you are drinking sodas or coffee in costume, be very careful not to spill anything on your clothing or shoes. Some costume people who have spent back-breaking hours designing and sewing the costumes will request a policy of "No eating or drinking (except water) once you are in your costume." If so, have your snacks and drinks before you dress.

Smoking is often not allowed in the dressing rooms because of the proximity to other people and costumes. In Equity companies, if there is no overriding theatre policy, smoking in each room may be determined by the individual actors, but if one person objects, smoking is prohibited in that dressing room.

Dressing Room Company

In many theatres, only actors are allowed in the dressing rooms—there is often just barely enough space for them, let alone visitors and family. If you have a very close friend or family member with you prior to the show, it is still inappropriate to bring him to the dressing room, unless you are a star with a private room. It may be OK to invite your guest into the green room for a pre-show chat; however, visitors should always leave at the half-hour.

After the show, friends and family gather backstage to offer congratulations, and it's usually pretty chaotic. Though a certain amount of spontaneity and joviality is anticipated, it's important to comply with your theatre's policy about visitors backstage. If the policy does not allow visitors in the dressing room, friends and family must wait for the actors in the green room. On the other hand, if the cast is small and you have plenty of dressing room space, it may be acceptable to receive your post-show visitors there.

I once shared a large dressing room with only one other actress. This was quite a luxury, but on a couple of occasions she had several friends in the dressing room immediately following the performance, and I had nowhere to change. Use good judgment and exercise consideration for your fellow actors regarding your visitors.

Opening Night and Reviews

Opening night is always an exciting and frantic time in theatrical performance. Get to the theatre early, because there are always cards to open, flowers to be unwrapped, and last-minute details to take care of. Nerves will be taut on opening night, so you need extra time to apply makeup with trembling hands. In some professional theatres the atmosphere backstage on opening night may be atypically subdued; actors may be more controlled than usual and likely to prefer silent concentration. It's important to respect this and keep your own merriment and excitement somewhat contained.

In many professional situations, actors exchange personal cards or little gifts on opening night. (In school and community productions, cards and gifts are usually not expected.) If you are unfamiliar with the tradition at your theatre, you may privately ask the stage manager what is generally done or what has been done in the past.

Opening night cards are easy to write: "It's nice to work with you, break a leg," or "Have a great opening," or any other message you wish to convey. Gifts are not required by any means, but if you have the time and a little money, the exchange of small presents can be a very nice ritual. Typical opening night gifts among cast members might include single flowers, local souvenirs, bath bubbles or hand soaps, coffee mugs, hard candies or chocolates, small bottles of champagne or liqueur, etc. (If you do receive booze, it should not be opened until after the performance.) Cheap little "gimmick" gifts may also be purchased, if that's your style. And if you do plan to get gifts or cards, do so well in advance of opening night, so you will not be running around like a crazy person frantically looking for notions and scribbling notes just before the performance. (A tip: Before you go out shopping for just anything, think about a small gift that would be appropriate to the show or the character. Just like Christmas shopping, it's a heck of a lot easier if you have something in mind.)

Actors often receive flowers for opening night, either in bunches or arrangements. If your dressing room is small and you have received a lot of flowers, you may wish to take an arrangement or two to the green room where more people can enjoy them and they will not take up valuable dressing room space. Many actors take fresh-cut flowers home with them after the first show.

There is some question about who should receive presents and when. The same card and/or gift you give to the cast members may also be given (if appropriate and desired) to the director and stage manager on opening night. For crew and other theatre personnel, it's appropriate to wait until closing night, when you may feel that you have many people to thank. Traditionally, actors give money or a personal gift to the dresser and hair maintenance person, if he or she has attended you throughout the run. Other people who have been helpful (including, for example, a crew member who was particularly supportive, an ASM who made the calls, a box office manager who gave comps) would certainly deserve a thank-you note. For running crews and/or construction crews, (if you are really feeling generous), a group gift is appropriate but completely optional. For example, at the end of one run, I gave crew members free tickets to the movies, and for the closing party at a summer stock company I bought a case of beer for the overworked interns.

IMMEDIATE BACKSTAGE

Whenever you are in the immediate backstage (also known as "offstage" or "in the wings"), you must move quietly and remain silent. If you have the opportunity before the show to go up and check your props, do so calmly and efficiently, even if the house is not open.

Immediate backstage is not the place to speak with the stage manager or any member of the crew or cast. If a prop is missing, take it up with the stage manager as far as possible away from the backstage area. (A good time might be when he or she comes to the dressing room for the calls.) It is totally inappropriate for actors waiting in the immediate backstage to have any personal conversations prior to the show, while waiting for an entrance, or during the scene breaks. Once "places" is called, the immediate backstage area should be cleared of all people except running crew and actors waiting to go on.

Allow plenty of time to get to the immediate backstage area prior to your entrance. Late entrances stumbling on stage out of breath are inexcusable. Avoid pacing or exercising just offstage, which might cause you to emit soft grunts or loud breathing. Another good reason for getting backstage early is that it allows you plenty of time in case you have forgotten something like a costume piece or prop.

If something goes wrong on stage, it is very common for actors to stagger backstage and immediately start joking or laughing (or yelling) about what happened. Don't forget that this kind of noise may not only be heard by the audience, it will be terribly distracting to the actors still on stage. Don't assume that scene break music will cover any whispering or laughing you do—it won't.

All movement that takes place in the immediate backstage area should be slow, quiet, and cautious. If you are involved in getting on or off stage in a blackout, it is imperative to *move slowly*. Many amateurs try to run as quickly as possible so they won't be "caught" when the lights come up. This can create all sorts of accidents and pose a danger to the entire cast. (In any case, the lights should NOT come up until the stage manager indicates that the stage is clear.)

To facilitate movement in blackouts, *glow tape* (tape that glows in the dark) should be placed at strategic locations on stage and backstage. It will highlight major places to avoid or to hang on to, and help you get oriented. (If there is no glow tape, you may request it.) In addition, the stage manager or a crew member may be available to shine a small flashlight onto the stage to aid the actors entering or exiting. (Of course, actors can also help each other.) People who are not entering or exiting during a blackout should freeze wherever they are backstage and not move again until the lights come up.

PERSONAL SUPERSTITIONS

Actors are generally fun, witty, gregarious, generous, intelligent, amiable, outgoing, personable, talented people. They are also very superstitious. In the words of a former President, "Make no mistake about this." The degree to which actors take superstitions seriously is certainly individual; however, there are some time-honored theatrical superstitions that most professional actors believe in and religiously uphold.

Rituals and Good-Luck Pieces

Experienced actors usually have a very specific ritual for setting up their dressing table. They bring in a small hand towel (just the right size for an individual makeup area) and then carefully arrange their makeup and other small items in exactly the same pattern established in previous productions. My personal good-luck hand towel was a gift from my sister; now well-worn, it's been used for many years in many shows. The actor may arrange the makeup in a precise order for practical as well as superstitious reasons. Small photographs or other good-luck mementos, such as ornaments, postcards, stuffed animals, or porcelain figurines, may be positioned carefully on the makeup table.

Many actors follow an identical ritual from the moment they come into the theatre in the evening to the moment they leave. This ritual will probably not vary much from show to show, and some veteran actors attach good fortune to following the set pattern. An enforced change in the ritual may even be considered bad luck.

Small personal good-luck charms are often carried on stage in a pocket or sewn into a costume. Examples: an earring, cuff links, rabbit's foot, four-leaf clover, lucky coin, religious medal, worry beads, tiny photo, strip of ribbon, playing card, or other small bit considered to be essential to a great performance or audition.

Through the years, famous actors have held unique and sometimes peculiar personal superstitions. Tallulah Bankhead, a walking encyclopedia of superstitions, used to say, "You name it, honey, I believe in it." She held that champagne was lucky and should be consumed in quantity before and during performances. (Let's face it, she was a drinker.) Visitors to her dressing room had to enter with the right foot first; the left was unlucky and offenders were sent out and told to re-enter correctly. The famous Barrymore family (John, Ethel, and Lionel) gave red apples to each other on their opening nights, but these perfectly beautiful specimens were never under any circumstances to be eaten. Jimmy Durante had a superstition about hats: they should never be placed on beds. The only antidote to the bad luck was to remove the offending hat, hang it up, and not touch it until the owner was wearing another hat.

Personal superstitions need not necessarily be agreed upon by all actors in a company, but in the interest of good public relations it's wise to be aware of who believes in what, and at least acknowledge and be considerate of others' personal beliefs. General theatrical superstitions, on the other hand, are regarded by the majority of veterans and professionals in the theatrical community as Holy Writ, and newcomers to the theatre are well-advised to beware.

THEATRICAL SUPERSTITIONS

Don't Quote the Scottish Play

There is one superstition so old, so all-consuming, and so intimidating that just about everybody in the theatre, no matter how cynical or pragmatic they may be, believes in it. This is the superstition about *Macbeth*.

As Richard Huggett says in his fascinating book, *The Curse of Macbeth*, "This play is considered the unluckiest play of the theatre and has for four hundred years carried in its wake a terrifying trail of disaster and bad luck." The play is believed to be truly cursed, and it is universally held to be extremely bad luck to quote from it while inside a theatre. Many actors are wary to mention it by name even outside the theatre, and if it must be discussed it is referred to as "The Scottish Play," "The Caledonian Tragedy," "The Comedy of Glamis," "Mr. and Mrs. M.," "That Play," or some other fictitious title.

Personally, I have not seen or heard of a production of this play that was not fraught with disaster. Since 1975, in New York City alone, numerous productions have come and gone, not one a success.

Phillip Anglim and Maureen Anderman starred in a production at Lincoln Center several years ago; rumor had it that the leads were so cautious that throughout the rehearsal period the director and entire cast referred to them as Mr. and Mrs. Johnson instead of the dreaded title characters. Still, the show was roasted by the critics and Mr. Anglim, fresh from his Tony award-winning triumph as the "Elephant Man" took a career beating from which he apparently never recovered. Another ill-fated production, this one at Circle in the Square, starred Nicol Williamson. Critics agreed that it was badly miscast and mis-directed (which was unfortunate for Mr. Williamson because he directed himself). One of the more memorable moments had the title character teetering above the audience atop a ladder-like tower, delivering the famous "Tomorrow" speech. Can you imagine?

Another production involving a group of experienced performers was done by a highly-respected Off-Broadway company. Word had it that the "professional" leads were at each other's throats the entire rehearsal and barely survived the run. Most recently, a production starring two of the theatre's greatest living lights went down in history as one of the worst productions ever to grace a Broadway stage—Glenda Jackson and Christopher Plummer's production was filled with conflicts and replacements on the road until after a great deal of bad publicity and worse reviews, it closed silently and ignominiously after a very brief run.

As if having a flop show isn't enough, various productions of this ill-fated and accident-prone play have turned up all sorts of disasters—actors dying during the play, accidental stabbings on stage, unexplained illnesses, and so on throughout theatrical history. John Houseman had an incredible experience with his 1935 production at The Negro Theatre Project of the WPA (Works Progress Administration) in Harlem, New York City. As Artistic Director of the Project, Houseman invited Orson Welles, whom he knew to be an innovative and creative director, to join the Project and select a play to direct. It was actually Orson's wife Virginia who came up with the inspiration to set the play in Haiti and call it the "Voodoo Macbeth."

For this all-black production, a troupe of African drummers, including a featured performer who was an authentic witch doctor, contributed real Voodoo chants and spells. Percy Hammond, well-known critic of the *New York Herald Tribune*, hated the production and attacked not only the show but the theatre, the government, the New Deal, and the WPA. The leader of the African troupe and his corps paid a visit to Mr. Houseman and declared that in their opinion the review was an evil one. To the troupe leader's question "The work of an enemy?", Houseman responded in the affirmative, and agreed "He is a bad man." That night the African drummers got together to do a little Voodoo number of their own. The critic became ill and died shortly thereafter—of pneumonia, it was said.

There are many theories about why this particular play carries such a history of incredible disaster and bad fortune. One is that the witches' cauldron scene contains an authentic black magic spell which, when spoken aloud, is the cause of the curse. Another poses that the play is inherently evil, and everything associated with it is cursed.

Antidotes to the Bad Luck

Young actors who are not aware of this superstition run the risk of being shouted at and/or bodily thrown out of the dressing room if they (no matter how innocently) mention the name of the play or quote from it. In order to cancel the bad luck, the offending actor may be required to leave the dressing room, turn around three times, knock on the door, and humbly beg to be re-admitted. (Some purists will require you to throw salt over your left shoulder after your third turnaround.) The offender may also be requested to recite "Angels and Ministers of Grace defend us," from *Hamlet* (I:4), which is supposed to have cleansing qualities. And another theory holds that profanity has a neutralizing effect—a stream of obscenities will banish any evil spirits within hearing.

Don't Whistle in the Dressing Room

It is considered very bad luck to whistle in the dressing room or anywhere in the backstage area. The danger of whistling backstage had at one time a very practical reason. In the 18th and 19th centuries the backstage crew members were recruited from the navy, and were responsible for raising and lowering (*flying*) the scenery, because they had experience with handling the hemp lines on which the scenery was flown high above the stage. Traditionally, the crew was directed by the stage manager, who whistled at them, one blast for "raise" and two for "lower." Any foolish actor or visitor whistling backstage could cause total confusion in the performance, or worse, end up with flying scenery on the head.

Another theory holds that whistling summons the Devil. Actors who do (even accidentally or unconsciously) whistle backstage may be requested to leave the dressing room and perform one or more of the antidotes described in the above section.

Don't Wear Green on Stage

Costume designers may not be elated about my passing this superstition on; nevertheless, here it is. In addition to green, there are some other colors that are considered marginally bad luck— yellow and black, for instance. Yellow was worn in Medieval productions by the Devil, and was therefore associated with evil. Black was also considered unlucky and to avoid wearing it, men had fabulous tuxedos in rich midnight blue tailor-made for their on-stage work.

But green is considered the unluckiest color of all, and according to superstition, you must not wear it or have it on the stage or anything connected with the play. There are a number of probable and some ingenious explanations for this one. Some say that it dates back to the days when actors performed outside on green lawns (hence the expression, "see you on the green"), and if an actor was wearing green he would disappear into the background. Another theory holds that the superstition arose in the 18th and 19th century when the spotlight that illuminated the actors was green. It was called the "lime," and limelight was particularly popular for villains in melodramas. If you were wearing green under a green spotlight, the two colors would cancel each other out and you'd be nearly invisible. Some who believe in this superstition hold that green is the special color of the leprechauns, and they become jealous and hostile if mortals wear it. One lighting designer put it more practically with, "Green is a real bitch to light, it always looks like muddy brown."

I have worn green once in my professional career. I was aware of the superstition, but the gown was a stunning floor-length satin number, perfect for the period and the character and the play, and anyway (I reasoned) it was such a dark green that it looked black under the stage lights. The production was a total disaster, and my personal reviews were dreadful. Most designers are aware of this superstition and will not plan for actors to wear green on stage, but sometimes it's unavoidable, so you may just have to grit your teeth and wear it.

If you must wear green, you may rationalize that the superstition came about when actors always provided their own costumes and carried them around in a trunk—even today you still hear the term "the actor's trunk." Since it was up to the actors to select their own costume colors, if an actor was stupid enough to wear green, he brought on his own bad luck. Today, because theatres provide the actor's costumes, if they insist that we wear green it might be reasoned that we weren't responsible for the decision.

Real Flowers, Real Money, Real Jewelry, Real Mirrors, Real Food

Real flowers, real money, real jewelry, and real mirrors are considered very bad luck to carry or use on stage. In many cases, practical considerations overrule any thought about whether or not the thing carries a curse.

For example, real flowers are thought to be bad luck, but they could present problems anyway. They must be kept in a vase with water, which might fall and create a mess all over the stage; they wilt; they are expensive and must be replaced every night; petals or dripping water could fall off and pose a serious danger of someone slipping and falling on stage; roses could prick someone who might bleed onto a costume, furniture, or another actor; they could cause a sneezing fit to a person with allergies, etc. It's no wonder real flowers are prohibited—today's artificial flowers look as good as the real thing anyway.

Real money and real jewels are also considered bad luck according to superstition and are forbidden on stage. This theory may have stemmed from the practical issue that real money or expensive jewelry might easily be stolen or lost. There is also the strange paradox that real jewels never look real; from a distance they look small and colorless compared to the masterpieces that a good prop master could come up with. Gertrude Lawrence apparently took this superstition very seriously indeed. When her co-star Douglas Fairbanks, Sr. substituted real diamonds for the paste ones she wore during the 1930 run of *Private Lives*, the horrified Gertrude threw them back in his face and refused to speak to him ever again.

It's unlucky to have real mirrors on stage—substitute a piece of polished tin or aluminum. If you must use a real mirror, the surface should be sprayed heavily to dull the reflection. This one also probably dates back to Medieval days when people believed that if you looked into a mirror you would see the Devil standing behind you. There is a fascinating legend about a production of Marlowe's *Doctor Faustus*. In one scene, six devils are supposed to appear reflected in a mirror. Apparently at this fatal performance a seventh devil was seen by the leading actor, who realized that it must be the Devil himself. The audience ran out screaming and the actor playing Faustus died of a heart attack.

A very practical reason for not having real mirrors is that they reflect light—a bright reflection from a mirror that is not dulled or sprayed will bounce around into the audience. It might also be posed that mirrors present a temptation to egotistical actors, who could conceivably become so involved in their own reflection that they lose concentration in the play.

The theory that real food cannot be used is somewhat confusing, because if actors must eat on stage they have to consume something. The superstition is that the food should not be what it is supposed to be. Bread may be substituted for an omelette, for example, or pasta for chicken parmigiana. It might be suggested that a clever crew was responsible for circulating this superstition because they didn't have the money, time, or ability to prepare the fabulous gourmet feasts called for in many plays.

Practicality usually rules the day with regard to food. For example, if the entire cast is sitting down to a table and eating an on-stage meal, and the production takes place in a large auditorium, almost anything edible can be used. But there are times when the real food simply must be used because it will read. If you're playing a small house and you're supposed to be eating an apple, nothing else will do.

Peacock Feathers

Peacock feathers, peacock fans, and peacock designs of all kinds (in any form, incorporated anywhere, including on curtains, wallpaper, pictures, or rugs) are taboo on stage or anywhere in the theatre. It is not known where this superstition comes from, but it may be because the design looks like staring eyes. Many actors hold that peacock designs and feathers signify general bad luck even outside the theatre.

Sir Henry Irving was manager of the Lyceum theatre in London from 1878 to 1903. Also a brilliant actor, he worked with leading lady Ellen Terry, and reigned as the dominant force of the British stage for many years. During a production of *Othello*, in which he shared the stage with the famous American actor Edwin Booth, Irving was told there was a woman with a peacock fan in the house. An usher was immediately sent into the audience with a letter that urged, "For God's sake, take the peacock fan out of the theatre to avoid disaster!" Sensing the seriousness of her faux pas, the woman held the fan out to the nervous attendant for disposal, but he was terrified and refused to take it. The woman eventually left the theatre and tossed the offending fan into a garbage pail, but not soon enough to save the show. It was one of the few total failures in Irving's long and glorious career, and after the scheduled run ended, he never played it again.

The peacock problem seems to have followed Edwin Booth around (besides, of course, the rather rotten luck of having a brother who assassinated the President). A friend gave Booth a stuffed peacock as a congratulatory present when Booth opened his huge and splendid theatre on Sixth Avenue in New York City. Reluctant to hurt the friend's feelings, Booth accepted it and placed it in the front lobby. The theatre was a complete failure, and within a couple of years Booth was personally bankrupt. Years later he quarrelled violently with the ex-friend, attributing the downfall of his managerial ambitions to "that miserable bird of malignant fate!"

Good Luck is Bad Luck

In a typical professional theatre you will never hear a veteran actor wish another "good luck." The superstition holds that "to wish good luck on another person is to part with it yourself." As a result, numerous curious replacements have been found, including the common, "Break a leg," derived from a European saying, which, literally translated means "may you break an arm and a leg." Usually actors say inane things to each other like "good show," "give 'em hell," "knock 'em dead," or simply "have a wonderful time out there." There's also "See you on the green," or "See you on the ice." In France the traditional good-luck greeting is "Merde."

ACTORS' SUPERSTITIONS

Superstitions associated with the theatre also cross over into TV and film production because so many actors start their careers in theatre and bring them into other media. And in addition to traditional theatrical superstitions, there are a number of common general superstitions that many actors uphold in their professional and personal lives. Though young actors may be just as skeptical and cynical about these superstitions as the others, the number of veterans who believe in them makes them worth knowing about.

Critics and Reviews

Many actors do not want to know when there is a critic or any other VIP in the audience. "Other" VIPS might include outside producers, the author (or any famous author), the mayor (or any other person of political influence), a local or national star, a TV or radio bigwig, a casting director or talent scout, a theatrical or film agent or manager.

Producers, directors and/or stage managers should NOT announce the presence of a critic or other VIP in the house. Actors should be very careful NOT to tell other actors when their agent or manager is in the house. Besides being superstitious, professional actors prefer not to know because they realize it will contribute tension and may affect their performance.

Some professional actors are very superstitious about reviews and refuse to read them. For this reason reviews (whether good or bad) should never be posted for viewing inside the theatre, nor should they be brought in by anyone for any reason. Out of consideration for those who do not read reviews, it is imperative for other actors to keep the information they may have read to themselves and not make comments or carry on discussions about reviews inside the walls of the theatre.

Lynn Redgrave, one of our finest stage actresses, shared a personal story with a group of fellow professionals to illustrate the effect that reviews can have. She was appearing in a Chekov play, and one critic raved about the brilliance she exhibited during a very quiet moment on stage. Lynn was flattered by the attention and the compliment, but that particular special moment was never duplicated again—from then on, she was always self-conscious about it. She never again read reviews.

Many professionals rightly conclude that reading reviews will not provide any constructive help. If they are good, the actor is likely to get carried away by his or her own confirmed greatness. If they are bad, the actor will become depressed and angry, emotions that can only be detrimental to performance. The time to read reviews, if at all, is after the show closes. Rave reviews and fabulous notices can then be given proper perspective; constructive criticism may be filed in the actor's memory for future improvement; pans may be quickly forgotten and quietly tossed in the garbage.

Talking about Auditions

Many professional actors are very superstitious about auditions—it is considered bad luck to mention anything about an impending audition to anyone. (This is quite the opposite of beginners, who take every opportunity to brag about their humorous auditions and interviews.) There are several reasons experienced actors do not like to discuss their auditions.

For one thing, auditioning and getting refused happens so often that actors learn to accept the rejection, but it's still not easy. It is hard enough for actors to deal with the constant stream of "No, thank you's," and telling others about auditions will only prompt follow-up questions such as, "How did it go?" or even worse, "Did you get it?" Most often, the answer is no, so the fact of the rejection is reinforced in the mind of the actor as well as the estimation of the "well-meaning" friend. In the profession, blabbing about auditions could potentially be dangerous—your greatest rival could get on the phone to his or her agent and finagle an audition (which is rare, but who needs the competition?).

If a professional actor's audition does not conflict with rehearsal, nothing need be said, but if the actor must be absent from scheduled scene work to go to the audition, someone needs to be told. Discreet stage managers keep this information to themselves, but sometimes word gets around, and when the poor actor returns, everyone knows. If this scenario happens in your company, do not ask the actor about the audition unless information is offered. Actors who hold to the superstition hate to be interrogated: "What for?" "A commercial?" "What's the product?" "Who's the client?" "Who sent you on it?" Each question answered, each bit of information given out curses the potential project more and more. And don't be offended if the actor simply says, "Sorry, I prefer not to talk about my auditions."

Superstitions about Comedy

Actors who do comedy are possibly the most superstitious of all—they may be positively adamant about their beliefs. Probably their most common superstition is: if something is working, do not talk about it. Colleen Dewhurst said, "You can learn lines, but then there is the mystery. If it works, you don't try to examine it."

Actors who do comedy and who are very funny not only don't want to discuss what's working and what's funny, they especially do not want to be complimented directly or even overhear a general comment about a particular line or bit of business in which they are involved. One very talented actress I worked with (so funny she stole the show in a supporting role) would plug up her ears and flee whenever the conversation became specific about certain bits or line readings she was doing.

Interestingly, within that same company there was an equally funny actor who believed just the opposite. He felt that all comedy was just technical, and that you could examine and analyze it and discuss it and talk about it forever, and it just didn't matter. Both schools of thought are probably valid. Just be aware that if you hold to the notion that discussing comedy is OK, there may be others who do not share your viewpoint. This goes for personal compliments directly to the actor, as well as general self-congratulatory remarks at intermission or immediately following a performance.

If you are working in a comedy (or you have attended a comedy and have a friend in the cast), be very careful about how you phrase your compliments. It is OK to say "You are very funny," or "That was a hilarious performance," but avoid specific comments like, "I just loved what you did with *that* line," or "*That* bit was the funniest thing I have ever seen." Some people may actually be offended by your attempts to be nice. To call inordinate attention to something that is particularly funny is to some actors akin to putting a hex on it. If it's working, don't mess with it.

Believe It or Not

Everyone who has ever worked in a play and had the experience of being backstage will agree that the atmosphere is very special. There is no doubt that there is more than a little magic associated with theatrical production and, by extension, all actors in all theatres. The mystery of live performance permeates the backstage area, and superstitions are considered by some to be part of the holy tradition of great theatre. You don't have to believe in superstitions, but having respect and consideration for those who do will certainly make life backstage easier and your theatrical experience more rewarding.

8
Acting as a
Career

If the burning desire to act for a living hits you at an early enough age, you can plan to attend a good school and major in theatre. Many of my students have asked whether or not college is even necessary (again, the impression that acting takes no brain power!), and I always strongly recommend that high school graduates attend a four-year college and get a degree.

For one thing, it's important to learn as much as you can about as many subjects as you can, which is something one does in college. For another, it takes the same kind of discipline and self-application to complete college as it does to perform, so having a degree is certainly meaningful to casting people and agents. Last, and perhaps just as important, a college degree should help prepare you for at least one other area in which you could make a living while you are preparing for stardom.

FORMAL EDUCATION

If you have already earned your degree in a college or university, you may wish to go on to obtain a Master of Arts (MA) or Master of Fine Arts (MFA). If you have a degree in another area, you may wish to attend some theatre or acting classes at a nearby college or university for your own knowledge and edification. The following is by no means an exhaustive list, and there are many institutions of higher learning where you could get a perfectly decent education as well as training in the theatre. This section is provided for those who are curious about what schools might be worth checking out, and/or those with good reputations that may be conveniently located.

Undergraduate Degrees

Many four-year colleges offer a major in theatre and/or speech. Even if you can't afford the college of your choice, it is still wise to attend junior college and then move on to another school at which you can receive your BA. It is appropriate to get your degree in theatre or speech, but not absolutely critical. If your school does not offer a degree in theatre, you can look into other avenues of theatrical performance while you are going to school, such as amateur and community theatre. Even those schools that don't offer a theatre degree usually do have a drama department and a theatre, and you can get your much-needed experience there.

In the not-so-distant past, there was a consortium of schools called the "League of Professional Theatre Training," which obtained grants and private funding in order to provide a forum for its students to enter the professional theatre when they had completed their formal education. Other schools outside the League cried "monopoly" because they felt their training was just as professional, and consequently the League was declared unconstitutional and disbanded. Because the League schools have been considered by some to be tops in the field of training actors for the profession, and in the interest of starting somewhere, here is a list of the schools that belonged to it: Boston University, Brandeis University, California Institute of the Arts, Carnegie-Mellon University, Juilliard, New York University, North Carolina School for the Arts, San Diego State University, Southern Methodist University, State University of New York (SUNY) at Purchase, Temple University, the University of Washington at Seattle, and Yale University.

Another group of recommended schools include the Ivy League colleges, good because of the back-slapping, glad-handing "old-boy" networking, which helps people connect with other graduates of influence. Meryl Streep and Brooke Shields went to Princeton, and Tony award-winning director Jerry Zaks graduated from Dartmouth. Non-Ivy League schools that have produced big stars and have reputable theatre departments include: Northwestern University in Chicago, Catholic University in Washington, DC, the University of Virginia, and the University of California at Los Angeles (UCLA).

There are also some professionally-oriented schools that offer a degree called a Bachelor of Fine Arts (BFA). This means that you do more concentrating on your particular chosen area and less on the more general liberal arts. Some of the top schools that offer a BFA include Juilliard in New York and the DePaul University Theatre (formerly the Goodman Theatre School) in Chicago.

At still other schools that offer theatrical training, you will receive an "Associate Degree" or a "Certificate of Completion." (These are not recognized as college degrees.) Some of the more notable of these theatre schools include the American Academy of Dramatic Arts (AADA), and the American Music and Dramatic Arts Academy, both located in New York City. There are two schools in London that are also well-known for their training programs: the Royal Academy of Dramatic Art (RADA) and the London Academy of Music and Dramatic Art (LAMDA). If you are interested in studying overseas, you will find that most of the top colleges and universities offer a semester of study in London as part of their curriculum.

Also a wise choice, if you know you want to study acting as a profession, is a school affiliated with a professional theatre. These include, for example, Syracuse University, which houses Syracuse Stage (Syracuse, NY), the University of Minnesota, allied with the Guthrie Theatre (Minneapolis, MN), Missouri Repertory Theatre located on the campus of the University of Missouri in Kansas City, Meadow Brook Theatre on the campus of Oakland University (Rochester, MI), and the American Conservatory Theatre (ACT) in San Francisco.

Studying at a college or university that supports a professional theatre does not mean that you will get a job in that theatre, but it will expose you to the process and give you the opportunity to observe experienced actors in the professional milieu. There are many repertory theatres throughout the country that are allied with colleges and universities, and there is probably one within your geographical area.

MFA Degrees

In addition to getting your Bachelor of Arts, you may wish to go on to obtain a Master of Fine Arts, which is the "PhD equivalent" degree for people specializing in the performing arts. There are numerous schools offering an MFA in theatre, including many of the colleges and universities already mentioned.

Several years ago Yale put itself on the map by forging a bridge between academic and professional theatre, and Yale Rep was set up on the campus. (Interestingly, at the time that Yale's MFA program was established, the school did not even offer an undergraduate degree in theatre, so the people who attended the MFA program were typically not Yale grads.)

Many schools now offer MFA degrees; unfortunately, the trend toward professionalism has gone so far that applicants at some schools are now preferred to have some professional experience (and even already be members of Actors' Equity Association) in order to be accepted to the MFA program. A complete listing of schools that offer MFA degrees may be obtained by sending for the "Directory of Graduate Programs" published by Warner Books and available through GRE in Princeton, New Jersey.

Schools in New York City

There are many other avenues of training for actors. Numerous actors who have obtained a degree in theatre move to New York City and begin to study at one of the many institutions there that offer specific acting training, though not a degree. These might include, for example, the HB Studio (Uta Hagen and Herbert Bergoff) or the Actors Studio. (Note: There was a time when the Actors Studio was considered one of the best; its followers and adherents are still numerous, but the audition process for acceptance is grueling.)

There are also numerous non-profit theatres in the city, which have attained good reputations and offer classes in everything from acting to directing to playwriting. Some of these are the Ensemble Studio Theatre, Playwrights' Horizons, and Manhattan Punch Line.

Private Teachers

Finally, actors may wish to study with individual teachers who have obtained a reputation in the business. Some of these people are quite well-known, and have achieved guru-like status to their students. The top ones even have a whole group of next-generation "certified" teachers who are proponents of their philosophies and teach their structured "systems." Among these are: Sanford Meisner, Stella Adler, Lee Strasberg, and Robert Lewis.

If you choose to study with an individual, either in New York City or in your hometown, select your teacher carefully. Try to audit a class before you plunk down your money, and get a feel for what is being taught. If you don't agree with what's happening in the class, or if you don't like the teacher, don't sign up no matter how good he or she is reputed to be. If the teacher claims to be a proponent of a particular method, try to obtain a book or pamphlet on that approach and read it to see if it appeals to you and if you feel challenged by it.

Once you have completed your degree, additional acting classes should be considered an "adjunct" to getting into the business. There was one private teacher, for example, who insisted that students NOT audition for any plays while they were taking and completing his two-year course. That's defeating the purpose—at this level, you should be allowed to perform while you are learning.

A word of caution: your acting classes should never be hurtful or painful. There has been a wave of teachers in the theatre whose treatment of students borders on the unethical. For example, one very well-known and highly-respected teacher in New York spent his classes browbeating and intimidating his students into revealing painful experiences from their past. Apparently, he believed that actors could not be "free" if they were carrying around unresolved traumas. While it might be true that you would be a better actor if you resolved your past traumas, this type of psychological work is not appropriate for an acting class and should be reserved for sessions with a qualified psychologist or psychiatrist.

You should be on the lookout for teachers who might take advantage of you or be abusive. Though it is not pleasant to recount, a teacher in New York was recently convicted of molestation of several female students. Never allow yourself to stay in a situation in which you may be asked to do something that compromises your principles. Never let a teacher talk you into doing a nude scene, for example, in order to "explore your abilities." (Avoid doing scenes in class that require nudity of any kind, particularly one that has been "suggested" by the teacher.) You can also say no to scenes that you find particularly violent or otherwise morally offensive. No teacher should ever be allowed to violate your sense of psychological or moral privacy. If you find yourself in a compromising position, get out of the class and report the teacher to the authorities.

THE ACTORS' UNIONS: EQUITY, SAG, AFTRA

After you've completed your degree, if you're serious about acting as a career, it would probably be wise for you to join the actors' unions. All the performers' unions are branches of the Associated Actors and Artistes of America (Four A's), the organization affiliated with the AFL-CIO, which determines the jurisdictional characters of each union. There are nine branches of the Four A's unions, also known as the "sister unions," which include: Actors' Equity Association (AEA or Equity), the American Federation of Television and Radio Artists (AFTRA), the American Guild of Musical Artists (AGMA), the American Guild of Variety Artists (AGVA), Screen Actors Guild (SAG), Screen Extras Guild (SEG), the Association Puertoriquena de Artistas y Technicos Del Espectaculo (APATE), the Italian Actors Union (IAU), and the Hebrew Actors Union (HAU). The union you join first is called your "parent" union.

Most actors belong to Actors' Equity Association, Screen Actors Guild, and the American Federation of Television and Radio Artists. Why do we need three unions? Because each one has jurisdiction in a distinct area and covers professional work with different contracts, minimum wages and governing rules. Most actors belong to Equity for theatre work, and SAG and AFTRA in order to work in commercials and film, radio and television.

If you are trained for opera or nightclub singing, you might enter the professional world through AGMA or AGVA. The American Guild of Musical Artists (AGMA) covers employment in opera and ballet, and the American Guild of Variety Artists (AGVA) covers cabaret and nightclub, variety and specialty acts. If you continue to perform in opera or cabaret, you will work under the jurisdiction of one of these two unions; if you cross over to theatre, film, and TV you will be required to join Equity, SAG, and AFTRA.

It is important to realize that the performers' unions do *not* operate like the Teamsters or any other typical organized labor union. Performers' unions neither obtain work for their members, nor do they offer employment "listings" or opportunities for paid-up and active people. You will not be "checking in" with the union and receiving your job assignment for the next week. Belonging to one of the actors' unions does not guarantee work to any performer in any area. The advantage of joining the union is the protection you receive by way of minimum wages, pension and welfare benefits, working hours, and on-the-job conditions.

Actors' Equity Association (AEA or Equity)

Equity was founded on May 26, 1913, by a group of actors in New York City. Prior to its establishment, all rules and wages were set by theatre managers, and actors simply did not protest, either individually or in a group. Because each manager set his own conditions, there was no minimum wage, no compensation for rehearsals (rehearsal time was unlimited with no guarantee of ever actually playing), members of failed companies were stranded on the road wherever the show closed, actors were required to perform numerous free matinees, all costumes were furnished for free by the actor, dressing rooms were unheated and filthy, and productions might close with no notice or cause or salary for actors. In short, exploitation was a permanent condition of employment.

Equity's beginnings were shaky, but the organization quickly gained strength, and in July of 1919 the American Federation of Labor (AFL) granted a charter to the Associated Actors and Artistes of America, of which Equity was the largest component. Today the union sets minimum wages for actors, restricts the number of hours actors may rehearse and the number of weekly shows allowed, establishes open audition/interview requirements for current productions, requires employers to contribute to health and pension plans, monitors working conditions for practicality and safety, fosters aggressive policies to help increase employment opportunities for minorities (non-traditional casting), and arbitrates contract disputes.

Actors' Equity Association covers work in *live* theatre. Equity administers contracts in the following areas: Broadway (Production Contract), National and Bus & Truck Tours, Resident and Non-

Resident Dramatic Stock (COST and CORST Contracts), Indoor and Outdoor Musical Stock, Dinner Theatres, Resident Theatres (LORT Contracts), Industrial Shows, Theatre for Young Audiences (TYA), Off-Broadway, Chicago Area Theatres, University Theatres, Cabaret Theatre, Letter of Agreement for Developing Theatres (LOA), Small Professional Theatres (SPT), and Guest Artists.

Screen Actors Guild (SAG)

In 1933 a small but brave group of actors founded a new craft guild to represent performers' interests in the growing film industry. Working conditions were appalling in the new Hollywood that was cranking out six hundred films a year. Actors were required to work six days a week with no limit on hours, which meant that one day's shoot could "wrap" at midnight and the actors could be called for 7 A.M. the next day, with no extra compensation. Meals were haphazard and breaks given only at the convenience of the producer.

In those days, powerful film moguls would put a large number of people "under contract" (hence, contract players) and for a set fee could use them wherever they deemed fit—in lead roles, in supporting roles, in "cameos," or as extras. Contract players were considered the property of the studio to be developed, groomed, improved, and lent out to other studios at a profit. They worked hard and worked often, and the formation of SAG occurred when the studio heads decided the contract players were getting too much money and should be cut to half salary. SAG Articles of Incorporation were filed on June 30, 1933, and within the year membership increased to two thousand. Four years later the producers finally accepted the guild's demands when the membership, now grown to five thousand, voted to strike. Scale was established at $25 per day.

Today SAG contracts govern: feature films, filmed series and mini-series for television, television commercials and voice-overs, industrial films, and stunt and extra work in film. The Guild also sets minimum wages for work, limits hours of work under a particular contract (or sets overtime rates), establishes meal breaks, requires sanitary and safe working conditions, and has a pension and health plan.

American Federation of Television and Radio Artists (AFTRA)

In 1937 the American Federation of Radio Artists (AFRA) was born. (There was no "T" because there was no TV.) Like the other unions, AFRA emerged out of outrageously unfair treatment and astonishing exploitation of artists by employers. In the 1930s, radio was big business. But because there were no minimum wages, jobs in a highly competitive industry were awarded to the performers who worked longer and cheaper than their colleagues. Actors might rehearse for three days for a single on-air performance, and the five dollars total pay was considered generous.

Networks and independent stations were making huge profits while performers sometimes got nothing at all after endless rehearsals. One employer demanded a 10% kickback from everyone who worked for him. As with other industries, payment was up to the individual producers, so actors never knew *what* they would be paid, *if* they would be paid, or how long they would have to work.

When AFRA was started up in 1937, the networks and stations resisted, but when the biggest stars of the day, including Eddie Cantor, threw in their lot with the union, the networks relented and AFRA won. In the 1940s, when television came into being, there were some questions of what union should handle employment, so the first network contract was negotiated by a group known as the Television Authority. In 1950 the Television Authority and AFRA merged, creating what is today known as the American Federation of Television and Radio Artists.

Today's AFTRA covers employment in network television broadcasting and syndication, commercials for radio (and some TV), network radio and syndication, phonograph recordings, closed-circuit television, public (educational) television and radio, and nonbroadcast material, including slide films and cassettes. Its membership consists of actors, news broadcasters, announcers, sportscasters, disc jockeys, weathercasters, analysts, panelists, and moderators who work in radio and television.

There may be some confusion about which union covers television work, SAG or AFTRA. A very broad generalization says: if it's film it's SAG, and if it's tape it's AFTRA. (Film usually has a softer quality, tape is a little harsher, e.g., the difference between a feature film and a soap opera.) For example, SAG jurisdiction covers: filmed commercials and voice-overs for same, filmed series, etc. AFTRA generally covers material that is taped, including taped series and voice-overs for same, taped commercials, and daytime series (soaps), and, of course, all news, sports, and weathercasts.

Joining the Unions

Should you join the union? This question is often asked by students, and the answer is: if you are serious about making a career in the industry, an unqualified yes. And the sooner the better. One important thing to be aware of before you join: you cannot accept non-union work after you have become a member of the union. This means, of course, that if you join SAG you would no longer be eligible to work for your local TV station doing a non-union commercial. And if you're a member of Actors' Equity, you will no longer be permitted to perform for free at your local community theatre. If you live in an area that does not have many professional opportunities for union performers, and if you are planning to stay in that area and get as much experience as you can, then perhaps you should postpone joining the union.

If you're planning to make a career of acting, you might as well start by making the commitment not to work for free. This will probably mean moving to a large city or a geographical area that provides enough working opportunities for you to make a living. The logistics of moving to an area like New York and forging a plan for yourself in the business are outlined in the book, *How To Be a Working Actor*, by former ABC Casting Director Mari Lyn Henry and Lynne Rogers.

One of the major reasons for joining the union is that your résumé may carry a little more weight with agents and managers. Many agents will not even consider a performer who is not a member of at least one union. So if you haven't listed the affiliation at the top right under your name, your picture and résumé go right into the garbage. The exception to this attitude may be found in agents who specialize in young performers; they might respond positively to a promising teen who doesn't belong to a union—yet. But for the most part, agents need to have some way to weed out people from the hundreds of pictures they receive every week, and one of the basic requirements may be union affiliation.

JOINING AFTRA: So how do you get into the union? Joining AFTRA is easy—it's an "open union," which means that all you have to do to join is come in with a check for the $700 initiation fee, and be willing and able to pay the minimum annual dues of $85. You do not need to have a job under AFTRA jurisdiction, and you can stay a member of the union without having any work. Again, remember that joining the union will not provide you with any guarantees of getting work.

SAG ELIGIBILITY REQUIREMENTS: The eligibility for joining SAG is: if you have been a member of either AFTRA or Equity for a year and have worked as a principal at least once in either union, you may apply for membership in SAG. To understand the designation of "principal" you need to know that all union work is done under a specific type of contract. Various union contracts include, for example, "Principal," "Chorus," "Extra," etc.

So to join SAG you need to have worked under a principal contract for a job in AFTRA or Equity. Please note that if you have worked as an extra for one day on a soap or in the box office at an Equity theatre, you are not eligible to join SAG. A Principal role might include, for example, a sizeable role in an Equity production, a radio commercial, or a day player in an AFTRA industrial film.

If you are not a member of another union, you would only be eligible to join SAG if you have a commitment for a role as a principal in a film commercial or filmed television show, or if you have proof of employment as a SAG-covered extra player at full SAG rates and conditions for a minimum of three work days. SAG's initiation fee is currently $862, and minimum annual dues are $85.

GETTING INTO EQUITY: For young performers who are really committed to becoming professional, joining Equity should be the first order of business. Equity eligibility requirements are as follows: you are eligible to join if you sign an Equity contract with a producer within the union's jurisdiction. You are also eligible to join by virtue of membership and employment in any of the Four A's unions—the nine unions listed at the beginning of this chapter. Applicants must be members in good standing of the "parent" union for at least one year, and they must have performed either as a principal or for three days of work comparable to an extra performer.

If this is beginning to sound like a "Catch-22," you're right, it is. "You have to have work to join the union, and you have to belong to the union to get work," is how some actors put it. In order to be eligible to join SAG, you have to have a SAG job, or you must have worked under the jurisdiction of Equity or AFTRA. In order to join Equity, you have to have an Equity job or you must be a member of and have worked under a SAG or AFTRA contract. You can get into AFTRA, but how do you get work?

Fortunately, Equity offers another very logical way to join by working as a "journeyman" or "apprentice." It's called the *Equity Membership Candidate Program*(EMC). Performers work as interns at a participating professional theatre, and for each week they work they receive one "point" towards membership. Participating professional theatres include many Equity Resident Theatres (LORT companies), Dinner Theatres, Chicago Area Theatres, and Resident and Non-Resident Dramatic Stock Companies. Equity Candidate positions, though they involve long hours, hard work, and little (if any) pay, are highly sought-after, and performers must usually audition along with numerous other hopefuls for these slots. After securing a non-professional position at a participating professional theatre, the actor must register with Equity as a Membership Candidate by completing the registration form and paying a one-time fee, which is credited against the initiation fee due when the Candidate is ready to join.

After forty weeks of work at accredited theatres, the Candidate may take a written test, and if the test is passed, the Candidate may join Equity. (Candidates who do not take the test are required to complete fifty weeks of work.) The weeks need not be consecutive, and may be accumulated over any period of time. But the Candidate may no longer work at an Equity theatre unless he or she signs an Equity contract after the fifty weeks are completed. A listing of theatres that have Equity Candidate Programs is available through your local Actors' Equity Association. The membership fee for Equity is $500, and the minimum annual dues are $52.

There are some professional theatres that do not pay the interns; rather they *charge* interns for the privilege of working and learning there. Though this hardly seems fair, it may be valuable if you can get accepted at a theatre that requires payment because these places are usually first-rate. The competition to get accepted as an intern is very tough, but the credit of working there may be worth it. If you are thinking of joining Equity through the Equity Candidate program, be prepared for long and difficult hours, work in every area of theatre *other than* acting (including construction, box office, props, backstage dresser, lights and sound, costume crews, etc.), and limited acting in the form of small bits and walk-ons. This is known as "paying your dues."

Your Professional Name

Are you aware that each of the unions allows only one member to have a specific name? Needless to say, if your real name is Tom Jones or Sally Smith, you're probably not going to be able to use it when it comes to join the union. You might be able to use your middle initial, but if the name is a common one, it's possible that your name with the initial is also "taken." If you are set on becoming a professional, it's important to do some research and think about a name before you get photos and résumés copied and send them out in the hundreds to casting people.

People used to change their names all the time, and numerous current stars were born with another name. On the other hand, you do see a trend today towards keeping the family name, unless it's terribly long, unpronounceable, or awkward. I was never advised to change my name, for example, and it is my family name. People tend to remember it, once they know how to pronounce it, because it's unusual. Of course, the slight difficulty with the last name is balanced by the simplicity of the first name. (If a casting director or agent mispronounces my name, I just simply say, "It's McTeeg," with no further comment.)

I have a friend named Dennis Sook who, when he first came to New York and joined the unions, took the name Dennis Austin. I don't know why he changed it in the first place; maybe he felt that Sook wasn't sellable. In any event, several years later he changed it back to Dennis Sook. (This can get expensive.) I met Jackie Zeman before she became a star on "General Hospital," when her name was Jackie Seaman. I know of another actor who was advised to change his last name from Rupprecht to Ruppert. He considered it for a while (and may have even changed it) but on his cable show, "Supermarket Sweep," he is using his original name.

You can research who has what names and find out if yours is "taken" by calling the membership department of each union. You may be able to use your chosen name in one union but not another. It would be practical if you could find a name that you could use consistently in all your union work. Having a name that's not "in use" also helps avoid confusion—agents and casting people should be able to associate you with your unique name.

REPRESENTATION: AGENTS AND MANAGERS

Franchised Agents

Who are these people and why do we need them? Agents are legitimate representatives of talent throughout the country. In return for setting up auditions and appointments and negotiating contracts, agents charge 10% of the gross the actor earns when they book a job. In order to provide theatres and producers with talent, agents must be *franchised* by the unions in which they are working. In other words, if they represent Equity actors working under Equity contract, they must have an Equity franchise; the same holds for SAG and AFTRA. If an agent does anything unethical or illegal, such as withholding checks from performers or taking too large a commission, he stands to lose his franchise.

Actors have different arrangements with their agents. They may be *signed*, which means that they have a contract that the agent will represent them exclusively either in a particular area or "across-the-board." Signed across-the-board means the agent represents talent exclusively in all union work. Actors signed in all areas may not work through any other agents in the business.

On the other hand, numerous actors work as *freelance* artists. This term goes back to Medieval days, when some knights would ride around from castle to castle offering to compete in tournaments for a fee. They weren't employed by just one castle, so they came to be called "free-lancers." Freelance actors are not signed with a particular agent, but may work with several. Actors may also be signed in one area and work freelance in others; e.g., you might have an exclusive contract with a commercial (SAG) agent but be freelance for Equity and AFTRA employment.

Should you sign with an agent? If you are lucky enough to get an offer from a franchised agent to work exclusively with him or her, and if you are relatively new to the business, by all means try it. Agents do not offer contracts to performers they do not believe in, so you at least know the agent thinks you can make money for the office. If a lengthy commitment puts you off, it may be some consolation to know that most agent contracts are for a period of only one year, and if no employment is obtained or the actor doesn't get any auditions, the performer can get out of the contract.

Personal Managers

What's the difference between an agent and a manager? Both are actors' "representatives," which means that performers pay them a percentage of their salary to set up auditions and appointments and negotiate contracts for them. Managers are not franchised by the unions, and are therefore somewhat more difficult to "track." Anyone with any kind of background in theatre, TV, or entertainment can set himself up as a personal manager.

There are two groups of people who would probably benefit most from having a manager: big stars and nobodies. Managers of big stars literally manage their time, setting up appointments and arranging schedules, and operating as a protective shield between stars and the public. They are also notorious for being tough negotiators, and may work as middlemen between a star and an agent.

A nobody might need a manager because he doesn't know anybody yet, and the manager is supposed to be "introducing" him to people in the business. Managers work closely with the actor on a far more personal and detailed basis than agents. They set up interviews *with* agents, provide advice regarding pictures and résumés, and generally promote the actor with every business method at their disposal. Yes, managers work with agents. Remember in the last section we pointed out that in order to get work for union members, an agent had to be franchised by the union? Well, managers are not franchised by the unions, so for any union jobs, the manager must work with a union-franchised agent.

Before you sign with a manager consider the following. First, managers usually require the actor to sign an exclusive contract for a minimum period of three years. Second, "exclusive" in this case means that even if the actor gets work independently, the manager still receives a commission. Third, if the manager sets up a booking through a union-franchised agent, you are responsible for paying *both* the manager's commission and the agent's commission. Fourth, agents are limited by law to a 10% cut, but because managers' fees are not set by any legal entity, they can charge any commission, usually 15%. The point is that if you book a union job through a manager you may be paying 25% commission off the top.

Actors are advised to use caution before signing an exclusive agreement with a manager. Check with the Better Business Bureau in your area, and talk with other actors you know who are represented by the manager. Find out if the manager is a member of the National Conference of Personal Managers, 210 East 51st St., 2nd Floor, New York, NY 10022 (212) 421-2670. If he is not a member, it doesn't mean he is not a good manager, but belonging to an association of this sort might reassure that this is not just a fly-by-night operation.

Read over the manager contract carefully: it should state that WHEN you get employment, you pay the manager an agreed commission of the gross. If you are requested to pay any money "up-front," or it is suggested that you simply MUST go to a particular photographer and spend a certain amount of money on pictures, or that the manager will "take care of" printing your résumés and charge you for it, do not sign a contract with that person. No legitimate manager will dictate where you should go or how much you have to spend on your materials.

Some actors rationalize working with a manager by saying, "I'd rather be paying 25% of *something* than 10% of nothing." And to be fair, there are some very good managers in the industry who really earn their fees, and who represent actors at all stages of their careers.

Showcases

How in the world do you get an agent or manager? There's another "Catch-22" in the business: you can't get an audition without an agent, and you can't get an agent unless they see your work. But how can they see your work if they aren't getting you work? You can do a showcase.

Showcase is the classification designated by Equity allowing members to work for free in hopes of getting representation and experience. Equity sets the rules by which directors and producers must abide, including: rehearsal hours are limited, actors are reimbursed for transportation, number of performances is limited, ticket price is limited, total seating capacity is limited. (The current showcase code allows for a total audience capacity of no more than 99.)

Should you do showcases? Sure, if you are new in town or don't have an agent. I happened to meet my wonderful agent as a result of doing a showcase. It was spring, I hadn't worked in a while, and an old acquaintance happened to be directing a showcase. I was at a slow point in my life and my career, and after reading the sides I was not that impressed with the material. When the director offered it to me, I almost said "no, thanks," but at the time I couldn't think of a reasonable excuse to get out of it. (I had, after all, auditioned.) My agent was in the house as a courtesy to the leading man who was a client of his; that's how he came to be there and see my performance. In fact, he later admitted to me that the play was the "worst piece of garbage" he had ever seen, but he liked my work.

RESOURCE MATERIALS AND ADVERTISING

East Coast and Regional Resources

So where do you start? The first thing you need is several resource materials that provide lists of theatres, casting people, agents, advertising agencies, production companies, and others who typically use talent. You also need access to the trade papers, which have casting notices and other pertinent information.

If your geographical area is New York City and/or the metropolitan area, you will want to obtain the weekly trade paper, *BackStage*. This lists Eligible Performer Auditions and Interviews (EPAs and EPIs) for future productions throughout the New York and Regional markets, and provides a cast breakdown along with location of the auditions. (Eligible Performers are those who have an Equity card or a requisite amount of professional experience.) *BackStage* charges a fee for non-union casting notices, so productions that are non-Equity are easily recognizable by the "... ADVT" at the end of the listing.

Needless to say, if you're going to respond to an ad in *BackStage* you need to be available to audition should you get a call, and to go into rehearsal if you get cast. If you are not ready to make this commitment, don't waste your valuable pictures and résumés. *BackStage* comes out weekly and is available at newsstands in the metropolitan area and in larger cities throughout the country. It may also be obtained by subscription. The *BackStage* office is located at 330 West 42nd St., New York, NY 10036 (212) 947-0020.

Another industry trade paper is *Variety*, which contains pertinent information about the entertainment business. Though it will certainly help educate you to what's happening in the industry, *Variety* does not provide any casting listings, and is therefore not as frequently read by actors as is *BackStage*.

One of the most valuable resource books for East Coast actors is *Ross Reports Television*, called the Ross Report. This little monthly publication is packed with comprehensive and up-to-date listings of the following New-York based companies: Advertising Agencies, Independent Casting Directors, Producers of TV Commercials, Television Talent Agencies, Literary Agencies, Non-TV Talent Unions, Network Offices and Studios, and Network Program Packagers. The booklet lists New York Musical & Variety Shows, Dramatic Serials (series), and Primetime Programs, as well as Los Angeles Dramatic Serials and West Coast Program Production Studios.

The Ross Report is available in single copy form at bookstores throughout the country. To obtain a copy or to order a subscription, write to Television Index, Inc., 40-29 27th St., Long Island City, NY 11101 (718) 937-3990.

For lists of theatres, check the bookstore. There is a book called the *Summer Theatre Directory* by Jill Charles, which lists both union and non-union summer stock companies. If you are a member of Equity, you can also obtain lists of theatres operating under various contracts at the local union office.

One of the most valuable theatre resource books I recommend is the TCG *Theatre Directory*, produced by Theatre Communications Group in New York. This small and inexpensive manual lists all the regional theatres in the country operating under an Equity Resident Theatre contract, the "LORT" theatres. The book comes out annually and can be obtained from TCG at 355 Lexington Ave., New York, NY 10017 (212) 697-5230.

TCG also publishes a large annual volume, which provides a more comprehensive listing of each regional theatre, including production photos and specific seasons. This is called *Theatre Profiles*, and can also be obtained from the TCG office.

For Broadway and Off-Broadway theatre news, the weekly publication called the *Theatrical Index* lists all shows currently in production, in rehearsal, or slated for the near future. Also listed are the star and the cast (if it's cast), the producer, the director, and the casting director. The *Index* is especially important for professional actors, and it is posted in the Equity Lounge at the union office in New York. It is also available through the larger theatre bookstores and by subscription at Price Berkley, 888 Eighth Ave., New York, NY 10019 (212) 586-6343.

West Coast Resources

Drama-Logue is probably the most helpful trade paper for actors on the West Coast. Similar to *BackStage*, it also has interviews with personalities, information on industry activity throughout the country, and numerous advertisements. (Ads can be a source for beginners, too: for photographers, answering services, coaches, picture and résumé copies, etc.) A weekly publication, *Drama-Logue* is available at newsstands throughout the Los Angeles area. You can obtain information about where it can be purchased by writing to *Drama-Logue*, P.O. Box 38771, Los Angeles, CA 90038-0771 (213) 464-5079.

Hollywood Variety and *The Hollywood Reporter* are daily publications that offer some juicy tidbits on who's doing what to whom and who's lunching where in the Los Angeles area. These papers do not contain casting listings, so they're not as widely read or as valuable for actors as *Drama-Logue*.

Advertising

Once you have your pictures, you'll need to do some self-promotion. If you are a member of Equity, AFTRA, or SAG, you can get listed in *Player's Guide*, which is a gigantic annual volume listing just about every actor in the business. You will have to decide what category you fit into (Young Leading Man/Woman, Leading Man/Woman, Character, etc.), complete a form, and pay a reasonable fee. Everyone listed in the *Guide* is given the same amount of space, about two inches by about eight inches. Your listing will include your name, phone number or agent, selected credits, and photograph. Be forewarned that credits may be checked, as will your union affiliation. For more information and an application, write to *Player's Guide*, 165 West 46th St., New York, NY 10036 (212) 869-3570.

On the West Coast, there is the *Academy Players Directory*. It's similar in format to the *Player's Guide*, but it comes out three times a year. To be listed you must be a member of a guild or signed with a SAG franchised agent. (You do not have the option of listing credits in the *Academy Players Directory*.) For more information, write the Academy of Motion Picture Arts and Sciences, 8949 Wilshire Blvd., Beverly Hills, CA 90211 (310) 247-3058.

PICTURES AND RESUMES

The first thing you're going to need to get started in the business is your picture and résumé, the primary "tools of the trade." The format for actors' pictures and résumés is very traditional and is to be followed strictly. You need an 8" X 10" black-and-white photo (also called an 8 X 10) on the back of which your one-page résumé is firmly attached. (When you turn over the picture you will see the résumé.)

Preferably you will go to a professional photographer to have your photos done. Agents and managers in New York and on the West Coast usually have several photographers they like to recommend, depending on what's in vogue. Specific professional photographers are preferred because their work is consistent and meets the requirements of industry people who are trying to get work for you.

Many beginners, however, are either not in the New York area, do not have an agent who can recommend a photographer, or cannot afford the $200 to $300 fee that even reasonable photographers charge. This may sound high, but don't assume you will be saving a lot of money by having a friend take a snapshot. A bad photo can do hundreds of dollars worth of harm. With that in mind, we can make certain generalizations about 8 X 10s, and you can at least follow this advice and share it with your local photographer or whoever is taking your pictures, if you are unable to follow the first recommendation.

Head Shots

Actors who are seeking work in the business will need two 8 X 10 pictures, one "legit," and one "commercial." These photos can (and should) be taken at a single session simply by a change of hair, makeup, clothing, and attitude. If you think of yourself as *only* a serious actor and not in need of a commercial picture, it is still advisable to get one because if you are lucky enough to meet any agents they are probably going to ask for your commercial head shot.

Do some research for your picture by studying commercials on TV. Find, borrow, or buy something appropriate to wear to your photo session—it should be casual, open-necked, and neat. Light colors (pastels) and medium tones are usually most appropriate for the commercial shot; for example, a light or patterned shirt with a medium-tone V-neck. Avoid red, dark blue, and brown (because they photograph black), and shiny materials that look too flashy. Your makeup (men and women) should also be light, meaning "not a lot." Your hair can be contemporary but should be reasonably neat (especially for commercials) and should not be hanging in your eyes.

Don't wear any jewelry, except small, tasteful earrings (for women only). Don't wear a business suit—the look will limit you to "spokesperson" or "business person." Avoid turtlenecks or blouses with ties that wrap around the neck; this wardrobe conveys a somewhat "up-tight" image, and is usually not flattering either.

Your "legit" picture presents the image you want to project for work in theatre, film, and soaps. On the more serious and (for women) glamorous side, the legit look is usually "stronger" than the commercial look. You may choose to wear darker clothing, and your makeup may be more pronounced. Women may wear tasteful jewelry, but it is not recommended for men. Clothing may be darker, dressier, and more dramatic. Again, you should not wear a business suit. Avoid wearing something that specifically reads "period," because casting people will think of you only for period plays. Try to find something that looks dramatic but does not make an extreme statement or limit your look to one type of play. Makeup can be more dramatic, but nowhere near as heavy as stage makeup (no false eyelashes for women). Another makeup tip: apply translucent loose powder liberally with a brush or your face will shine.

A special note about "legit" pictures. Don't forget that this is your photo for the legitimate theatre. I am aware that "sex sells," but you sometimes have no control over who might get your picture or what their reaction may be. One of my students, for example, was talked into doing a head shot in which she *appeared* to be wearing nothing (of course, it was just from the top of the shoulders up.) But this is not the kind of image you want to project. Most legitimate agents and casting directors will not be taken in by a risqué photo; on the other hand, if your picture is a "come-on" you may get a response from someone just waiting to take advantage of you.

Both your commercial and your legit pictures should be well-lit (no half-in-the-dark faces, please). Some photographers like to take pictures outside because they don't have to spend any money on studio or lights; personally I do not recommend this because you have much less control over how you will look in sunlight. You can sweat easily (which causes makeup to shine), you'll squint if you have sensitive eyes, and the wind can blow your hair all over the place.

RESEARCHING THE PHOTOGRAPHER: If you live in an area where there may be several photographers from which to choose, narrow down the list by asking for recommendations from your agent and people in the business. Select three or four photographers in your price range, then call each and arrange an interview appointment. All reputable photographers should be able to spend a little time with you up-front; if they are reluctant, then you probably don't want to work with them. At the time of the interview, you may look at the photographer's previous work to see if you like it (their portfolio or "book") and ask questions, including, "What do you charge for the session?" "How many pictures will you take for that money?" "How many finished prints will I get for the fee?" "Do you do the hair and makeup?" "How do I select my wardrobe?" "What types of wardrobe shall I bring?" "Where will you be photographing me?" "Do you do your own retouching?" and "What happens if I don't get my shots in the session?"

Regarding hair and makeup: many photographers do not do the hair and/or makeup but can recommend someone who will do so at your session. The hair and makeup may *not* be included in the session fee, so find out what that separate charge is going to be before the session. Be especially careful with hair: if you can't duplicate the "do" you will be in trouble when you're told your picture doesn't look like you.

Good photographers will not mind answering your questions and putting you at ease. The charge for professional photographs can range from $100 to $700 for the session. The photographer should take several rolls of film so you have a good number of pictures from which to choose. You should be able to discuss what types of wardrobe to bring and specific pieces you have that will work for the commercial look or the legit look. You should be able to discuss how your hair and makeup will look for the two shots. Most photographers I have worked with do their own retouching; you shouldn't have to run around trying to find a specialist who can do that for you. You should walk away with at least two different (a "legit" and a "commercial") retouched finished prints.

SELECTING THE PICTURES: After your session, the photographer will provide *contact sheets*, which contain your "proofs." These are little prints of each frame of film from which you select your final photos. When you are going through your contact sheets making your selection, be sure to use a little magnifier. Getting a closer view will definitely influence your selection.

If you have a mentor or an agent or advisor, show him or her the contact sheets and get an expert opinion. What are agents and casting directors looking for? First, they want a picture that looks like you. Next, agents and casting people talk about the picture that "pops," the one that has the most expression in the eyes, the one that shows your unique personality the best, the one that says "Hire me, I'll be fun to work with."

Here's an important bit of advice from a professional: ALWAYS SELECT PICTURES THAT YOU LIKE. You must be happy with your pictures, and you must be proud to send them out to agents and casting people. Some advisors (for some strange reason) will select the most unusual or bizarre picture of you they find, and just because it's different, tell you that's the one they like and the one you should have copied. (This has happened to me, more than once.) Watch out for this. You *must* feel that your photo is flattering and exciting as well as an accurate representation of yourself.

What if you get your contact sheets and you don't like any of the pictures, or you like the face but not the clothes? This is where going to a good photographer can help you enormously in the first place. If you simply cannot find even one photo that's acceptable, you should be able to schedule another session with the photographer at no extra charge (or for a minimal charge). This is called a *retake*. Don't forget that if you have paid extra for the hair and makeup person you may have to pay this fee again, if you use him or her again. While working with a reputable photographer can help you avoid the need for a retake, these things happen, and good photographers have the means to deal with them.

COPIES OF YOUR PHOTOS: So you've had a wonderful session with a terrific photographer and you've walked away with two great retouched finished prints. You then take these pictures to a photo reproduction place and get copies. (Avoid photographers who charge you for the session and a certain number of prints; you will have to keep coming back to them for more prints, and reproduction places can usually do them cheaper.)

Here's how photo reproduction works. You take your finished original prints in, and they make a negative and reprint the ordered quantity, usually 25, 50, or 100. Though most professionals order a hundred, you can certainly start with a smaller amount, but the fewer you order the more costly they are per photo. (Also, check out the *Ross Report*, there are HUNDREDS of agents and casting people out there.) On the other hand, don't get thousands—if you are young or new to the business, you may wish to get new photographs in a year or two.

If you are in a large photo reproduction place, you will be asked to select a type font for your name. ALWAYS have your name put on the front of your picture. The photo place makes up a separate negative, called a "name slug," which has your name on it. It will cost a little extra, but it's critical that your name be identified with your face. The name slug can be used for both your photos, and reused whenever you get more prints.

Other considerations are the format: do you want border or no border, on glossy paper or matte? Most professionals use the borderless, matte format, but if you're new to the business it may be wiser to go the slightly cheaper route. It doesn't really matter all that much as long as you have a good picture.

In New York, copies of 8 X 10 pictures at the larger places cost about fifty cents each (excluding the cost of the negative and name slug, but those are one-time charges). If your pictures are costing you much more than this, it may be a good idea to send your carefully packaged originals to a reputable place in New York or another large city, and have the photos copied and returned. (Be prepared to pay shipping charges.) Two possibilities are Ideal Photo at 145 W. 45th St., New York, NY 10036 (212) 575-0303 and CopyArt at 165 West 46th St., New York, NY 10036 (212) 382-0233. Write to them for price lists or call for information about ordering by mail.

POSTCARDS: Most professional actors also have their 8 X 10 shot(s) made into 3 X 5 postcards for sending to agents and casting people on a regular basis. This is a good advertising tool, and considering the number of people who don't like to be called on the phone and the number of agents whose offices you can't get into in person, it's wise to think about using the mail to sell yourself.

The format for the postcard is a 3 X 5 card: your photo is printed on one side (the long way) with your name, union affiliations, and phone number in a white border beneath it. (Again, never send out a postcard without your name and phone number—it's a waste of money!) Turn the photo over and address the card, write your note, stick a postcard stamp on it, and drop it in the mail.

You can get postcards made at the same place you have your 8 X 10s reproduced, but I don't necessarily recommend it because they are expensive. Of course, they're printed on card stock, and the quality is good, but you'll pay thirty-five cents for each. If you are going to send out postcards, you should have enough to cover your whole list and also do a number of mailings. There are places that offer cheap postcard reproduction, say under $100 for a thousand. The quality is not as good (they use a process called Velox), and the card stock is not as heavy, but for the purpose they are OK as long as the reproduction is acceptable. (Acceptable Velox is not too grainy, not uneven, not too dark.)

You can find out about the places that do this sort of inexpensive postcard reproduction by looking for ads in the trade papers. Don't forget that every time you do a mailing, it's going to cost quite a lot for the postage alone, so if you can save on the postcards you're ahead of the game.

Résumés

When you are setting up your résumé, the first thing to remember is that it needs to be "cut to fit" your 8 X 10 photo. The standard size of typing paper is 8 ½" by 11". If you get the entire thing nicely typed up and centered and duplicated on the wrong size paper, you're going to be spending a lot of time with the scissors. Before you even sit down at the typewriter or word processor, cut the paper to 8" X 10", and set your margins accordingly. Type the résumé to be centered on 8" X 10" paper.

As mentioned, the résumé must be firmly attached to the back of the picture, facing out. This means four staples (in each corner), or glue. I have found that rubber cement works best because if the résumé changes, you can remove the old one and replace it with the new without ruining the photo. You can also use spray glue to stick the résumé on, but this is a more permanent adhesive. Some places offer printing directly on the back of the picture, but I don't recommend this for the simple reason that if your résumé changes you can't get it off.

You should always attach your résumé to your photo before you even go on an interview or audition; in fact, do several at a time and have them handy. If your picture and résumé is not in the proper format, that may be reason enough for an agent or casting director to "file it in file 13" (which is the trash).

Your résumé should always begin with the following information, in this order:

Your Name: (in large type centered at the top)
Union Affiliations: (AEA or Equity, SAG, AFTRA)
Your phone number: (service or machine)
Height: Hair: (color)
Weight: Eyes: (color)
Age Range: Voice: (singing range)

Needless to say, don't forget your name at the top and NEVER, EVER send out a résumé *without* a phone number on it. This seems so obvious, but it's done all the time. How in the world are people going to contact you if there's no phone number?

Your phone should be a 24-hour answering service or a number that has an answering machine attached. Indicate this by (service) or (machine) after the number. Agents will not try again if they call your number and get no answer at all; they do not have time. Do not rely on your family or friends to relay your messages, it's too risky. As a professional you will be expected to stay in touch with your service or your machine on a regular basis (every couple of hours) to check for messages and get back to people.

Your height and weight should be actual, and list your color of hair and eyes. This is logical information to provide if your photo is the traditional black and white. Unless you are looking for modeling jobs, it is not necessary to list your size (your height and weight take care of that). It is also unnecessary to list your Social Security number.

Do *not* list your date of birth; instead give an age range. (Some casting people feel this is *not* important because the picture should look like you at the age you are.) Most people can play at least a five-year range, so if you're really 23, you could list your range as 20-25. If you are tall, or if you look older than your age, you may list yourself a little older, say 21-26.

"Voice" means your singing range and type, e.g., soprano, mezzo, baritone, tenor, etc. If you are a dancer you may also wish to list the types of dance you specialize in right up here at the top in a separate category titled "Dance."

Now we come to the body of the résumé, your credits. In the next three sections you will include your theatre, film, and TV credits. The area in which you have your strongest credits should be listed first. For example, if you have the most experience in television, list those credits right at the top. If credits in all three fields are about the same, the category you list first might depend on your base. If you're in New York, for example, you would list your theatre credits first, and if you're in Los Angeles you'd list your film credits first. In whatever order, the next sections will include these three categories:

> Theatre
> Film
> Television

Within each section, always list your credits in order from most important to least (not in chronological order). Be sure to put the name of the character you played and the place where you did it, even if it was a high school or college production. For film and TV, some people would advise you to list only credits in which you played a specific role, not extra work. Do not list any commercials under this "TV" section, but only work you did for television, including day-time shows (soaps) and series. If you have few TV and film credits, you may combine these two categories.

The question of what to include on your résumé brings up an important point: should you lie? In a word, no. It is particularly dangerous because some of the casting people you meet will know the truth. Agents do not want to work with dishonest people. Period.

On the other hand, you needn't belittle your credits. If you worked in the chorus on a musical, and if your character had a name, it's OK to put that name as a role. If asked, of course, you may say that you really had a great time being in the chorus. Some beginners list their extra experience because they have no other credits. Rather than place these "credits" under a category titled "Extra work," it may be better to simply list them under the Television and Film category. If asked, you don't have to say "Oh, it was nothing, it was only an extra." But be honest: "I really learned a lot because it was the first extra job I did."

The next sections of the résumé are:

> Commercials—List on Request
> Special Skills/Sports
> Education/Training

Regarding commercials, most professionals have the category listed if they have done principal work on commercials, followed by "List on Request." (This means that if someone requests a list of your current conflicts you can provide one. Another way this may be worded is "Please ask for current conflicts.") If you have done commercials, *do not list the products*. The reason for this is that, under SAG commercial rules, you may represent only one product of the same kind at any given time. If you already have a commercial for a particular type of product, it's called a *product conflict*. This protects the clients by ensuring that the same person is not touting conflicting products. For example, the Rice Krispies client wouldn't want you showing up on TV doing a spot for Kix Cereal.

If you are a high school or college student or recent graduate, you may list another section, which I call "Activities, Honors, and Awards." I feel this is important for young beginners because, though not directly related to performance, it does give agents and casting people some idea of who you are and what you've done. Here you may list your school teams and clubs (if you were an officer, mention that), Student Council or Dean's List Honors, and other special awards you've received.

The last section contains a very broad category called "Special Skills and Sports." You can list here the musical instruments you play, other languages you speak or accents you specialize in, and sports you do well. (If you have listed a team or an award related to a sport in the previous "Activities" section, mention the sport again here.) Don't forget to list the things you can do that many people take for granted, such as swimming and skating. If you play an instrument, list only the ones you play well. If you specialize in many sports and do several very well, you may wish to list them in a completely separate section beneath this one titled "Sports."

There is the story about the young woman who was asked if she could ride a bike, and she responded "yes, of course." She booked the commercial, the clients and ad reps and production people were all set up to shoot the commercial on location on a remote country road, and the talent couldn't ride the bike. Keep in mind that if you list something in the Special Skills or Sports section, you must be able to do it all day for the hundreds of rehearsals and takes and retakes that commercials require. So if you're going to list "jogging," be sure that you actually do jog on a regular basis. Again, be honest.

Before you have your résumés printed, check your master carefully for spelling errors or typos. Shop around for the best prices on résumé copying, and order the same number of résumés as you have photos (both shots). You may want to select a finer quality of paper for printing your résumés (heavier stock or a color other than white) but I don't recommend that you have it printed on hot pink or lime green. Acting is a business—you want to present a quality product.

When you go to get copies, don't forget that you now have an 8" X 10" paper, and most copy places use standard-size paper. Align your 8" X 10" page to the *upper left* corner of the larger paper, do not center it. (It may even be a good idea to paste it up.) This way you need trim off only two sides rather than all four. Some copy places have 8" X 10" paper, but be sure you take a photo with you before you consent to printing on this size. The paper should be just a little smaller than the photo. (Many pictures are exactly 8" X 10" or a little *smaller*, so you will still have to trim the 8" X 10" paper to get it to fit neatly on the back of the photo.) I usually have my résumé printed on standard paper and trim it myself with a paper cutter (available at most copy places).

Sending it Out

Now that you have your photo and résumé, you can begin to send them out: to theatres, agents, and casting people. Mail photos and résumés to one person at an agency (not the entire company), and always include a cover letter. It is very helpful if you have a "recommendation"—meaning someone of influence has recommended you. If you can get someone to recommend you to a theatre where his name means something, or to an agent who works with him, so much the better. Agents always like to know that a "friend of a friend" sent you. Always ask the person who is recommending you if you may use his or her name in your cover letter. Do not say, "I was recommended by Bruce Willis," when, in fact, you worked as an extra on a Bruce Willis film.

What to say? Keep it short. If you have done your research you can make mention of your own recent experience with the potential employer or agent. For example, "I very much enjoyed the way you directed 'Three Sisters' at the Studio Playhouse." Or, "I was impressed with the originality you expressed in your casting of 'Twelfth Night.'" You do not need to tell the casting person all about yourself in the cover letter—let your résumé speak for itself. Tell them what you want: "I would like to arrange an interview to meet you." This may be followed by, "I will call in two weeks in hopes of arranging an appointment." Be brief, be positive, get to the point.

Your stationery for your cover letter should be smaller than your picture and résumé. The cover letter should be neatly typed or legibly written, and attached to the picture and résumé with a paper clip.

Envelopes just the right size for an 8 X 10 photo are sold at the large photo reproduction places, and you may also purchase card-board to insert with the picture. (Warning: I have heard that some agents and casting directors hate cardboard, though I don't know why. It does keep the photo from getting crumpled and wrecked.) The cost of 100 envelopes with cardboard is a little over $10.

One final note: Don't send pictures and résumés to areas that are not accessible and that you can't get to for auditions. If you are in Los Angeles, concentrate on the West Coast and don't waste your money on New York. If you are in Chicago, concentrate on that met-ropolitan area. Wherever you send your picture, you should be willing to get there at your own expense for auditions and interviews (unless you know that a particular theatre holds auditions in *your* city). If you are a student, don't send your picture out until you are ready, willing, and able to meet with agents and casting people and to go on auditions in their locale.

PROFESSIONAL WORK AND THE FLOW OF CASTING

There are many areas available for talented actors to work. The trick is getting to the people who can help you get the jobs. Because there are so many people in the "Flow of Casting," I've made up the following charts so you can see the relationships of the major players involved. The first chart involves print work, commercials, and saps/series.

Chart 1: Flow of Casting for Print, Commercials, Soaps/series

In Chart 1, the three categories (Print, Commercials, and Soaps/Series) all have a common ancestor: the client. The client is the company (e.g., General Mills, Procter and Gamble, the Upjohn Company) that has a product to sell (Cheerios, Ivory Soap, Motrin). The client hires an advertising agency to help them invent, organize, and execute campaigns, in the form of print and commercial advertising. The ad agency then determines the logistics of each job.

If the job is a print shoot, the ad agency hires a photographer to produce everything needed for that particular project. The photographer, in turn, puts out the call to print agents, who then obtain the models and actors for go-sees. Go-sees are usually held in the photographer's studio.

The ad agency also oversees commercials: they hire a director and a production company to shoot the commercial. Note that commercial production companies and directors do not work for the ad agency but are contracted to shoot a particular spot or spots. The director may be present at auditions, will certainly view the tapes, and often has input into the casting.

The casting department is in charge of setting up all auditions and providing the agency with the right talent. "In-house" casting simply means that casting personnel within the ad agency handle the logistics of casting, and the auditions are held at the advertising agency. Independent casting means that a casting director outside the agency will be in charge of casting, in which case the auditions are held at the independent casting office. In commercials, the casting director contacts agents who arrange appointments for the talent.

For many soaps and series the client is certainly important: this is the sponsor. TV production can also work the other way around, i.e, the network signs an agreement to produce a show, and then goes out and gets advertisers (sponsors) for it. Either way, we wouldn't have network TV without the client. Networks may have producers or packagers for a show, who take charge of all the production elements. It is the producers or packagers who hire the casting people to get the talent. And the casting people call the agents, who call the actors.

Other areas offering work for actors are the public television and cable markets. The flow of casting is very similar to that of the networks; the difference is that instead of having to deal directly with a client or sponsor, the cable or public TV station has to answer to its paid customers or subscribers.

Chart 2: Flow of Casting for Industrials

At the top of the Flow of Casting for Industrials is the company or corporation. If they do not have their own in-house production staff, they hire a production company and director. Some companies that do a large number of industrials might have their own in-house casting; if not, an independent casting director is hired. Then calls go out to the agents, who call the actors.

Chart 3: Flow of Casting for Feature Films

The Flow of Casting in Feature Films is quite simple, belying the difficulty of getting work in features. Here the studio wields most of the power. They hire a director, who does *not* always have input into the casting. Though there may be a casting director, studios negotiate directly with agents for stars. Separate casting offices usually handle principals and extras.

Chart 4: Flow of Casting for Theatre

The Flow of Casting in Theatre is fairly self-explanatory. The producer and artistic director oversee the theatre or production. In the case of regional theatre, the artistic director may work with the producer (or managing director) to select a director for the show. In the case of Broadway, the producer may or may not have such a position of power, and the director may be independently arranged. The director then contacts the casting director; if the theatre or show has its own in-house casting director, auditions will often be held at the theatre. If the theatre or show uses an independent casting director, auditions may be held at his or her office.

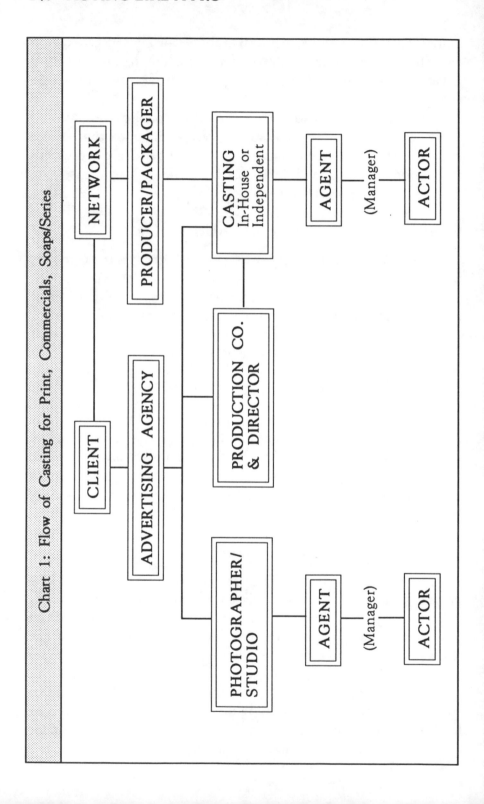

Chart 1: Flow of Casting for Print, Commercials, Soaps/Series

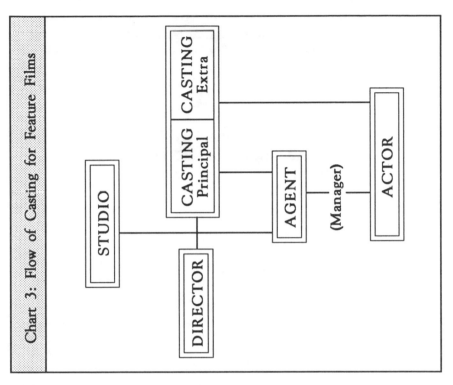

Chart 3: Flow of Casting for Feature Films

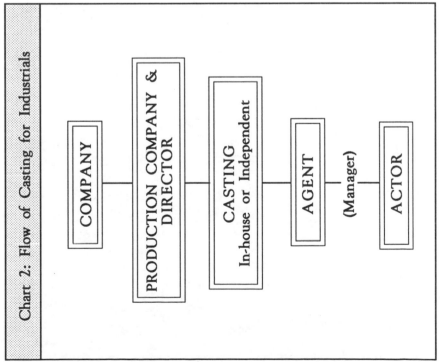

Chart 2: Flow of Casting for Industrials

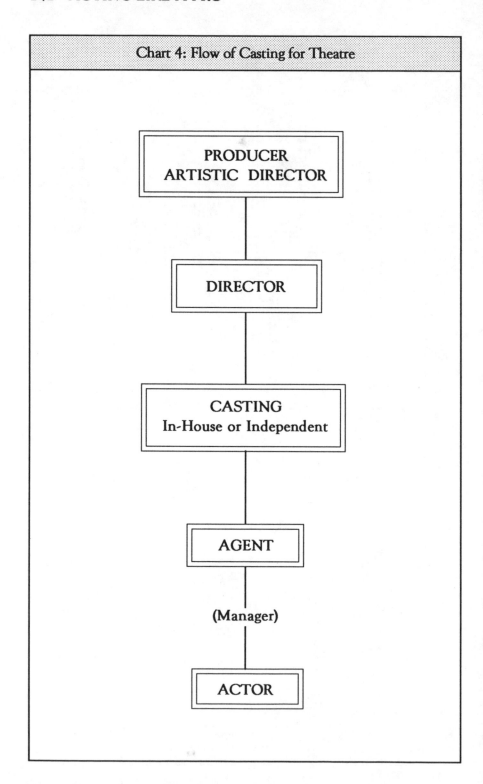

Chart 4: Flow of Casting for Theatre

PRODUCER
ARTISTIC DIRECTOR

DIRECTOR

CASTING
In-House or Independent

AGENT

(Manager)

ACTOR

THEATRE WORK

This area may be the most difficult in which to actually get paid employment. And the pay, except for Broadway and stars, is notoriously low. But that should not discourage you from working in theatre. Most actors come back as often as possible to the "real thing" because there is no better medium to keep up your skills and practice your craft. Look at Farrah Fawcett—even after she was a big TV star she agreed to do an Off-Broadway production called *Extremities*. It not only gave her a new reputation in the business, it led to the movie.

We've already mentioned going the Equity Candidate route, and this is a good way to get your union card. Don't forget too that Equity operates under all sorts of contracts, in numerous cities throughout the country. It may be easier for you to audition for and obtain work in Children's Theatre, Dinner Theatre, or Summer Stock in Kansas City or Minneapolis instead of plunging into the huge markets in Los Angeles or New York.

Remember, you have to start somewhere in this maze of the business. It's better to plant your feet in one geographical location and work at getting work for a year, than to skip around all over the place. For beginners, I recommend starting in slightly smaller areas, simply because the competition isn't as tough. Most of the time your persistence will pay off—maybe you won't get the first job you audition for, but after several auditions a director might just give you a chance.

I began my professional career working for a satirical theatre in Omaha, Nebraska. As a result of crazy kind of comedy I was doing, I was able to finagle an appointment with the artistic director of the local Equity theatre. Apparently he knew my work by reputation, because after a short chat he offered me two leading roles in the upcoming shows, and offhandedly mentioned, "Oh, yes, you'll have to sign an Equity contract." And that was that.

Many people get their first Equity job under a Children's Theatre (TYA) Contract. Dinner theatres are not quite as popular as they once were, but the ones that are still in operation have fairly solid reputations. Summer stock may be just as hard to get into as any other kind of stock, but there's so much more of it around.

A number of beginners have this question: should I continue to do non-union work, and to seek non-union paid employment? One thing you may acquire is credits towards "eligibility," meaning that when you have met the requirements, Actors Equity Association would recognize you as eligible and you would be allowed to attend EPIs and EPAs. And, of course, you will gain experience, wherever you work.

On the other hand, there is a whole group of non-union theatres and non-union performers who seem to make a career of non-union work. This will not accomplish a great deal for you, with the possible exception of the privilege of traveling around wherever the work is and doing lots of shows. Because Equity does not have jurisdiction, there may be no recourse if the producer doesn't pay your salary, rehearses for very long hours, or doesn't provide decent conditions in which to work.

INDUSTRIALS AND COMMERCIALS

Industrial Shows and Industrial Films

An *Industrial Show* is a live show sponsored by a particular company, for a limited period of time, for a restricted audience (usually only company employees). For example, Burger Bites might want to present a flashy show for their employees at the annual convention—that's an industrial. Some of these companies have big bucks, and they are willing to part with some of them to get the best talent they can find. The Pepsi industrial, for example, has a reputation for being spectacular.

Much of the time you need to be a triple-threat performer to do industrial shows, because they love to have a dancing, singing, and talking hamburger or other product. But don't laugh. Industrial shows can pay very well and may involve travel (which means a per diem in addition to salary). Professional industrial shows fall under the jurisdiction of Equity. Your agent may call you with an audition or you can consult the trade papers.

A typical industrial show audition is conducted in a fashion similar to musical theatre auditions. Be prepared for the possibility of a singing call-back, a dance call-back, and/or a reading call-back. (Equity does allow a certain number of call-backs, so grin and bear it.) Industrial shows can be a lot of fun and a good credit.

Industrial Films are in-house films produced for a particular company, usually made to provide information or training to company employees, and for internal use only. Many of you have probably seen industrial films at one time or another—you just didn't know what they were. Through an industrial film, for example, a company might explain the medical and dental plan, or train employees on how to use a new technology. In the industrial film area, available work for actors is primarily non-musical; they are hired as spokespersons or principal characters in the film.

Don't forget to sign in when you arrive for your audition appointment. (If you do *not* have a specific appointment, it is even more important to sign in.) In a typical industrial film audition, you will be asked to read on-camera from the script. If the character is described as "executive," "professional," or "spokesperson," they are looking for a business suit. Otherwise, dress according to the character description you are given.

Industrial films also pay a decent rate, and you may be hired for a number of days or weeks. There are union as well as non-union films produced throughout the country. Both SAG and AFTRA have industrial film contracts, so the union that has jurisdiction will depend on the signatory agreements of the production company. My first SAG job was an industrial film, and I have worked frequently in the field over the years.

Commercials

Whether or not you aspire to doing commercials, if you are interviewing in any major city that has any amount of commercial production, you should certainly investigate the possibilities in this highly lucrative area. If your geographical area is large enough to have agents, and if the agents think you're the right type, they'll see dollar signs the minute you walk in.

What is the right type? Almost any type, these days. There used to be a typical P&G (Procter and Gamble) look, which meant: fair skin, blonde (or red) hair, and blue eyes. It still helps, but there is room for all types in the commercial marketplace—just watch commercials to see what I mean. As we mentioned in the section on commercial pictures, the "look" for commercials is generally neat and somewhat preppy. But if you're a character or blue-collar type, it can be almost anything.

Some casting directors will tell you that you have to decide exactly what "type" you are and then cultivate that image. For example, are you a young mother/dad, a glamour gal/guy, a fashion model, a "real person," a professional/executive, a comedian/enne, a character person? If you're interested in exploring this further, and learning how to enhance a specific image, Vangie Hayes' book, *How to Get Into Commercials*, provides detailed breakdowns of various marketable commercial types and what they should look like.

GETTING A CALL: What if you get a call for a commercial audition? If it's a union job, you'll usually be called by an agent. If not, you may be called in by the producer, director, or almost anyone connected with casting. While they are on the phone, try to get as much information as possible about the role you are going up for. If they say "professional," that's very specific, but if they say "housewife" (what an archaic term that is!) then you should ask, "Blue-collar or up-scale? Casual or dressy?"

The more information you can obtain about the specific spot you are going up for and the role you are playing, the better. But don't bug the agent. If they say "20s casual young mom at home," or "character construction worker on the job," that should be enough. If you're a popular and busy commercial person, your agent may ask you if you have a product conflict, which we discussed in the section on résumés.

Commercial tip: dress for the role. If you're told you're going to be a young mom, don't come waltzing into the ad agency in low-cut leather. Many professionals I know carry around big tote bags with changes of clothing and props to create a different look: eyeglasses, bow ties, hard-hats, plaid shirts, sweaters, scarves, earrings, etc. Be aware that what's most important is what you wear from the waist up, because that's the part of you that will appear on camera. (You may have some terrific fisherman's boots just perfect for Mrs. Paul's Fish

Fillets, but unfortunately they probably won't even show. Wear a hat.)

THE COMMERCIAL AUDITION: Most commercial auditions in the major metropolitan areas take place at an advertising agency or casting director's office. Be on time, of course. If it's a union (SAG) commercial, there will be an official *sign-in*. The very first thing you should look for on the sign-in is the name of the product listed at the top. Make sure you are signing in for the correct product, because agencies may be casting more than one spot at the same time. The sign-in is a formal record of all the people who auditioned for a particular spot, and it is submitted to the union after the casting call.

This is the information you will be asked to complete on the SAG sign-in: Name, Social Security number, Agent, Time of Appointment, Actual Time In, Actual Time Out, Initials, and Interview Number. Because these forms are used by SAG to help monitor who is auditioning for what, you may also provide voluntary information on the sign-in, which includes your age range, sex, and race.

Use your professional name, and have your social security number handy when you sign in. Never list a manager's name under "Agent." (If you have a manager, he should tell you the name of the agent he is working with on this call.) Your time of appointment is the specific time the agent gave you for an appointment.

The "actual time in" is the time on the clock when you enter the agency or casting office, and the "actual time out" is the time you are finished with the audition. (Most commercial auditions are actually very short, from the time you get into the taping room to the time you're done.) The reason that you are asked for your initials is to ensure that you actually signed yourself in and out at the times recorded, so be sure to complete this box. Next, circle the appropriate number corresponding to the total number of times you have auditioned for this particular spot, choices being 1, 2, 3, or 4. (SAG members must be reimbursed for auditioning after a certain number of callbacks.)

On a voluntary basis, you may complete the rest of the information, including your sex, age range, and race. (The age is either under or over 40, so it's not that specific.) Use the codes provided to circle your appropriate race classification letter. This section is entirely up to you and not completing it will not jeopardize the job.

The first thing you ask the receptionist after you sign in is for the *copy*. This is a sheet with the commercial script or lines on it. (There may be no copy, meaning you would be on camera but have no speaking lines. If you are hired as a principal it's the same money.) Take time to look at the copy, and (are you ready for this?) read for comprehension. At many agencies the *storyboard* may be available or posted for actors to view. This is a series of little cartoons that show the action of the commercial.

You will study the copy from the piece of paper. You may take this into the audition with you, or you might be requested to leave it behind if they have made up a card. This is a large, poster-size card with the copy printed in large letters, which is strategically placed in the taping room so you can read from it. You will be taped on camera for most commercial auditions. You are usually talked through the actions of the spot, and then you get one rehearsal. The casting director will then turn on the camera and ask you to "Slate, please." To *slate* simply means to identify yourself by saying "Hello, I'm (your name)." Then you do your audition and you're done. Note: SAG members may not be requested to "ad lib" unless there is no copy.

Important point #1: You need almost no volume for commercials, so keep your volume down and your energy up. (No small feat!) Important point #2: Use your talent. Most actors new to commercials use a fakey, sing-songy approach and end up sounding like Barbie and Ken dolls. The people who cast commercials are looking for actors who can give some life to their performance. So use your brain and try to do something exciting and interesting. It doesn't hurt for you to show a sense of humor too.

Don't call your agent after the audition, and don't call her in two days to ask whether or not you got it. Professional actors do not usually follow up on commercial auditions. Though you may not hear anything at all, it's important to maintain a positive attitude about your work, and many experienced actors consider it a successful audition if they feel they did a good job and gave it their best.

Like theatre, commercials also have call-backs. You should wear exactly the same thing you wore before, and look exactly the same. You may be wondering, if they have put you on camera, why they need to see you in person again after such a short time. Good question. They just want to make sure that you are reliable, both in terms of getting to the audition and in terms of delivery. They may want to direct you in a different way. They may want to see you with other people. Don't ask, just go.

If they are interested in booking you, they will put you on what's called *first refusal*. This means that you should not take a booking from someone else until you first check with this client through your agent, to be sure they don't want you. After several days of anguished waiting, you may be released from the booking, meaning they don't want you. Of course, you might just book it. If you do, congratulations! You're on your way!

SAG commercials pay *residuals*, which are the money the actor gets each time the commercial *airs* (runs on-the-air). Residuals are where the "lucrative" part comes in. If the commercial is a "non-air demo" or a non-union spot, you may be offered a flat, one-time fee called a *buy-out*. If the spot is a non-air demo, it cannot be aired anywhere, and that should be in the contract. But if it's a non-union buyout, they can use it forever without paying you an additional cent. This is why we have a union.

If you are in a metropolitan area, check out the video schools, which will provide you with a much greater in-depth study of commercials and experience on camera. One of the oldest-established video schools in the New York metropolitan area is Weist-Barron, which offers video classes for young performers (ACTeen), as well as adults.

PRINT WORK AND VOICE-OVERS

Print Work

Almost every major city has opportunities for print work—wherever there are advertising agencies and photographers and clients. Print jobs are still-photography work, in which the actor poses in a picture used in an advertisement for a product or client. (Look in a magazine —see those people who are playing the moms and dads, the "real people," the "company employees," in the ads?

Those are paid actors in print jobs.) This is not to be confused with modeling, although you may be competing with models for these jobs. Many of these jobs require a certain type of expression or acting, and these assignments are called "commercial print work." If you're not a runway model or a fashion model or a glamor model, you could still be a "commercial print model."

In print work you are hired by a client to represent a product for the print media, which includes newspapers and magazines. Some agents and managers who do commercials also handle print work, but there are also specific agencies that deal exclusively with print.

If you consider yourself primarily a model, you should, of course, start out with a portfolio and composites. But if you are primarily an actor, you don't need these tools right away. A print agent or manager might say "Well, you're just not properly prepared," in which case you explain to them as nicely as possible that you are trying to get work as an actor and that though you do not consider yourself primarily a model, you are certainly willing to go up for print jobs. Most reputable agents will send you out anyway, if they think you have potential.

Print agents who are *not* reputable may suggest that you have to spend $500 for a composite session and another $500 for the prints, and they know exactly where to send you. (They are probably recommending a friend with whom they have a deal and receive a percentage of the fees.) Obviously, you do need to have at least one photo, but your commercial head shot should do. (P.S. Many photographers don't even want a head shot, they just use the Polaroids.)

PORTFOLIOS AND COMPOSITES: If print work turns out to be a little gold mine for you and if you book a number of jobs, you can then think about reinvesting some of it in the business by getting a portfolio and composites. Your *portfolio* is the book you carry around to "go-sees." It contains photos of you in different poses, with different expressions, both close-up and full-length. If you have done some work, the "tear sheets" (prints from actual jobs) can be included; if not, you may need to hire a photographer to shoot portfolio shots. Portfolio books used to be 11" X 14", but now some are as small as 5" X 7".

The composite is a single page photo reproduction (usually on Velox), which has your head shot on one side and two or three different poses on the reverse. Some fancier composites are a two-page fold, and even feature color shots. If you are experienced, you can use prints from actual jobs you have done for your composites.

Another advertising tool is the Agent's Head Sheet or Book, which is the compilation of all the talent the agency works with. Usually agencies expect their exclusive talent to fork over $200 to $300 to be included in the annual book.

GO-SEES: Your agent or manager will call you with a "go-see." On the phone, you should be given the same sort of information you need for commercials. If the character description is not specific enough, you can ask for more details. Instead of a specific appointment, you will be given a range of hours for the call. For example, "Go anytime between 10-1 or 2-4."

Go-sees are usually held at the studio of the photographer who is shooting the job, and they are not called auditions, they are called go-sees, because that's exactly what you do. You physically present yourself at the office of the photographer, complete an information card, and he or she will probably take a Polaroid. Many print calls take just a few minutes, but in other situations there may be lines of people waiting. It's hard to judge, so the best thing to do is go when you know you will have time to wait, if necessary.

BOOKINGS: You may be put on *hold* for a couple of days, and if you get *booked*, congratulations! For your work, you will receive a fee, usually a dollars-per-hour figure. The current rate in New York for professional commercial print people is $250 an hour. That may sound like a lot, but most print jobs are only one to two hours. On top of that, there is no union governing commercial print work, so the agencies can and do take 20 to 25% (or more) of your fee. And most print jobs don't pay for at least three months. Other than that, it's a great way to make money in an acting-related field.

The booking fee received for a print job does not typically include usage everywhere, so to protect themselves many people write in a qualifying usage clause right on the *release*. (The release is the paper you will be asked to sign on the job, which gives the client permission to use your picture.) If it is not spelled out, you may write on the release: "No posters, billboards, point-of-purchase, packages, labels, direct mail, or TV." If they want to use your face for any of these other things, they will have to get permission and pay you more.

JUST TESTING: You have to be a little cautious about who you go see, when, and the types of jobs you take. Always go through an agent or a manager. Don't take evening appointments—legitimate photographers have office hours during the day. Unfortunately, many photographers work and live in the same space the studio is in, which may be an apartment building, so you can't really eliminate all the possible go-sees at the photographer's home. But if you have any reason to be suspicious, don't go to the call, or take a friend with you.

Never let a photographer talk you into doing shots you don't want to do, no matter how much money he says they are paying. You should never be requested to remove any article of clothing (except an outer coat or jacket) in order to have a Polaroid taken.

Some models who are new to the business and don't have any photos of themselves sometimes work out a deal with a photographer: in exchange for the model's free time, the photographer will take some pictures as "tests," and the model receives free prints as payment. Warning: Don't get taken in by the promise of "test shots." Unless you are referred by your agent or manager to a specific photographer, test shot sessions could be detrimental to your health. In most cases you're better off paying for your shots, if you really feel that you need them.

Another warning: don't respond to Want Ads in the Employment section of the paper that say: "Models wanted—No experience necessary." They are also traps.

Voice-Overs

Voice work or voice-over work is essentially that which does not require your on-camera presence. It is a highly lucrative field (again, residuals!) for a small percentage of the working professional population. The reason this market is so difficult to break into is that people who do voices do *all kinds* of voices and accents, they are hired and rehired because they are known, and they can *look* like anyone at all as long as the voice is right.

Voice work is done throughout the country on a local level that might be available for the beginner. I booked my first Chicago radio commercial just by walking into a studio with a well-known and well-respected performer who, unsolicited, talked the producers into giving me a chance.

The voice market includes all radio spots, voice-over filmed commercials, cartoons, industrial films, and TV narration. In New York, the competition is stiff and actors may be "sent up" for voice work, which means going into the agency to do a taped audition. If you want to go into voice work, cultivate a number of distinct voices and accents. I know one highly specialized voice-over woman in her fifties who can still sound convincingly like a two year old.

If you're serious about this end of the business, you'll need a *demo tape*, which is an audio tape of your voice work. Experienced professionals have their best representative work spliced together into a very polished demo presentation. Beginners have to start from scratch by selecting copy and hiring a studio to record and edit the tape. (Don't try to record yourself on your little Sony, it won't work.)

There are many consultants in this field, and it is probably worth it to find out who specializes in helping actors put together a demo. The fee is not cheap, but as with pictures, quality counts. You'll have to get several copies of your demo tape, because you need to be able to give it away to people. There are also production houses that offer discount prices for "dupes" (duplicates).

FEATURE FILM, SOAPS, AND SERIES

Feature Films

Feature films are currently shot all over the country, and work may be available if an actor happens to be in the right place at the right time. Getting a speaking role in a feature film is tough. Unless you're a very special type, the competition is not only tremendous, often there aren't even any auditions held for film work. There are many "unadvertised specials" in the industry, which are deals called "packaging." This means that if a top agent has a major client starring in the film, the agency has an agreement with the producer to provide ALL THE ADDITIONAL PRINCIPAL ACTORS on the film. Ouch.

Aside from that, the work that's available in features may include: Principal Role, Day Player, Stunt Player, Stand-In, Special Business, and Extra. The principal roles and the day players are usually cast by casting directors, so you or your agent will need an entree to the movie casting people.

In Hollywood, most principal roles are played by experienced people who are also known quantities. If you are a relative unknown, or if the role is something you're not usually associated with, you may be requested to do a *screen test*. This means that you have already had a couple of good auditions and they want to put you on camera. You will arrive at the studio several hours before your screen test for hair, makeup, and wardrobe. Then your scene will be blocked and re-hearsed (with or without a partner), and on "Action!" the cameras will roll.

The one-line roles on feature films (principals) are not usually screen-tested, but they will be auditioned. You will probably need to work through an agent for any principal work including Day Player.

Stunt Players are some of the hardest workers in Hollywood, and those who are good (and careful) work fairly regularly. Stunt actors are used in all scenes in which there may be physical harm to an untrained actor if he were to do the action. So a stunt person might do anything from a fatal car crash to a slap on the cheek. Stunt pay is good, but you must be highly trained, and there are still risks. If you are interested in stunt work, there is a book called *The Stunt Guide*, by John Cann.

Stand-Ins are the people who literally "stand in" for the stars. The process of making a movie is painstakingly slow, so the pro-duction company hires actors who are about the same size and coloring as the stars to "stand in" for them while they set up the shot. Stand-ins are paid a little more than extras, but they do not appear on camera. They are sometimes referred to collectively as the "Sec-ond Team," the stars being the "First Team." The Second Team gets to freeze in the cold and suffocate with the heat while the First

Team is relaxing, but it is work.

Extra work on feature films is available to members of SAG and SEG. SEG, the Screen Extras Guild, operates primarily on the West Coast, and is the union that specifically represents Extras. Most SAG actors can also work as Extras on films under SAG jurisdiction, so you need not join SEG unless you live in Los Angeles and plan to make a career out of doing extra work (which some people have done).

Sometimes the stand-ins are selected from the group of extras. Sometimes extras are given important silent bits on camera, which are referred to as *Special Business*. Chances are that this type of bit will not have been auditioned, but the director will select someone from the available extras on the day of the shoot. A special business pays a little more than an extra and, of course, carries a "great deal" more prestige.

You will not be requested to audition for extra work; however, don't assume that you'll get a job just because you belong to the union. You must usually send a picture and résumé and/or register with the casting office handling the extra work. If something comes up that you're right for, you will be called directly by the casting office and booked for a certain day or day(s). Sometimes they ask for a day plus a "rain day" or another additional "avail day." This means that you must be available to work on the additional day(s), in case they don't get the shot, or it rains, or they are inordinately delayed, or the star is sick.

The name of the game when doing extra work is our old friend, "Hurry up and wait." You have to have a lot of patience to do film work, because the tiniest shot takes forever. My most memorable film experience paid me for 2½ days of principal work to go out to Long Island to do one line. The film was *Masquerade*, starring Rob Lowe and Meg Tilly. I was requested to take a bus to the location on the far tip of Long Island, and upon arrival at the deserted resort I discovered that there wasn't a soul around. I checked into the very nice accommodations they had provided, and after several hours one of the ADs told me to "hang loose," because I wouldn't be needed until around noon the following day.

Naturally I stayed up late, and got a call at 7 A.M. "We need you *now!*" I screeched into the shower and pulled on clothing, rushing out to find a chauffeured car waiting. I was taken to the location, rushed into makeup and costume, hustled onto the set, did my one big line, and was temporarily excused. I was assigned a lovely and comfortable bedroom suite in what could only be described as a mansion, and there I rested and read for several hours. By noon I was getting bored, so I left my room to walk into a totally dark hallway. Slight change of schedule: The truck with all the lights had inadvertently left the location. On the spur of the moment they had decided to do a night scene in the middle of the day by covering all the windows.

A whole busload of extras had arrived that morning, and they also were sitting around through all of this. Finally at about 6 P.M. we were called into a main downstairs room to do the final scene of the day. By now it was dark out, but that did not faze anyone as they set up bright lights outside the living room and created warm "sunlight" for this daytime scene.

When the movie came out I discovered with some disappointment that my "scene" had been cut from the final edit. Oh well.

Soaps (Daytime Television)

Soaps are, of course, daytime television. If you are going to try to get work in a soap, you will obviously need to be available to work in either New York or Los Angeles, because that's where all the soaps shoot. When you send in your pictures and postcards, you will usually use your "legit" picture; however, I've heard at least one casting person say they like to see different shots of people. So you could conceivably send your commercial picture the following week or month, and so on.

I have the greatest admiration for actors who play the regulars on soaps. They work long hours; they sometimes have to learn long speeches or scenes in just twenty-four hours; and they work with some of the worst material known to the literate world. (Pity the poor writers too, they're cranking out a whole script a day!) The soap people who are any good and who have some longevity invariably rise to the occasion (of course they get paid very well) by developing the ability to truly "make something out of nothing." This is gimmicky "shortcut" acting that regulars cultivate to make the material work. And it usually does.

Because soap opera reaches its tentacles to the far corners of the world, your typical TV viewing audience may get the impression that soap acting is really good. It's not, but not because the actors are not talented and hard-working. The actors are terrific, the material is just not there. There's no consistency of character, people die and come back to life, there's no dramatic build to a climax, and there's no end. Is this good drama?

The chances are very slim that you will get a *contract* role on a soap. Not impossible, but slim. Contract players are regulars on the show. They have a legal commitment to work for a certain period of time, usually one to three years. Contract work is cast by the soap's casting director, and an audition will usually involve a screen test.

If you do get the opportunity to read for a contract role, pick up your sides as soon as they are available. You may also receive a character background sheet or synopsis, which is supposed to provide you with some glimpse of the character's past on the show. You can also research your audition by reading every *Soap Opera Digest* you can get your hands on and tuning in to the show every day until your appointment. Study the way good actors work on daytime TV and try to do that in your audition.

The smaller roles and extra jobs in soaps can be a good entré to the business. Besides the contract players, available work would include the following non-contract categories: Recurring Principal, Principal, Under Five, and Extra. A *Recurring Principal* player is one who is not on a contract but who appears on the show on a fairly regular basis, such as a nosy neighbor or the friendly bartender at the local eatery.

A *Principal* player is one who has more than five speaking lines, and who may be hired for a day or a number of days or weeks. The *Under Five* classification designates a role in which the actor has less than five lines. *Extras* have no lines but are important for dressing the "background."

The names and addresses of the casting directors of soaps are listed in the Ross Report. Usually the casting director handles contract and principal players, and an assistant casting director is in charge of under fives and extras. It's important to be persistent in your contact with the casting offices, because they do tend to hire actors who "keep in touch."

Of course, there's the story about the beautiful young woman who was hired as an Extra on a soap for a tennis scene. Looking "simply smashing" in her shortie tennis whites, she was noticed by the producer, who requested her to audition for a contract role that was coming up. The rest is history.

Series Work

Any discussion of series work will be closely tied up with where you live, because most series work shoots in L.A. This leads to the decision of which coast to choose—East or West. Almost everyone will agree that New York is the Mecca for theatrical work; Los Angeles has the bulk of the series filming; and both shoot about the same number of commercials. In order to be available for whatever might come up, some actors who can afford it are bi-coastal, traveling to and living in the place that offers the most work opportunities for any given "season." ("Pilot season" is hot in L.A., for example.)

In making your decision about where to settle, you should consider your personal lifestyle as well as your background. For example, if you tend to be primarily interested in cultural opportunities as well as good theatre, go to New York. If you are an outdoor kind of person who loves swimming pools and warm climates, go to L.A. In New York you will pay $1,000 a month for a studio rental; Los Angeles isn't that much cheaper but you might get a little more space. In New York everything is as crowded as the proverbial sardine-tin, while in L.A. everything is all spread out. New Yorkers don't usually drive or own cars, but rely on public transportation to get around. You would be a fool if you didn't have a car in L.A. These are important considerations in helping you decide what's best for you.

One other very important thing is this: in New York it *is* possible to get work without an agent, in Los Angeles it is *not*. With that in mind you may wish to be sure you have a darned good contact out on the West Coast before you pack up and move there.

Los Angeles actors are expected to have a *demo reel*, which is a reel of film representative of their work. Like the demo tape, there are consultants in this field to help beginners present themselves in a good light (again, no home movies), and to help select material that is appropriate and exciting. Your demo reel needs to be professional to compete, so you should just set aside the (considerable) money it will take. You will need duplicates of your demo reel, which can be done at video production companies at a discount for volume.

These are the common classifications of actors working on series: Weekly Players (Regulars), Day Players (less than a week), Stunt Players, and Extras. Guest stars may be on a weekly or day-player principal contract, depending on the total work commitment. If you are being considered for a Regular (Weekly Player), you may have a screen test, which will be similar to the one described in the section on feature films. As in features, prime-time requires auditions for all speaking roles, even if the actor has only two lines.

Though you do need an agent to get principal (weekly or day player) work, it's possible to get employment as an extra by contacting the extra casting office or attending one of their casting calls or registrations.

WRAP

At the official end of a commercial, print, soap, or film job, the final word is, "That's a *wrap*." Meaning, of course, that's it, the end, go home, and thank you.

In the industry there is yet another well-worn story about the man at the circus who took care of the elephants and, to put it bluntly, shoveled elephant dung. That's what he did, day in and day out for twenty years. Finally an old friend came by and said, "Harry, this can't be much of a life for you. All you do all day is shovel elephant dung. Why don't you stop?" To which the astonished Harry replied, "What!? And QUIT show business?"

Once you get hooked, it's hard to leave. As with your work in theatre, try to maintain a perspective as a human being. Realize that you are "worth it," as Cybill Shepherd is fond of telling us, and maintain your integrity and sense of responsibility. "Get a life," which means try to be as normal as possible within the confines of a business that can be very hard on the personal side as well as the psyche. Don't rule out all the things you have always wanted because of the business; rather, try to find a balance between your lifetime goals and what you can realistically expect if you choose to make acting your profession.

In that same circus there's a man who has spent his entire career getting shot out of a cannon. Finally, after twenty years, he goes to the ringmaster and says, "I've had it. I've been shot out of the cannon for twenty years. I'm tired. I quit." To which the ringmaster responds, "Oh, that's terrible! Wherever am I going to find a man of your caliber?" If you're good, you'll get hired for work in the industry, and I hope the information provided here will help ease your way into the exciting experience of life in show business.

Additional Reading

Arlen, Michael J. *Thirty Seconds*. New York: Farrar, Straus & Giroux, 1979.

Barton, John. *Playing Shakespeare*. London & New York: Methuen, Inc., 1984.

Bates, Brian. *Way of the Actor*. New York: Random House, 1988.

Brandreth, Gyles. *Great Theatrical Disasters*. New York: St. Martin's Press, 1982.

Caine, Michael. *Acting in Film*. New York: Applause Theatre Books Publishers, 1990.

Callow, Simon. *Being an Actor*. New York: Grove Press, 1984.

Carr, Kate. *How You Can Star in TV Commercials*. New York: Rawson, Wade Publishers, Inc. 1982.

Chekov, Michael, and Charles Leonard. *To the Actor*. New York: Harper Collins, 1985.

Cohen, Robert. *Acting Professionally*. New York: Barnes & Noble Books, 1983.

Gielgud, John. *The Ages of Gielgud*. New York: Limelight Editions, 1984.

—.*Gielgud, An Actor and His Time*. New York: Clarkson N. Potter, Inc., Publishers, 1980.

Goldman, William. *Adventures in the Screen Trade*. New York: Warner Books, 1983.

—. *The Season*. New York: Limelight Editions, 1984.

Hagen, Uta. *Respect for Acting*. New York: Macmillan Publishing Co., Inc., 1973.

—. *A Challenge for the Actor*. New York: Charles Scribner's Sons, 1991.

Harrop, John, and Sabin R. Epstein. *Acting with Style*. New York: Prentice-Hall, 1990.

Hay, Peter. *Theatrical Anecdotes*. New York and Oxford, England: Oxford University Press, 1987.

Hayes, Vangie, with Gloria Hainline. *How to Get Into Commercials*. New York: Harper & Row Publishers, 1983.

Henry, Mari Lyn, and Lynn Rogers. *How to Be a Working Actor*. New York: Evans & Company, 1986.

Herman, Lewis, and Marguerite Shalett Herman. *Foreign Dialects*. New York: Theatre Arts Books, 1943.

—. *A Manual of American Dialects*. New York: Theatre Arts Books, 1947.

Hinman, Charlton. *The First Folio of Shakespeare* (The Norton Facsimile). New York: W.W. Norton Co. and The Hamlyn Group, 1968.

Houseman, John. *Final Dress*. New York: Simon & Schuster, 1983.

—. *Front and Center*. New York: Simon & Schuster, 1979.

—. *Run-Through*. New York: Simon and Schuster, 1972.

Huggett, Richard. *The Curse of Macbeth*. Great Britain: Picton Publishers, 1981.

Laban, Rudolf. *The Mastery of Movement*. Boston: Plays, Inc., 1975.

Leonard, Charles. *Michael Chekov's To the Director and Playwright*. New York: Limelight Editions, 1984.

Lewis, Robert. *Advice to the Players*. New York: Stein & Day, 1980.

—. *Method or Madness*. New York: Samuel French, 1958.

—. *Slings and Arrows*. New York: Stein and Day, 1984.

Meisner, Sanford. *Confessions of an Actor*. New York: Simon and Schuster, 1982.

Richardson, Ralph. *An Actor's Life*. New York: Limelight Editions, 1982.

Rigg, Diana. *No Turn Unstoned*. New York: Doubleday & Company, 1983.

Shanks, Robert. *The Cool Fire*. New York: Vintage Books, 1976.

Shurtleff, Michael. *Audition*. New York: Walker & Company, 1978.

Stanislavski, Constantin. *An Actor Prepares*. New York: Theatre Arts Books, 1967.

Glossary

ACCENT COACH—An accent or dialect specialist who attends selected rehearsals, gives accent notes, and coaches actors; may also work individually with actors.

ACTORS' EQUITY ASSOCIATION (AEA or Equity)—The union that covers professional employment in live theatre and industrial shows.

AFFIRMATIVE ACTION CASTING—Use of a non-traditional type in a role commonly played by another sex, race, age; formal term used to ensure that minorities and women are given opportunities to audition for appropriate roles.

AGENT, THEATRICAL—Business person who represents actors in exchange for a percentage of their professional employment earnings (limited by law to 10%).

ALEXANDRINE—A line of verse having six feet (twelve beats).

AMERICAN FEDERATION OF TELEVISION AND RADIO ARTISTS (AFTRA)—Professional actors' union covering radio and television employment including: daytime TV (soaps), live TV, video-taped commercials, news/sports/weather broadcasts, radio commercials, disc jockeys, industrial films, etc.

ARENA STAGE—Stage surrounded on all sides by audience; also called "theatre in the round."

ARTISTIC DIRECTOR—Person who oversees all the artistic decisions in a repertory theatre or stock company; influential in selecting plays for the season, hiring the directors and resident actors.

ASSISTANT DIRECTOR (AD)—1) In theatre, person who assists the director. 2) In film, ADs perform functions of theatre stage managers: keep track of actors, call them in for work, act as spokesperson for the director, etc. If more than one, called "first AD, second AD," etc.

ASSISTANT STAGE MANAGER (ASM)—Assistant to the stage manager; if more than one, called "first ASM, second ASM," etc.

ASSOCIATED ACTORS AND ARTISTES OF AMERICA (4 A's)—Organization affiliated with the AFL-CIO, of which all actors' unions are branches, including: AEA, AFTRA, AGMA, AGVA, SAG, SEG, APATE, IAU, HAU.

AUDITION—Reading from a given script for a play, commercial, voice-over, film, industrial, etc.

AUTHOR—Person who wrote the play (also called the playwright); in a musical, person who wrote the book.

AVAIL DAY(S)—Date(s) actor must be available for shoot.

BACKSTAGE—Area encompassing 1) all the dressing rooms and common rooms for actors in a theatre production; 2) the area immediately behind the set not visible to the audience, also called "off-stage" or "in the wings."

BACKSTAGE—Trade newspaper in the New York metropolitan area, with casting listings for East Coast and regional theatre.

BIO—An actor's condensed biography, used in theatre program.

BIT—In blocking, a small piece of on-stage business.

BLOCKING—The physical movement of all the actors on stage.

BOOK—1) (noun) In musical theatre, the sections that are spoken are known collectively as the book. 2) (verb) To definitely confirm employment on a specific job, e.g., "They want to book you for 2-4 Wednesday."

BOOK OUT—Term used to mean not available, e.g., "I'm going on the road, book me out for the next six weeks."

BOOKED—Having confirmed employment on a specific job e.g., "You're booked." Once booked, a minimum payment to talent must be made even if the shoot or job is cancelled or rescheduled.

BOOKING—A confirmed job in the industry; usually refers to print work, commercials, voice-overs, other jobs of a relatively short nature.

BOX OFFICE MANAGER—Person in charge of all ticket sales.

BREAK-AWAY—Costumes constructed with Velcro® or snaps, designed to rip apart easily for on-stage bits or quick changes.

BREAKING THE FOURTH WALL—Delivering a line or speech directly to the audience. In proscenium theatre, sets are composed of three walls; the invisible fourth "wall" is the one through which the audience views the play. (Example: An "aside" in a Shakespeare play.)

BUILD—In costumes, to create from scratch.

BUSINESS—In blocking, a small piece of action on stage.

BUSINESS MANAGER—In professional theatre, the person in charge of business procedures and paying salaries.

BUY-OUT—One-time flat fee for a job.

CALL TIME —The time you are expected to be at rehearsal, theatre studio, or location; may differ from actor to actor.

CALLBACK—Second (or more) audition for a play, a commercial, or a radio or TV project; if more than one, termed "second callback, third callback," etc.

CALLING THE SHOW—Calling the warnings and cues for actors, lights, sound, curtain, etc., for the entire production; the stage manager usually calls the show.

CALLS—Known as "the calls," i.e., half-hour, fifteen minutes, five minutes, and places; the stage manager or ASM makes the calls.

CAMEO—A relatively small but highly visible role.

CAMERA LEFT—Appearing on camera to the left of the screen; to adjust to camera left, move to your right.

CAMERA RIGHT—Appearing on camera to the right of the screen; to adjust to camera right, move to your left.

CASTING DIRECTOR—Person in charge of screening actors and selecting appropriate people to audition; works closely with the director to cast the show.

CHEAT, CHEATING—In blocking, 1) to move one's body or face out to the house slightly; or 2) slight movement in any direction to give focus or balance the stage picture.

CHOREOGRAPHER—Trained expert who stages the dances in a musical, or the special movement in a play; fight choreographers stage the fights or special physical actions.

CLOSED—Not open to the public; most professional play rehearsals and jobs are closed, guests not permitted.

COMMERCIAL—Radio or TV job in which the actor represents a commercial client such as Procter & Gamble, Colgate, etc., in a filmed or taped TV or radio advertisement.

COMP—1) (theatre) Abbreviation for complimentary ticket. 2) (modeling and print work) Abbreviation of composite.

COMPOSER—The person who wrote the music.

COMPOSITE—A group of photos on a single page showing a variety of poses, characters, and/or expressions.

CONFLICT—1) (verb, accent on second syllable) To pose a scheduling problem, i.e., "I have a booking that will conflict with rehearsal." 2) (noun, accent on first syllable) Prior commitment, i.e., work, school, or class, that would pose a scheduling problem, e.g., "I have a conflict on Tuesday."

CONFLICT, DRAMATIC—(noun, accent on first syllable) Inherent struggle between characters, or within a single character, representing two opposing sides or views.

CONFLICT, PRODUCT—(noun, accent on first syllable) Having a current commercial promoting the same type of product, therefore unable to accept commercial employment in that area.

CONTACT LIST—List of names, addresses, and phone numbers of cast members, stage management, director, et. al.

CONTACT SHEETS—Photographic sheets on which all the negatives from a shoot or session are printed; used to make selections of photos.

CONTRACT—Legal agreement between actor and agent granting exclusivity to the agent; legal agreement between actor and producer or client spelling out terms of employment, including length of time and financial arrangements. Actors sign contracts for all professional jobs.

CONTRAST—The striking differences created in drama; can be generated between characters or within a particular character's own emotional sense. Use of contrast is also called "playing the opposites."

COPY—The script or lines in a commercial.

COSTUMER—Person in the costume department who builds the costumes.

COUNTER, COUNTERING —In blocking, counter-crossing, i.e., moving in an opposite direction from another actor in order to balance the stage picture.

CROSS, CROSSING—In blocking, physically moving from one place on stage to another.

CUE-TO-CUE—A rehearsal that works only entrances and exits, light and sound cues, skipping most of the acting and script.

CUED—Refers to lights or sound that are not practical but come from the light/sound booth, triggered (cued) by an on-stage line or action (see PRACTICAL).

CYCLORAMA—Curved canvas "wall" at the back of the set used to give an illusion of space and distance and for sky and cloud effects.

DANCE CAPTAIN—In musical theatre, a dancer under contract in the show designated to run brush-up rehearsals and fill in for the choreographer when necessary.

DEMO REEL—Film or videotape demonstrating actor's on-camera capabilities.

DEMO TAPE—Audio tape demonstrating actor's voice-over capabilities.

DEPUTY—Professional actor under contract in a production elected by other members of Equity to communicate problems and represent actors in disputes with management.

DESIGNER—Artist who creates the specific look or tone of the production in a particular area, e.g., costumes, lights, sets, sound.

DIRECTOR—The person who makes choices about theme and concept for the entire show, and who orchestrates the actors to achieve a desired result. Directors work closely with all designers and (in a musical) with the choreographer and musical director.

DRAMA-LOGUE—Trade paper that lists casting calls for the Los Angeles area.

DRESS PARADE—Rehearsal designated for actors to dress in costumes and "parade" on stage for the director, costume designer, et al.

DRESS REHEARSAL—Rehearsal in which costumes are worn; also called simply "Dress." FULL DRESS includes all costumes and makeup; TECH-DRESS includes costumes, lights, and sound; FULL-TECH-DRESS includes all costumes, makeup, lights, and sound; FINAL DRESS is the last before opening (usually full-tech-dress); INVITED DRESS has an invited (non-paying) audience.

DRESSER—Costume or other crew person responsible for helping the actor get into or change costumes.

ELIGIBLE PERFORMER AUDITIONS (EPAs) and ELIGIBLE PERFORMER INTERVIEWS (EPIs)—Open auditions or interviews required and monitored by Equity to ensure actors an opportunity to be seen for an Equity production; "eligible" is a term defined by the union.

ELISION—In verse, contraction of two syllables into one. Example: heav'n.

ENSEMBLE—Cast members working in harmony to serve the interests of each other and the play; ensemble often results from actors working together over time, but can also be achieved in a single play.

EQUITY MEMBERSHIP CANDIDATE (EMC)—Person earning points toward Equity Membership by serving as an apprentice or intern in professional theatres.

EXEUNT—Latin plural of exit, meaning "they go out."

EXTRA—Union designation for talent working on-camera but not in a principal role; also called "background talent."

FALSE—Scenery or set piece that does not actually work, but is merely painted on; not "practical."

FARCE—Comedy that depends on physical action, ludicrous situations, and unexpected happenings; also called Low Comedy.

FAVORED NATIONS—Clause in an Equity contract stating that no other person in the company is receiving higher compensation than that particular actor.

FEMININE ENDING—Verse line considered regular but having an extra (eleventh) unstressed syllable at the end.

FIGHT CAPTAIN—Actor under contract in a show designated to ensure that fights and physical business remain as originally choreographed.

FIGHT CHOREOGRAPHER—Person who stages the fights and

other physically demanding scenes and/or bits, and who coaches and rehearses same.

FINAL DRESS—Last dress rehearsal before opening, usually a full-tech-dress.

FIND THE LIGHT—1) To determine the place on stage where the lights have been focused. 2) To find the place in an audition where the best available light is.

FIRST REFUSAL—In commercials, a term used to mean "we have first option on your services and you should not take another job until you hear from us, one way or the other"; similar to "Hold."

FOCUS—1) The place on stage where the audience is looking. 2) Technical term for adjusting lights after they are hung.

FOOT—An iamb, composed of an unstressed syllable followed by a stressed syllable (see IAMBIC PENTAMETER).

FOOT, IRREGULAR—In verse, a foot that is not composed of the regular unstressed followed by stressed pattern. Types of irregular feet are: trochaic, anapestic, dactylic, spondee, pyrrhic, and dipodic.

FRANCHISE—Legal agreement; usually refers to agents franchised by Equity, SAG, AFTRA.

FRENCH SCENES—Breakdown of the play into small scenes for rehearsal purposes; if used, the director or stage manager will determine and give the French scene breakdown.

GENERAL AUDITION—Auditions prepared in advance by the actor, always memorized and blocked, usually monologues; audition to show ability, as opposed to specific audition for a play.

GO-SEE—In print work, designated time for actors to go and see a photographer, who usually takes a Polaroid for a specific upcoming print job; not called an audition.

GOING UP—Forgetting your lines. Example: "I really went up in the second act. Thanks for saving me."

GREEN ROOM—Common room backstage for actors and crew.

HANDLE—A specific approach to a character, e.g., an accent, a character trait or mannerism, a posture, etc.

HIGH COMEDY—Work that draws characters from the upper strata of society, in which much of the humor is dependent on verbal wit; also called comedy of manners.

HOLD—In print and extra work, a request to reserve time; not yet a definite booking, e.g., "you are on hold for Tuesday."

HOUSE MANAGER—Person in charge of ushers and seating.

IAMBIC PENTAMETER—Type of verse made up of five iambs (feet), each composed of an unstressed syllable followed by a stressed syllable.

INTERVIEW—Face-to-face meeting with an agent, a casting person, a director, etc., but not an audition.

LYRICIST—In a musical, person who wrote the words to the songs.

MANAGER, PERSONAL—Representative for actors who oversees all career decisions; works with agents to book jobs for actors; takes a percentage of actor's earnings (usually 15% or more).

MANAGING DIRECTOR—Person who oversees all business aspects of a theatre and who works in concert with the artistic director; also called general manager or business manager.

MASTER SCRIPT—Copy of the play marked by the stage manager with all blocking and cues; used to run the show.

MOCK-UP—Reproduction of a costume using the design but made out of inexpensive material, often muslin.

NON-WORKING—Prop or set piece that is there but doesn't really work. Example: on-stage sink, but water doesn't come out.

OFF BOOK—Having lines memorized and able to perform without script in hand.

OFF-CAMERA—Work not appearing on film or tape, also called

voice-over.

OFF-STAGE—1) Backstage immediately behind the set and not visible to the audience, also called "the wings." 2) Heard but not seen, as in "off-stage noises."

ON-CAMERA—Appearing on film or tape.

PACE—Individual rhythm of the character; picking up pace means "go faster."

PERIOD—The timeframe in which a production is set, established by the author or the director.

PERIOD PLAY—Play set in a timeframe other than contemporary.

PHOTO—Actor's professional photographs are 8 X 10 black-and-white head shots; models and commercial print actors may also use composite shots and/or other photographs in their portfolios.

PICK UP CUES—Leave no space between previous actor's last line and the beginning of yours; distinguished from PACE.

PLAY THE HOUSE—Usually in comedy, performing for a particular audience at an appropriate pace depending on their response.

PLAYS, TYPES OF—Tragedy, comedy (high or low), drama, melodrama, and satire.

PORTFOLIO—Model's book containing examples (tear sheets) of previous work and photographs exhibiting potential.

POST-REALISM—Theatrical style (also called post-modernism) representing a revolt against realism, characterized in numerous forms. See: POST-REALISTIC MOVEMENTS. Elements include: combinations of realistic and presentational styles; breaking the fourth wall; poetic or formal language mixed with slang.

POST-REALISTIC MOVEMENTS—Symbolism, neo-romanticism, expressionism, constructivism, surrealism, stylization, theatricalism, formalism, epic theatre (agitprop), and absurdism.

PRACTICAL—Actually working on stage; can refer to lights, props, sound, appliances, parts of the set, etc.

PRE-SET—Props, costumes, lights set on stage before the beginning of the play, act, or scene.

PRESENTATIONAL—Theatrical style that dominated theatre from ancient Greece to the Modern period. Elements include: actors play directly to audience; conventions such as asides, soliloquies, and enlarged movement; language is poetic.

PRINCIPAL—Actor category designating a role of significance, usually with lines but not necessarily; each union may define "principal" in a slightly different way.

PRINT WORK—Work that utilizes actors for still camera advertisements and editorials, including 1) fashion—still-camera ads for clothing and designers; 2) glamour—still-camera work for makeup, perfume, etc.; 3) commercial—still-camera work utilizing actors in "roles" and character work.

PRODUCER—1) Person who oversees everything in the entire production, including how and where the money is spent. 2) "Angel," or person who contributes money for the show or the theatre.

PRODUCTION PHOTOS—Pictures of a theatrical production, taken during a dress rehearsal, performance, or after a performance.

PROPERTIES—All moveable things on stage; abbreviated props.

PROPS, PERSONAL—All items an actor carries or uses on stage, and costume pieces that are removable.

READ—Appear to the audience as what it is supposed to be; used in reference to props, costume pieces, bits, and business.

READ-THROUGH—Reading of the entire play from start to finish with the complete cast, without movement or blocking.

REGIONALISM—1) Mispronunciation of word or words reflecting common usage in a particular geographical area. 2) Misplacement of the voice reflecting a particular locale (example: nasality). 3) Idiomatic expression native to a particular area.

RELEASE—1) A polite refusal following a hold or first refusal, e.g. "We are booking someone else so you are released from the hold." 2) In print work, a legal agreement giving a client permission to use the picture of you they have taken during the shoot for advertising purposes.

RENDERINGS—Sketches drawn by the costume designer of proposed costume designs.

REPRESENTATIONALISM (REALISM)—Theatrical style in which the audience presumes to be watching realistic events. Elements include: actors play to each other; asides and soliloquies are eliminated; movement and language is everyday.

RESIDUALS—Payments made to union actors for reuse of commercials, films, etc.

RESUME—One-page listing of actor's experience, attached to the back of 8 X 10 head shot.

RUNNING CREW—The crew people who are actually at the theatre and working the show during performances.

RUN-THROUGH—Rehearsal in which the entire play is performed without stopping. Actors may be on or off book, but are expected to be in place and ready to go on directly from scene to scene and act to act. Run-throughs are often timed.

SCAN—1) To break down verse into the regular and irregular "feet" in order to decide correct interpretation of the poetry. 2) To mark text accordingly.

SCANSION—The process of analyzing verse into metrical feet and rhythmic patterns.

SCREEN ACTORS GUILD (SAG)—The professional actors' union governing work in film, e.g., feature films, series, commercials, industrial films, related voice-overs, etc.

SCREEN TEST—On-camera audition for film or TV job.

SERIES—Television show that airs regularly, usually once a week.

SHTICK —A bit of (usually) funny business on stage.

SIDES—Photocopies of the scenes from a play which will be read at auditions; a single "side" includes one scene for a specific character.

SOAPS—Dramatic TV shows that air during the day; also called "daytime television."

SPECIAL BUSINESS—Designation in SAG films, in which the actor does silent bit and is paid slightly more than an extra.

SQUAWK BOX—Intercom that goes from the stage into the dressing rooms and green room, allowing actors to hear the show and follow its progress; also called "monitor."

SLATE—To identify yourself by name at on-camera auditions.

STAGE LEFT—To the left of the actor as he/she faces the audience.

STAGE MANAGER—Person who oversees the entire production and works closely with the director; attends all rehearsals and keeps the master script; writes down all blocking and business; during the run makes the calls (half-hour, etc.) and calls the show (all cues); in professional theatre, maintains the show by calling necessary rehearsals and using disciplinary measures where required.

STAGE RIGHT—To the right of the actor as he/she faces the audience.

STANDARD AMERICAN SPEECH—Speech most newscasters use, which has no discernible accent and excellent diction; used for classics in the U.S.

STAND-BY—In theatre, the person prepared to go on in a role if another actor is unable to appear; as opposed to understudy, the stand-by does not otherwise appear in the show, whereas an understudy performs on stage in another (usually smaller) role (see UNDERSTUDY).

STAND-IN—In film, the person hired to stand in for a star or principal player while lights and background are set; stand-ins do not appear on camera.

STOP-AND-GO—A technical run-through, which stops at technical cues, works the cue, and then goes on.

STORYBOARD—Depiction of the action of a commercial in cartoon-style sketches, usually in several "frames."

STYLE—The manner or fashion of presentation. Two basic types of style are: period and theatrical.

STYLE, PERIOD—Style in which the fashion of the day (the period) is translated into thetheatrical fabric of the production.

STYLE, THEATRICAL—A particular view of the theatre and the nature of theatrical creation. The three main categories of theatrical style are: presentational, representational (realism), and post-realistic.

SUBURBANISM—Incorrect pronunciation of a word distinct to a specific suburb or small geographical location.

TAKING STAGE—1) Physical and emotional "set-up" when the actor prepares to begin on stage. 2) Dominating and/or using the entire stage, as in a long monologue.

TALENT—In film and television, the actors (as opposed to the crew) are often called the talent.

TEAR SHEETS—(pronounced *tare*) Advertising agency term for finished copies of print jobs; models request tear sheets after the shoot for their portfolios.

TECH-DRESS—A technical rehearsal with costumes.

TECHNICAL DIRECTOR—The person in charge of the crew and making sure all sets, lights, sound, etc., are working.

TECHNICAL REHEARSAL—Rehearsal specifically for technical aspects of the show, including lights and sound.

TELEGRAPHING—Giving away the joke before the punch line or playing the ending so the audience knows what is going to happen; also called "anticipating."

TEST SHOTS—Photographs given in exchange for free modeling time; not recommended unless set up by a reputable agent or manager with a known photographer.

THRUST STAGE—A stage surrounded on three sides by audience.

TYPING OUT—Audition process (usually for musicals) by which people are lined up and chosen or eliminated simply by looks and type.

UNDER FIVE—In daytime TV, the category in which the actor has five lines or less and is paid accordingly; not considered principal.

UNDERSTUDY—Person prepared to go on in a (usually) larger role if another actor is unable to appear; as opposed to stand-by, understudy performs in another role in the show, but the stand-by does not. Also called "cover," as in "I'm covering (or the cover for) the two female leads."

UNIONS—Branches of Associated Actors and Artistes of America (4 A's) including: Equity, AFTRA, AGVA, AGMA, SAG, SEG, APATE, IAU, and HAU.

VALUABLES—Things of value, either monetary or sentimental, collected by the stage manager at the half-hour and locked up during a performance.

VOICE-OVER—Work in which the actor does not appear on camera, but the voice accompanies film or tape, as in a commercial or an industrial film.

WARDROBE SUPERVISOR—Costume person in charge of maintenance.

WINGS—Immediate backstage, spaces to the right and left of the stage.

WORK-THROUGH—A run-through that allows for stopping and working various sections; distinguished from a stop-and-go (which is a technical rehearsal), work-throughs are primarily for acting values.

WRAP—In film, TV, and print, word signifying the end of the job; professional actors may not leave a job or location until they are officially "wrapped."

Index

About the Author

Mary McTigue has been an active member of Actors' Equity Association, Screen Actors Guild, and the American Federation of Television and Radio Artists for over twenty years. She has appeared in numerous professional theatre productions in New York City and throughout the country, and has played principal roles in network TV and radio commercials, industrial and feature films, daytime TV (soaps), and commercial print jobs.

As a teacher, Mary worked with hundreds of young adults in the ACTeen division of Weist-Barron, a professional school in New York specializing in film and video acting. She taught Acting Technique, Basic and Advanced Commercial Technique, and Film and Soap Scene Study.

Mary's writing experience includes several years with a New York City-based public relations firm. Between professional acting jobs, she currently develops and writes material for Creative Training Concepts, a consulting firm which designs and produces instructional programs for major corporations such as PaineWebber, Motorola, and Sea-Land Services.

A native of Minnesota, Mary attended Clarke College where she earned a B.A. in theatre (summa cum laude and Phi Beta Kappa). She has done post-graduate work at the Royal Academy of Dramatic Arts in London, and is currently completing her Master of Arts in Theatre. Mary lived for many years in New York City's Upper West Side; now a resident of Montclair, New Jersey, she is married and has one son.